CW00675132

Bader's
Duxford Fighters

The Big Wing Controversy

Dilip Sarkar

Ramrod Publications

Other books by Dilip Sarkar:-

SPITFIRE SQUADRON
THE INVISIBLE THREAD: A SPITFIRE'S TALE
THROUGH PERIL TO THE STARS
ANGRIFF WESTLAND
A FEW OF THE MANY
BADER'S TANGMERE SPITFIRES: THE UNTOLD STORY, 1941

Ramrod Publications is always pleased to receive readers' views on Dilip Sarkar's work. Dilip spends much time and effort helping others in their quests for information, especially the relatives of those who died on active service. In view of the author's heavy commitments, however, please keep your questions concise and realistic, and *always* enclose a stamped addressed envelope - due to the sheer volume of correspondence Dilip now receives annually, unless this courtesy is observed letters can no longer be answered. Also the volume of work involved now dictates that in certain cases an hourly research fee will be levied, proceeds being donated by the author to the Douglas Bader Foundation.

Dilip Sarkar's personal research process remains ongoing, and he would welcome contact with readers in possession of *any* previously unpublished contemporary photographs of either RAF or *Luftwaffe* origin. He is at present researching 'JOHNNIE'S' KENLEY SPITFIRES, as a joint-authorship project with Air Vice-Marshal JE Johnson, and is particularly keen, therefore, to hear from anyone stationed at Kenley in 1943. Dilip and the Air Vice-Marshal then propose a second title, 'JOHNNIE'S' D-DAY SPITFIRES: THE GREAT ADVENTURE.

Ramrod Publications is also pleased to take bookings for Dilip Sarkar's lecturing services, specialising in his published work. For further information, or for inclusion in our mailing list, please contact me, Anita, on (Tel) 01905 767735, (Fax) 01905 424533.

Bader's Duxford Fighters: The Big Wing Controversy

© Dilip Sarkar 1997

All rights reserved. No part of this publication may be reproduced, stored in a retrieval system, or transmitted in any form or by any means without prior permission in writing from the publisher.

First published in 1997 by Ramrod Publications, 16 Kingfisher Close, St Peter's, Worcester WR5 3RY

ISBN: 0 9519832 4 5

Designed and Typeset by Ramrod Publications
Printed in Great Britain by Aspect Print & Design, 89 Newtown Road, Malvern, Worcs WR14 2PD

Bader's
Duxford Fighters
The Big Wing Controversy

Introduction

Some years ago it became apparent to me, from extensive background reading and interviews with many survivors, that the Bader story, particularly with regard to the air combats of both 1940 and '41, was not necessarily as popular legend would have us believe. Having researched in detail the individual biographies of numerous of the Few, and related squadron histories, for a variety of reasons I then became increasingly interested with Fighter Command's Non-Stop Offensive of 1941. Research indicated that there were significant errors and omissions connected with this part of the Bader legend, and in the case of 'Reach for the Sky', the romantically embellished but nevertheless suitably inspiring story of Douglas Bader by Paul Brickhill, the truth had been deliberately distorted in several instances. It became clear that there was room for the publication of accurate historical references.

Concurrently with the preparation and publication of my fifth book, 'A Few of the Many', in 1995, I continued my research into 1941, and in particular regarding the exploits of Wing Commander Douglas Bader's famous Tangmere Wing. In connection with this research, much new fascinating information came to light, not just about the air battles but also accurate details concerning Douglas Bader's service life. In September 1996, 'Bader's Tangmere Spitfires: The Untold Story, 1941' was published (see Bibliography); as previous publications had not been relied upon for reference, but my own original research, much new ground was broken. It is a fact that 'Bader's Tangmere Spitfires', released in September 1996, represented the most significant work on the subject published for many years.

The 'Bader's Tangmere Spitfires' project attracted immense international publicity, not least as a result of our search for the remains of the Spitfire abandoned by Wing Commander Bader over France when he was captured in August 1941. I was consequently contacted by a television company seeking to produce a Bader biographical programme for Channel 4's *Secret Lives* series. At the time I was already working towards a similar goal with another company, and so declined involvement; the *Secret Lives* project was therefore shelved, but when I withdrew from my original arrangements and offered my services, the idea was reactivated. I was appointed Official Consultant, but despite having provided all of my research and contacts, which provided the basis for the wartime section of the programme, my name was omitted from the credits. In view of my *essential* contribution, which included the provision of unique and otherwise unobtainable information, the reader can appreciate that I was unimpressed. I was equally so when newspaper leaders proclaimed that the *Secret Lives* programme, broadcast in December 1996, 'broke brave new ground'; that was untrue, as the foregoing paragraphs indicate.

Immediately the research for 'Bader's Tangmere Spitfires' was complete, however, I commenced researching the Big Wing in great detail for this natural sequel volume. Again, during the course of this research it was discovered that numerous inaccuracies, omissions and incorrect interpretations existed in many previously published works. I had already covered the story of 19 Squadron, one of the Big Wing's units, during the Battle of Britain in my first book, 'Spitfire Squadron', published in 1990 (see Bibliography), but had touched upon the controversial tactics only as background to the daily events affecting the squadron concerned. From responses received from survivors, however, it was abundantly clear that many held strong and differing views about the subject, even when from the same squadron.

As a serving police officer with CID experience, I have a professional interest both in impartiality and thorough research. This background means that I have a natural aversion to myths and legends, but an unashamed bias towards facts and the truth, and interpretations based therefore upon evidence. It is a fact that the authors of many previous works connected with Group Captain Sir Douglas Bader have been either emotionally or personally involved. Few have been historians, the majority journalists. With all due respect to those concerned, such a combination does not necessarily make for an accurate and objective assessment. It must be appreciated, however, that when many of these accounts were published during the 1950s, authors had no or limited access to official records, which were largely not made available until the mid-1970s. I am confident that this book, however, which has not been subject to such emotions or restrictions, will provide the basis for further *accurate* research and a lasting reference to the *facts* of the Big Wing Controversy.

Another intention is that this story will be brought to the attention of a new generation, and the previous imbalance of credit rectified to some extent. In particular, I hope to have illuminated the names of both Air Chief Marshal Sir Hugh Dowding and Air Vice-Marshal Keith Park, the true victors of the Battle of Britain.

My main interest has always been the 'human' rather than technical side of war, and I think that this will be apparent to the reader from the quantity of first-hand interviews and quotes from personal papers which punctuate the text. One thing worth mentioning is that I never use the prefix 'Bf' when referring to either the Messerschmitt 109 or 110; the abbreviation may be *technically* correct, but I have *never* found such a reference in any pilot's individual combat report. Indeed, Flight Lieutenant Keith Lawrence DFC, a 10 Group Spitfire pilot in 1940, and amongst those pilots featured in 'A Few of the Many', once said to me, 'Dilip, when writing your books please do not use the term Bf; we never used it ourselves, but always referred to the *Me*'. Equally, the late Hans 'Peter' Wulff, a former *Luftwaffe* pilot who flew both fighters and bombers operationally, always referred to, for example, the '*Messerschmitt* One hundred-and-ten'; that, as they say, is good enough for me.

An interesting thing is that, contrary to my six previous books, this title has no foreword. It was decided that as the contents were so unique, from a security viewpoint it was unwise to allow the manuscript out of our hands until publication. 'Bader's Duxford Fighters' therefore stands on its own merits - or otherwise!

Dilip Sarkar
Worcester,
May 1997.

Contents

Dedication   1
Introduction   2

Chapter   1 The Scene is set   4
Chapter   2 Bader   28
Chapter   3 Gunsmoke in the sky   45
Chapter   4 Tally Ho!   75
Chapter   5 Big Wing   84
Chapter   6 Battle for London   106
Chapter   7 Autumn Leaves   131
Chapter   8 Meeting of Infamy   147
Chapter   9 A Political Disgrace   179
Chapter 10 The Great Experience   186

Index   211
Acknowledgements   214
Bibliography   216

Dedication

In 1982, Group Captain Sir Douglas Bader died prematurely. Today, the story of this legless pilot continues to inspire the general public, especially the disabled and aviation minded. It is appropriate that his inspiration and unique fighting spirit should live on through the charitable work of the Douglas Bader Foundation (information on which can be found in this book).

This book is dedicated to the inspirational memory of

Group Captain Sir Douglas Bader.

CHAPTER ONE

The scene is set

For the biographical details of those RAF commanders with whom we are concerned in this book, I would refer the reader to the bibliography. However, there are certain details and background events which are relevant to our account:-

Hugh Caswell Tremenheere Dowding was born at Moffat on April 24th, 1882. His father had founded a preparatory school in Scotland, and the Dowdings' was a dutiful Victorian middle-class background. In 1899, Dowding entered the Royal Military Academy at Woolwich, later being commissioned as a Second Lieutenant in the Garrison Artillery. In 1912, Dowding attended the Military Staff College at Camberley, during which time he learned to fly privately at Brooklands.

In 1914, war was declared on Germany for the first time this century, and as Dowding was a qualified pilot he was required to serve in France with the Royal Flying Corps (RFC). By July 23rd, 1915, Major Dowding was Officer Commanding (OC) of 16 Squadron, at Merville, which was largely engaged in artillery observation work. During this period, Dowding complained to Major-General Hugh 'Boom' Trenchard, the General OC the RFC, that his squadron had received a batch of wrong-sized propellers. Trenchard objected to Dowding's 'pernickety primness' and ordered him to fit the airscrews which had been delivered. The propellers' unsuitability was later proven when Dowding himself undertook the first test-flight, and was nearly killed in the process. Trenchard felt that the issue indicated Dowding's 'self-righteous stubbornness'; Dowding later considered the incident 'typical of Trenchard's technical stupidity'.

On June 18th, 1916, Lieutenant-Colonel Dowding returned to France where he was given command of No 9 (HQ) Wing, comprising four squadrons, at Fienvillers, near Doullens, ready for the infamous first battle of the Somme. Throughout this time the RFC suffered heavy losses, due to the so-called 'Fokker Scourge'. Nevertheless, Major-General Trenchard insisted that the offensive must be maintained, and even forbade his aircrews to wear parachutes, believing the life-saving silk umbrellas to be 'bad for morale'! The high casualties troubled Dowding deeply, however, and so after further differences with Trenchard he was posted home on New Year's Day, 1917.

Hugh Dowding shortly after being commissioned in the RAF.
(Author via Lady Odette Dowding)

It was much later to become significant that Dowding's replacement as OC 9 Wing was the 30-year-old Temporary Lieutenant-Colonel Cyril Newall. With 9 Wing, Newall was to gain experience of long-range bombing and reconnaissance prior to assuming command, in October 1917, of 41 Wing, a unit dedicated to countering the German night attacks on London. By the Armistice, both Dowding and Newall were Temporary Brigadier Generals, but the latter was also Trenchard's deputy.

On April 1st, 1918, the Royal Air Force had been born, with Major-General Trenchard the first Chief of the Air Staff (CAS) and known as 'Father' of the junior service. The Cadet College at Cranwell trained the service's officers, whilst technical training was provided by such schools as Halton. The RAF Staff College groomed future senior officers and the Central Flying School (CFS) set the high standards demanded of qualified flying instructors. Could the friction on the Somme between Trenchard and Dowding explain why the latter was not given a permanent commission as a Group Captain in the new service until August 1st, 1919? Nevertheless, by 1930 destiny was calling Dowding: on September 1st, he was appointed Air Member for Supply and Research. It was from this point onwards that 'Stuffy' Dowding started fighting the Battle of Britain.

Between April 1926 and February 1931, Air Commodore Cyril Newall, Trenchard's protégé and the first 'Bomber Baron', had served as both Director of Operations and Deputy Chief of the Air Staff (DCAS). On January 14th. 1935, Air Vice-Marshal Newall took on some of Air Vice-Marshal Dowding's duties as Air Member for Supply and Organisation, the latter's department then becoming Research and Development.

On the subject of between-the-wars aerial strategic thinking, it is worth quoting the following at this juncture:-

Marshal of the RAF Sir Hugh Trenchard, 1921:-

It is not necessary for an air force, in order to defeat the enemy nation, to defeat its armed forces first. Air power can dispense with that immediate step, can pass over the enemy navies and armies, and penetrate the air defences and attack direct the centre of production, transportation and communication from which the enemy war effort is maintained. It is on the destruction of enemy industries and, above all, in the lowering of morale of enemy nationals caused by bombing that the ultimate victory lies.

Trenchard also said that:-

The aeroplane is the most offensive weapon that has ever been invented. It is a shockingly bad weapon for defence.

In fact, Trenchard thought so little of defensive aeroplanes that he considered their worth only:-

.... necessary to have some defence to keep up the morale of your own people.

Stanley Baldwin, 1932:-

I think it is well for the man in the street to realise that there is no power on earth that can protect him from being bombed. Whatever people may tell him, the bomber will always get through. The only defence is offence, which means that you have to kill more women and children more quickly than the enemy if you want to save yourselves. I just mention that... so that people may realise what is waiting for them when the next war comes.

Hugh Dowding did not endorse the view that 'the bomber will always get through', or indeed that spending on the bomber force was necessarily the priority. On the contrary, he considered that although the fighter force should not be expanded at the bomber's expense, a powerful bomber force would be useless unless the fighter force was strong enough to ensure that its commander did not lose a decisive battle before the bomber force commander had time to fight one; Trenchard, said Dowding, had 'forgotten that "security of base" is an essential prerequisite.' It was fortunate for Britain, to say the least, that Air Marshal Dowding, Air Member for Research and Development, not only took this viewpoint but was also prepared to fight anyone who opposed his efforts to prepare a sound defence for these islands.

At the time of Dowding's appointment as the Air Member for Research and Development, the RAF's fighter squadrons remained equipped with biplanes. Constructed largely of wood and fabric, and generally armed with two machine-guns, the performance of these machines was little better than the fighters of the Great War. In 1912 Jacques Schneider, of the French armaments family, had instituted the Schneider Trophy, to be awarded to the victor of an international seaplane race. The experience gained by aircraft designers during the course of this competition, which was a matter of fierce national pride, was later put to good use in the creation of modern warplanes. Although Dowding had been against government funding of Supermarine's winning S.6B entrant, he did appreciate that Reginald Mitchell's designs held enormous promise for fighter aircraft. In 1930, the Air Ministry consequently issued specifications for a modern day and night fighter, capable of being flown by the average squadron pilot, to replace the RAF's existing obsolete biplanes. The Air Ministry's requirements were for higher speed and an enclosed cockpit in conjunction with eight-gun armament. It was in line with these specifications that the Rolls-Royce engined Hawker and Supermarine fighter projects progressed, leading to Specifications F.36/34 and F.37/34 then being drafted around the designs which were to become the Hurricane and Spitfire, respectively.

Gordon Mitchell, only child of the Spitfire designer Reginald Joseph Mitchell, with the prototype fighter, K5054.
(Dr. Gordon Mitchell)

The RAF air exercises in August 1934 had shown the weaknesses of the 'early warning system', which depended largely upon the Observer Corps. This obviously meant that the 'early warning' of hostile aircraft could only be given when they ventured within sight and earshot. Even when practising with the 80 mph Vickers Virginia at 7,000' the warning provided was inadequate. Trials had proved acoustic locators to be of little practical use, although the Chandler-Adcock system of radio direction-finding had made promising progress, enabling defending fighters to be 'fixed', 'plotted' and controlled from the ground. However, this system was also fundamentally flawed as it relied upon regular transmissions from the fighters concerned; hostile aircraft were likely to be much less obliging! A more general means of detection was therefore much required but yet to be discovered. Within the Air Ministry, Mr AP Rowe, the Assistant to the Director of of Scientific Research, felt so strongly about the matter that in June 1934 he reported to his chief, Harry Wimperis, that 'Unless science finds some new method of assisting air defence, any war within 10 years will be lost.'

As early as 1932 work by the Post Office had shown that aircraft reflected radio signals. In February 1935, at the request of the Tizard Committee, which had been formed to address the problems of air defence, Robert Watson-Watt submitted his report entitled 'Detection & Location of Aircraft by Radio Methods'. Recognising the significance of this detailed study, Wimperis and Tizard immediately requested £10,000 for experimental work, but the Air Member, Air Vice-Marshal Dowding, advocated caution and requested a practical demonstration: 'Let us first see if the system works'. Later that month, the 'Boffins' proved that it did.

Further developments were to be undertaken in secret on the Suffolk coast, under the guise of RDF - radio direction-finding. The creation of radar had completely transformed the ability of the defences to anticipate and thus defeat a bomber attack. The days of Trenchard's doctrine, 'the bomber will always get through', were over. Watson-Watt's inspired memorandum of February 1935 had identified three areas for research: the re-radiation of radio waves (to detect aircraft), radio-telephone communication between fighters and ground controller (to enable defending fighters to be directed towards hostile aircraft) and a means of transmitting coded signals from aircraft (to identify friend from foe). It was this technology, together with the modern, fast, eight-gun monoplane fighters, which was to form the cornerstone of the Radar-Based System of Early Warning, Interception and Control. A new chapter in aerial warfare, in which Dowding was playing a major role, had begun.

For more than a decade, all functions of air defence had been overseen by the Air Defence of Great Britain (ADGB), although the Commander-in-Chief was responsible for both the bomber and fighter forces, a system which Dowding found altogether 'ponderous'. The Expansion Scheme led to common-sense prevailing, and in 1936, five separate Commands were born: Fighter, Bomber, Coastal, Training and Maintenance. Dowding's experience as a Great War fighter Wing Commander, as a commander of the RAF Inland (Fighter) Area during the days of ADGB, and more recently, as Air Member for Supply and Research (the latter position having made him familiar both with the new monoplane fighters and RDF) made him the *perfect* choice for Fighter Command's first Commander-in-Chief.

Air Marshal Sir Hugh Dowding was 54 years old when he took up his new appointment as Air Officer Commanding RAF Fighter Command on July 14th, 1936. The new Command's HQ was located at Bentley Priory, a large country house situated to the north of London at Stanmore. He discovered there to be 'some lamentable deficiencies to be made good'. His immediate aim was to create the 'Ideal Air Defence' system, and his experience to date uniquely positioned him to succeed. Upon formation, Fighter Command consisted of two groups, 11 and 12, and for administrative purposes, No 22 Army Co-operation Group and the civilian Observer Corps. 11 Group had been formed in June 1936, its primary function being the defence of London and the south-east, whilst 12 Group was created in May 1937 to defend the eastern region from attacks approaching from the North Sea. Of course at that time any attack from Germany was expected to come from the east, without fighter escort (the range of which was of course limited). During the mid-1930s, no-one could foresee Hitler's unprecedented advance to the Channel coast in 1940, which thus put even London within the range of his single-engined Me 109 fighters. Prior to that occurrence, therefore, 12 Group, defending the industrial Midlands and the north, represented a crucial responsibility.

Under Air Marshal Dowding (who was promoted to Air Chief Marshal on New Year's Day, 1937), Fighter Command's 11 Group was first entrusted to Air Marshal Leslie Gossage. On December 14th, 1937, Air Commodore Trafford Leigh-Mallory became 12 Group's Air Officer Commanding.

Air Vice-Marshal Trafford Leigh-Mallory
(Author via Mr Ben Longridge)

Trafford Leigh-Mallory was born on July 11th, 1892, at Mobberley, Cheshire, his father being rector of the Anglican church there. On March 26th, 1911, Leigh-Mallory won an Exhibition scholarship to Magdalene College at Cambridge University where he read History. During the Great War, Lieutenant Leigh-Mallory served in France with the King's Liverpool Regiment, receiving a leg wound in June 1915. During the course of his recuperation, Leigh-Mallory volunteered for the RFC. By July 7th he was en route to join 5 Squadron, equipped with B.E.2d observation aircraft, at Droglandt.

At this time, the RFC's job was largely to act as the Army's scouts, providing advance information on German troop movements in addition to spotting for the artillery. On May 10th, 1917, Temporary Major Leigh-Mallory became OC of 15 Squadron, then, six months later, of 8 Squadron. With both units he flew further army co-operation flights. Previously published evidence suggests that Leigh-Mallory was not a popular squadron commander, being isolated, aloof and snobbish, and apparently more concerned with logistics than men's lives.

With 8 Squadron Leigh-Mallory was to significantly increase his experience of army co-operation, that unit carrying out the first air-to-tank liaison. The airmen's task was to warn tank commanders of enemy positions, but communications were difficult. Already having some experience of wireless telegraphy, Major Leigh-Mallory enthusiastically threw himself into solving the problem. The Armistice came on November 11th, 1918; for his wartime service, Major Leigh-Mallory received a DSO. His leadership of 8 Squadron, together with the extensive experience in army co-operation arising, laid the foundations for his subsequent RAF career.

Unlike that of Hugh Dowding, Leigh-Mallory's name appeared in the first 200 permanent commissions for the peacetime air force, published on August 1st, 1919. After training and staff appointments, in 1933 Group Captain Leigh-Mallory was sent to the Imperial Defence College (IDC) for a year. The IDC is the most senior of all the services' staff colleges, and Leigh-Mallory's selection to study there indicated that he was destined for Air rank. In 1937, Air Commodore

Leigh-Mallory became the AOC of 12 (Fighter) Group, and with his wife, Doris, set up home at Woodborough Hall, Hucknall, Nottinghamshire. Thus an army co-operation expert, with significant experience of training and administration but none of fighters, become entrusted with the aerial defence of the Midlands.

For Air Chief Marshal Dowding, one of the biggest problems of air defence remained the provision of a facility to give defending fighters sufficient warning to get off the ground and make interceptions. Just how crucial this was can perhaps be best appreciated by considering that the closing speed of the then modern fighter aircraft was reaching 500 mph. Having already grasped the potential of Watson-Watt's experiments whilst Air Member for Research and Development, Dowding was able, as Commander-in-Chief of Fighter Command, to integrate RDF into the System of Air Defence. In 1936, approval was given for building RDF stations, the first being constructed along the eastern approaches to the Thames. By the summer of 1940, the radar chain around the United Kingdom consisted of 22 Chain Home stations, supplemented by 30 Chain Home Low stations. Each was positioned to ensure, at least in theory, that every aircraft approaching Britain from the east or south would be detected by a minimum of two stations. RDF therefore became the keystone of Dowding's defence, with its network of stations, together with Observer Corps posts and centres, sector operations rooms, radio-telephony transmitters, landlines and ancillary devices all comprising the 'System'.

All of the RDF stations (except those in the later-formed 10 Group, which reported to the Western Filter Room at Group HQ) passed their information by direct landline to the underground Filter Room at Bentley Priory. There the information received was sifted by filterers and filter officers, a gridded map providing a visual display. The filtered information was then passed by tellers through closed speech circuits to the adjacent Command Operations Room and on to the appropriate Group and Sector Operations Rooms. It actually took just five minutes between a radar operator observing a plot to its appearance in the operations rooms.

It was impractical for the whole of Great Britain to be protected by two unwieldy groups, and so 13 Group became responsible for both the north of England and Northern Ireland, whilst 10 Group, which did not become operational until July 8th, 1940, protected the West Country and South Wales. The groups were then sub-divided into sectors, the main airfield in each being known as the Sector Station. Once the RDF information had been processed at Stanmore the details for the relevant area were received by a Group Operations Room. The 'plot' would then be displayed on the Group Operations Room map, but this did not include the overall Fighter Command picture, as did that at Stanmore. Nevertheless, with the information thus provided, either the Group Commander or Group Air Controller would then decide how best to meet the incoming raid given his available forces. Each airfield had its own control room and Controller who guided his fighters by radio telephone, based upon information and orders received from Group. Significantly, Dowding believed that tactical control of his 'System' should not be exercised from Bentley Priory, nor even from Group during hectic action. In establishing this system, which was excellent given the technology available at the time, Dowding in effect ultimately saved the country. This far-sighted delegation of tactical control, however, was to have very negative political consequences for him during the Battle of Britain itself.

When he became Commander-in-Chief of Fighter Command, Dowding initially had aspirations to succeed Marshal of the Royal Air Force Sir Edward Ellington as CAS. Right from the outset at Fighter Command, however, Dowding had resolved to do whatever was necessary to make the 'base', Britain, safe. He had to virtually start from scratch, and time was greatly against him. As we have seen he opposed the generally accepted view that the 'Bomber will always get through', and instead believed that the home base had first to be made secure. His unshakeable belief in this principle, indeed that it 'overrides all considerations', led to an obstinate insistence that his demands be met. He was to find himself in almost continual dispute with the Air Staff, where, he would later write, his name 'stank'. In June 1935, whilst still at the Air Ministry, Dowding was unaware that Air Vice-Marshal Newall was already being groomed to take Ellington's position. That the job as head of the service went to Newall, junior in rank and younger by four years, cut Air Chief Marshal Dowding to the quick. Newall, the choice of Lord Swinton (the Secretary of State for Air), had taken Dowding's place in France 20 years before; had Dowding left Fighter Command before the Battle of Britain, the consequences would probably been catastrophic not only for Britain but also the free world. He was the *only* man capable of making the home base safe.

From February 1938 until April 1940, the Assistant Chief of the Air Staff (ACAS) was Air Vice-Marshal Sholto Douglas. Born in 1893, Douglas was reading 'Greats' at Oxford in 1913, but his studies were rudely interrupted by the outbreak of war and he went to France with the Royal Horse Artillery. In 1915, he volunteered for observer duties with the RFC; his first flight, from Merville with 2 Squadron, was, in fact, on an operational mission! Shortly afterwards he was accepted for pilot training and within three months was back in France, flying two-seater, single-engined, Bristol Fighters during what was the early period of the 'Fokker Scourge'.

Air Vice-Marshal Sholto Douglas   *The gun turret of the controversial Defiant fighter*
(Both: Author via Mr Norman Jenkins)

In June 1938, Douglas informed Dowding that he must form nine squadrons of Defiants for day-fighting. The Defiant was a two-seater, but its only armament was four .303" machine-guns situated in a power-operated turret. How was a pilot, himself unable to aim directly, supposed to position his aircraft so that his gunner could open fire at a target which he (the pilot) could not necessarily see? Furthermore, the extra weight imposed by a second crewman and a gun-turret upon an airframe powered by the same Merlin engine as the lighter Hurricane, which was in service by that time, made for a considerable reduction in performance. Nevertheless, the Air Ministry had ordered some 450 Defiants in the very mistaken belief that the type would emulate the Bristol Fighter's success in the Great War. As an exponent of the latter type, Douglas was an enthusiastic supporter of the Defiant, arguing that 'for work over enemy territory a two-seater fighter is best'. What he, and the others involved, had overlooked was that the Bristol Fighter's success was largely due to its forward-firing armament, something which the Defiant lacked.

Dowding, as ever, recognised the incompetence of the Air Staff in respect of this matter and was understandably angry that such an important decision had been taken without his consultation. Douglas was supported by Air Vice-Marshal Sir Edgar Ludlow-Hewitt, the Commander-in-Chief of Bomber Command, and Air Vice-Marshal Donald Stevenson, the Deputy Director of Home

Operations. Despite the obvious facts, the latter believed that the Defiant was 'slightly faster' than the Hurricane! However, by June 1939, Stevenson had doubts and informed Dowding that Fighter Command must have nine, rather than the original 15, Defiant-equipped squadrons. Dowding still fought the issue, and although his initial response that Defiants should be confined to training was rejected, only two operational squadrons were formed. Unfortunately Dowding was only to be proved completely right by the virtual annihilation of those two units during the early stages of the Battle of Britain, after which the Defiant was withdrawn and reserved for night-fighting.

In July 1938, Air Chief Marshal Dowding received a new Senior Air Staff Officer (SASO) at Bentley Priory, Air Commodore Keith Park. In this loyal and tough New Zealander fighter 'ace', 'Stuffy' Dowding was to find the perfect right-hand man.

Air Vice-Marshal Keith Park
(Author via Mr Keith Park)

Keith Rodney Park was born in Thames, Auckland, on June 15th, 1892. In 1914, he joined the artillery as a Lance-Bombardier. Park fought at Gallipoli with the New Zealand 'Big Guns', and in July was commissioned as a Second Lieutenant. In August 1915, he became a regular officer in the British Army, continuing to serve as an artilleryman in the Dardenelles. In 1916, the Allied forces were evacuated from the peninsula and six months later Park was plunged into an even greater hell: the first Battle of the Somme. On October 21st, 1916, a shell exploded beneath Park's horse, killing the beast and wounding him. Invalided back to England, there Park later effected a transfer to the RFC, his wounds having graded him as 'unfit to ride a horse'.

Park went on to gain his pilot's 'wings' and by the time he was posted to 48 Squadron at La Bellevue in 1917, had some 135 flying hours; this experience ensured that he was well prepared for combat. Park was already a mature, battle-hardened officer who understood what was happening on the ground and knew what was expected of him in the air. To his credit Park even took personal care of his aircraft's machine-guns and sights, in addition to taking an interest in the technical aspects of both his flying machine and engine.

On July 24th, 1917, Park and his gunner, Second Lieutenant AW Merchant, were attacked by three Albatross scouts near Middelkerke. After the battle, Park's combat report claimed one destroyed, and two probables, although in fact he and Noss had also damaged a fourth enemy aircraft. For 'dash and tenacity', Park and Noss were immediately awarded the Military Cross. In 26 days, Park and his gunners destroyed seven more enemy aircraft, and damaged at least five others. Brigadier Becke recommended him for the DSO, but Trenchard decreed that a Bar to his

MC would suffice.

As a fighter pilot and leader, Park had not only earned respect, but had also learned important lessons about the conduct of fighter warfare. In 1922, reflecting on his Western Front experiences, Park maintained that in a future war, squadrons should be widely dispersed when on the ground, ground-strafing would be best conducted by small, fast, agile scouts with forward-firing armament, close escorts would not be effective when opposition was encountered, and that finally, tactics should be studied well in advance, on the ground, rather than 'on the spot'.

After returning from France, Park received two training commands before commencing a course at No 2 School of Navigation and Bomb Dropping. There the commanding officer encouraged voluntary long-distance flights. Consequently, at the end of April 1919, Park and a Captain Stewart flew a circuit of the British Isles: 1,880 miles at an average speed of just 66 mph! This was only the second time such a flight had been undertaken, and so it achieved much publicity. In June, Park was awarded the DFC, ostensibly for the aforementioned flight, but in reality to console him for a catalogue of bureaucratic incompetence which had deprived him of promotion. The episode, understandably, infuriated Park, now a career officer now with much ground to make up, and embittered him against the Air Ministry.

On August 1st, 1919, he received a permanent commission and became a Flight Lieutenant commanding a reserve of surplus aircraft at Hawkinge. In 1920, a display of RAF aerial prowess took place at Hendon. Squadron Leader Sholto Douglas suggested a daring low-level flypast by three Handley Page V/1500 bombers, of a type included in Park's store. Douglas arranged with the latter that three would be made ready, with each of them flying one, and another pilot the third. The display transpired to be Hendon's highlight, but the CAS, Trenchard, was less impressed with the low-level exhibition and rebuked Douglas, another career officer. Park and Douglas remained ever-distant after this incident, which may help to explain certain matters involving them both some 20 years later. In 1922, the pair joined another later RAF notable, Squadron Leader Charles Portal (to become Marshal of the Royal Air Force the Viscount Portal of Hungerford), at the RAF Staff College. Although the rift between Douglas and Park failed to heal during this time, Park found an ally in Portal who would later speak up for him at several critical moments.

In September 1923, whilst serving in Cairo, a medical examination decided that Park was fit to fly for no more than two hours a day, and only at altitudes below 5,000'; his previous medical history indicated that he would not cope well with stress. How wrong he was to prove that doctor in 1940! In June 1926, Park was summoned home for yet another medical, which found him A1B (fit for all duties in his branch of the air force). He was not to return to Egypt, however, since a chance meeting in London with Air Commodore Holt, Chief of Staff to Air Marshal Sir John Salmond, Commander-in-Chief of ADGB, lcd to an appointment on the latter's staff at Uxbridge. Park was given command of a department, known as 'Operations, Intelligence Mobilisation and Combined Training'. As ADGB had only been formed a year previously, Park was involved with planning this Britain's air defence almost from the outset.

In November 1927, Squadron Leader Park was rewarded with command of his own fighter squadron, 111. On New Year's Day 1929, he was promoted to Wing Commander and upon leaving the Squadron in March was posted to HQ Fighting Area at Uxbridge for staff duties. Typically, Park drove himself so hard that he made himself ill again; in 1930 a medical board sent him on leave for a month, advising him to have a complete break from RAF work, words echoed by the Fighting Area's commander: Air Vice-Marshal Hugh Dowding. It is generally little known that the association between these two officers commenced a decade before the Battle of Britain.

Between January 1931 and August 1932, Park served as Station Commander at Northolt; by the time that command expired, he had six years' experience in front-line home defence. However, the next five years were spent in posts removed from fighters and home defence, such as being Chief Instructor at the Oxford University Air Squadron. It might have been considered that Park needed to broaden his social experience prior to climbing further up the ladder. This he certainly did at Oxford, and again in 1934, when, as a 43-year-old Group Captain, he became Air Attaché in South America. In December 1937, Park returned to fighters when he was made Station Commander of RAF Tangmere, near Chichester. There Park enjoyed a last fling as a biplane pilot, flying Hawker Furies, before promotion to Air Commodore on July 1st, 1938, bringing with it the job of Dowding's SASO at Fighter Command. Destiny had now also called Keith Park.

From the foregoing, it can be readily appreciated that Air Commodore Park was not only a fighter 'ace' in his own right, but also a man with great experience of fighters and related tactics. Air Commodore Park immediately grasped Fighter Command's planned method of operation, as implemented by his chief, and went on to help Dowding improve it. Fortunately for Britain, these two men probably knew as much about fighters as anyone else in the world at that time.

Air Commodore Park was largely concerned with fighter tactics whilst at Bentley Priory, and the first major issue with which he was involved concerned the Defiant question. As a result of this he and Dowding upset Air Vice-Marshals Douglas, Stevenson and Ludlow-Hewitt. It was an early indication that, to perfect the 'System', the Commander-in-Chief and his new SASO were going to have to fight hard against incompetent interference.

Park recognised various deficiencies in Air Ministry policies and tactics. After the Munich Crisis, he reported on the shortcomings identified in the arrangements made to meet the threat. Fighter Command was short by some 10 squadrons, and only 25% of the existing units were monoplane-equipped. The Sector Control System required expansion in both Scotland and south-western England, and more airfields were needed, beyond those already in service requiring various improvements. Even more RDF stations were required, together with increased general manpower. It is doubtful whether such a critical, although accurate, report was well-received at Whitehall.

A report in October 1938 from Air Vice-Marshal Leigh-Mallory was even less well-received at Bentley Priory. In this memorandum, regarding the air defence of the United Kingdom north of London, he made no mention of monoplanes, and the emphasis was upon local, as opposed to area, defence. No appreciation was shown of other aspects of the System, such as a requirement for an increased number of searchlights and improved wireless telephony. For this plan, however, 12 Group's AOC requested 29 of Fighter Command's 41 squadrons, thus leaving 12 for the rest of the country, including London! Dowding and Park were horrified at what amounted to a complete misunderstanding of the basic principles of fighter defence.

The monoplane fighters remained in short supply, so much so, in fact, that few squadrons were equipped with them by this time. With so little experience in their operation, the problem of how best to employ them tactically posed a very difficult question. The Air Fighting Committee at the Air Ministry considered such matters as the best methods for attacking enemy aircraft, including the types of formations to be used in order to maximise the concentration of fire. Experiments were conducted by the Air Fighting Development Establishment (AFDE), and as a result the suggested basic fighter formation was the 'vic' of three aircraft, flying in close formation, the idea being that 24 machine-guns could be brought to bear simultaneously. However, during the Spanish Civil War of the mid-1930s the Germans had discovered that such formations were useless for fighter combat as they were too inflexible. Each pilot had to concentrate too much on formation flying and thus spent precious little time searching for the enemy. The *Luftwaffe* fighters therefore flew in a loose, stepped-up formation of four aircraft in line abreast, known as the *Schwarm*; when battle was joined, the formation split into two fighting pairs, each known as a *Rotte*, consisting of a leader and wingman.

The Fighter Command Manual of Air Tactics stipulated that a fighter could only attack from directly below or astern. Park realised that some 'latitude' was required, and in January 1939 he wrote to the Air Ministry openly criticising its fighter tactics. Far-sightedly, he remarked that 'The possibility of bombers having fighter escorts even in attacks on London should not be overlooked.' The following month he issued new instructions, 'Fighter Command Attacks, 1939' which again, however, concentrated upon attacks against perfectly formated bombers, and *assumed* that combined fire power was advantageous. In Park's favour, he stressed that the instructions were *not* a drill to be inflexibly followed, as formation leaders were to use their initiative in the air (having first been guided to the target by the Ground Controller).

An important question was the overall size of the intercepting formation. On April 3rd, 1939, Air Marshal Gossage, AOC 11 Group, sent a memorandum to his station and squadron commanders:-

Fighter Attacks - 1939

The Air Officer Commanding-in-Chief, Fighter Command has stated that his policy in regard to the engagement of enemy bomber formations, is to match a fighter against each bomber of the enemy formation so far as this is a practical proposition.

2.   In Fighter Command Attacks, 1939, it will be noted that this policy does not find its fullest expression in that the largest number of bombers which are simultaneously engaged by fighters is six. This limitation is at present occasioned by the following considerations:-

i)   Some squadrons have not had their monoplane fighters long enough to be able to employ them efficiently in formations greater than sections or flights.

ii)   In Air Exercises the best and most economical use has to be made of the target-aircraft which can be obtained for interception practice. For instance, if 60 bombers are available they are best used in flights or sections in order to give the maximum practice to as many fighter flights as possible, as opposed to operating the bombers in two masses of 30 or five formations of 12 aircraft.

iii)   It is desirable, from the point of view of training junior leaders, that interception exercises shall be carried out by flights or sections so that the maximum amount of practice, initiative, and experience can be obtained.

Thus it will be seen that training in the tactical handling of the formations of squadron strength has not been pursued as much as it might have been.

3.   The Air Officer Commanding-in-Chief holds the view that the squadron is likely to be the largest tactical unit employed in the simultaneous attack of a large enemy formation and that if two or more squadrons have to be despatched to engage such a raid, squadrons would attack in succession, as individual units, acting upon the initiative of their squadron commanders when interception had been made.

4.   Progress should now be made with the investigation of the problems which the performance attacks present. The AOC-in-C. intends that the pioneer work in this respect should be carried out under the auspices of the A.F.D.E. at Northolt, but he is, at the same time, desirous that other fighter stations should direct their training to this end also as soon as station commanders are satisfied that the state of their units permits this being done. Station commanders are therefore requested to notify these Headquarters and ask permission for the squadron or squadrons

concerned, pending the issue of further attacks by Fighter Command, to commence their training in the simultaneous attack of formations in excess of six bombers. For this purpose other fighter aircraft on the station should be used as targets, deployed at reasonably wide intervals to represent Bomber conditions.

At the time of Air Marshal Gossage's memorandum, it can be seen that the entire tactical thinking was geared towards small fighter formations, more training having been undertaken in respect of the flight, of six aircraft, than as a cohesive squadron of 12. There were also problems in obtaining realistic practice intercepts in training because of antagonisms between Fighter and Bomber Commands. In December 1938, Air Commodore Park had written frankly to the Air Officer Commanding-in-Chief of Bomber Command, Air Chief Marshal Sir Edgar Ludlow-Hewitt, criticising the fact that, in respect of training requirements, the latter ignored testing fighters and, therefore, the System of Air Defence. Ludlow-Hewitt much resented such a rebuke from an Air Commodore, but fortunately Dowding, as the senior officer, supported his SASO.

From July 8-9th, 1939, 11 Group conducted a simulated defence of southern England against an 'attack' by Bomber Command. 12 Group did likewise the following week in relation to a 'raid' on northern England. A conference on July 24th at Bentley Priory noted that 11 Group's success rate was a reasonable 60%. 12 Group's was less, but this was a result of Air Vice-Marshal Leigh-Mallory's fighters having started practising the new interception techniques later than Gossage's south-eastern squadrons, and the Group's RDF being less reliable. The exercises continued to be unrealistic, however, owing to the small number of bombers allocated by Air Chief Marshal Ludlow-Hewitt.

In August 1939 a further exercise was conducted using a larger number of bombers. The results were somewhat embarrassing for Air Vice-Marshal Leigh-Mallory. A low-level raid had surprised certain of 12 Group's sectors, which thereafter forced the AOC to mount constant standing patrols. Dowding and Park considered that these patrols were too extensive, and therefore an overreaction; too many fighters had been diverted from the primary task of intercepting bombers attacking vital targets and were instead employed in the defence of their own bases. Furthermore, during a night attack, the 12 Group Operations Room was evacuated for 10 minutes. Dowding consequently directed Leigh-Mallory that neither Group nor Sector operations rooms were to be evacuated unless dictated by damage. Clearly, without the Operations Room, the System broke down. With the benefit of hindsight, it is difficult to understand why officers of Air rank were promoted to commands in which they had no previous experience. Such appointments were acceptable in *peacetime*, however, for career officers to broaden their experience.

On August 9th, 1939, the Air Ministry wrote to Air Chief Marshal Dowding on the subject of 'Tactics v Massed Bomber Formations'. To quote selectively therefrom:-

On the one hand it is said that the air fighting problem does not really extend beyond the tactical situation involved in combats between units of squadron size, because a massed attack of the type envisaged will, in fact, take the form of a number of squadron formations in quick succession, possibly some hundreds of yards apart. Furthermore, to meet such an attack it is unlikely that a fighter formation exceeding squadron strength will be mustered and operated as one tactical unit before interception, and the chances of more than one fighter squadron attacking at the same moment are very small. The air fighting problem, therefore, is covered adequately by the investigations of the Air Fighting Development Establishment by formations of squadron strength.

Wing Commander GM Lawson, a member of Park's Operations staff, provided the following information to assist the Commander-in-Chief's reply:-

It is considered that a fighter tactical unit consisting of more than one squadron would not be able to carry out the role of interception and attack as efficiently as a squadron formation. It would take longer to climb to the height of the enemy formation, and it could not manoeuvre as quickly into position for the attack. In all probability, unless the enemy was intercepted at very close range, the Wing fighter formation would have to split up in order to close quickly with the enemy bombers. It would probably be necessary in any case for the Wing fighter formation to split up into squadrons or flights in order to bring effective fire against the greatest number of bombers at the same time. Attacks in Wing formation would be impracticable in conditions of heavy cloud, bad visibility, or at low height.

The school of thought which is in favour of large formations suggests that the aim should be to concentrate in strength before attacking.

It is considered that time is the important factor in interception and attack. The aim should be to attack the enemy as soon as possible, and not to wait until we have concentrated in strength before attacking.

The Memorandum gives particulars of the area covered by a large bomber formation. It is improbable that this represents a true war picture. It ignores the probability of dispersion after a long flight over the sea, after heavy AA fire, and after attacks by our fighters. The enemy bomber formation would almost certainly be dispersed over a larger area, and in Groups which would be unable to support each other by rear gunfire when the fighters attacked. These dispersed groups of bombers could be dealt with more effectively by fighters operating in flight or squadron strength.

Apart from the operational objections referred to above, it is suggested that peace training must be regulated to war conditions. It might be possible to train our regular fighter squadrons in wing tactics in peace, but it is doubtful whether it would be practicable to maintain that high standard in war.

On August 19th, 1939, Dowding replied to the Air Ministry:-

It is only a year ago since there existed a considerable body of opinion to the effect that high-speed monoplane fighters would not be able to deploy and deliver a simultaneous attack against an enemy formation owing to the danger of collision and of shooting one another.

2.   These fears, although not groundless, are proving to be exaggerated, and sections and flights are now habitually deployed for attack and we are working towards the habitual deployment of complete squadrons.

3.   The training required for these tactics, however, is by no means inconsiderable and, although I am glad to say that no collision has yet occurred in aircraft deployed for straightforward attack following a direct approach, I have observed several instances in which one fighter has flown into the cone of fire of another when the target aircraft have adopted the rotating method of avoiding action.

4.   While, therefore, I do not discount the possibility of mass deployment at some future time, I can say without hesitation that even tentative and experimental work in this connection would be premature at present.

5.   My own opinion (which I do not want to over-stress at the moment), is that the squadron will always be the largest tactical unit which it will be practically expedient to employ.

6.   The main object of simultaneous and combined attack is to secure superiority of fire, and each individual fighter has at present so great a superiority of fire against its "opposite number" that the situation may be considered satisfactory, and we ought not to sacrifice the speed,

flexibility and safety of our deployment for theoretical advantages which are likely to be illusory in practice.

7.   I agree that, on the evidence available, the *Geschwader* of 27 or 30 aircraft is the most likely formation in which the Germans would deliver their attacks, but I should propose to operate against such a formation at the present moment by flights in succession and, probably, later by squadrons.

8.   A further point is that under our present organisation, squadrons use different wavelengths, even when they are in the same Sector, and cohesion of attack would be difficult to ensure unless all aircraft were working on the same wavelength.

9.   I should make it clear that the above remarks apply to the fixed-gun single-seater fighter. If, and when, multi-seater fighters are adopted in the Service, the problem must be reconsidered on its merits.

Already, the size of intercepting formations were causing debate. Certain points raised by Air Chief Marshal Dowding are interesting. Firstly, his fourth paragraph indicates that he remained receptive to 'mass deployment', should circumstances dictate, although his personal view was that 'the squadron will always be the largest tactical unit it will be practically expedient to employ.'

In September 1939, the same month during which war was declared on Nazi Germany, Air Vice-Marshal Leigh-Mallory caused further concern at Bentley Priory. Dowding had expressly told his Group commanders not to issue their own local instructions in addition to Fighter Command battle orders, which covered the movement of squadrons. Dowding fully appreciated that to reflect changing military situations squadrons would have to move freely about the Command. Local orders only served to confuse the issue, a standard operating procedure being required. Despite having been told to cancel his local orders of September 5th, Leigh-Mallory wrote further to his sectors, and Dowding, on September 26th, concerning the disposition of squadrons:-

In view of the small number of squadrons in any one sector, and taking into consideration the fact that the Germans may deliver large scale raids on such important places as Birmingham, Derby and Sheffield, it is highly desirable that it should be possible to concentrate aircraft from as many other sectors as possible on to the front of the threatened target.

On October 1st, 1939, Air Chief Marshal Dowding replied:-

Dear Leigh-Mallory,

I have been reading your 12G/S.1292 dated 26th September, 1939, on the subject of lateral reinforcement.

2.   I find your paragraph 2 very difficult to understand. I take it that you mean that in some circumstances Digby would require strong reinforcements, and in other circumstances Wittering.

3.   In the former case you would have five squadrons at Digby, and in the latter no less than seven squadrons at Wittering.

4.   Now I have delegated tactical control almost completely to Groups and Sectors, but I have not delegated strategical control, and the threat to the line must be regarded as a whole and not parochially. The units at Debden and Duxford may be urgently required at short notice for the defence of London and, although they have been put under you to balance the number of stations

in groups, this function of theirs must not be overlooked. (You will remember there is an emergency order "Concentrate on London", which involves action by these two stations).

5. Then again, I do not wish normally to operate more than three squadrons from one aerodrome, or four squadrons under one Sector Commander. Aerodromes must not become too crowded, and our organisation allows only four wavelengths to each Sector. This of course does not prevent formations flying and fighting in another sector so long as they are operated by their own Sector Controller.

6. I note that you have made arrangements to operate a fifth wavelength in a Sector by means of the R/T Tender, but this was not the purpose for which R/T Tenders were provided.

7. The last part of your letter is also a little difficult to understand. I imagine that the crystals referred to are for the groundsets only.

8. Please do not think that I am criticising you in this letter. I admire the energy and foresight which you are bringing to your task. I would only ask you to remember that the Fighter Command has to operate as a whole, and reinforcements and readjustments may have to be made between groups and not only within them. We require a simple and flexible system which can be put into effect at short notice and with the minimum of preliminary arrangement. My idea is that I shall never put more than four squadrons into a sector, that crystal and control arrangements exist for this to be done in such a way that any squadron, and not only a previously selected squadron, can be moved, and that if more than four squadrons have to intercept and fight in any one sector they will do so under the control of neighbouring Sector Commanders.

The Commander-in-Chief's letter clearly lays down both his strategic thinking and what was expected from his Group Commanders. Significantly, in view of later events, Dowding indicated that there was every intention to utilise Duxford squadrons in the defence of London (Debden was a part of 12 Group until August 1940). The letter did not, however, prevent the ambitious and insubordinate Air Vice-Marshal Leigh-Mallory from later contravening the fundamental instructions contained therein. On October 3rd, 1939, Leigh-Mallory responded to Dowding, claiming that his previous letter 'concerning lateral reinforcement cannot have been a very good memorandum as it misled you regarding my intentions.' He went on:-

2. This matter has been frequently discussed by me with my Sector Commanders, and this type of reinforcement has been practised during some of my Group Exercises, so that my Sector Commanders are fully conversant with my ideas. This is why the whole scheme was not more comprehensively explained in my memorandum.

3. What I have in mind is a German mass attack of say 300-400 aircraft being delivered against one of the important objectives in the Midlands. in any one Sector I have only 24 aircraft for day operations, and consequently if such an attack develops, I must be able to bring in aircraft from adjoining sectors to counter it.

4. I can assure you that there is no intention on my part to upset the strategic situation in the Command, but only to make the greatest tactical use of the units in my group. This scheme provides purely for air reinforcement, and it is not intended that any aircraft should land at an aerodrome other than their own, so that the times during which squadrons would be away from

their parent aerodromes would vary between about 40 minutes, in the case of Digby reinforcing Wittering, and Wittering reinforcing Digby, and about an hour and a quarter for Duxford reinforcing Digby.

5.   As it is purely an air reinforcement the Duxford squadrons would be in R/T touch with either their own ground station or with one working their wavelength at Digby, by which it would be possible to recall them in the event of a threat developing further south.

6.   You will see from the above remarks that I have no intention of departing from what you say in paragraph 5.

7.   In regard to paragraph 6 of your letter, if you remember, last autumn, when it was laid down how the R/T Tenders should be allotted, they were sited so that sectors could operate on the front of adjoining sectors. With this end in view, the R/T tenders in the Wittering Sector, for instance, were sited at:-

     a)   Wainfleet All Saints, from which aircraft from Wittering could fly up as far as Donna Nook, and

     b)   West Raynham, from which it is possible to operate as far as Great Yarmouth and Honington into the Duxford Sector.

8.   To take a concentrated attack on Rolls-Royce at Derby, as an example, as how I was proposing to carry out this type of reinforcement. Digby would carry out the first interception about Skegness. Wittering then intercept about Horncastle, working with their R/T Tender at Wainfleet All Saints. Digby would carry out a third interception in the neighbourhood of Digby; the Duxford squadrons, as they have furthest to come, would intercept in the area Newark, Bottesford. The Germans might very easily direct a mass attack of 300-400 aircraft against Derby, and even with this method of reinforcing I would only bring 60 fighters into action against them.

9.   With regard to paragraph 7 of your letter, the crystals referred to are for ground sets only as with this type of reinforcement there would not be time for aircraft to land and change crystals as the opportunity would be lost.

10.   I can assure you that in any operations of this nature I shall always be watching the situation to the south of me most carefully, as I realise the reinforcement of London may, in certain circumstances, become my primary task. With this end in view I have arranged not only to concentrate the Duxford and Debden squadrons for that purpose but for Debden to hold a crystal for No 213 Squadron, which they could operate on their fourth R/T set, and 213 Squadron could thus be utilised to operate in the vicinity of Harlow.

The AOC 12 Group's response appears to have satisfied his Commander-in-Chief, who responded a week later, observing that:-

I had misunderstood your former letter, and, if one Sector Commander does not try to handle more than four squadrons the plan ought to work all right.

The chief difficulty might be from jambing between wave-lengths of units in adjoining sectors, but I see that you intend to operate units one after the other and not simultaneously.

In the example you give in paragraph 8, do not overlook the possibility of some of the earlier squadrons being able to land and rearm quickly so as to be able to have a second go on the return journey.

Despite this correspondence, Air Chief Marshal Dowding actually had more pressing matters with which to deal, being concerned principally with the number of squadrons available to defend Britain. On September 16th, 1939, he had written to the Under-Secretary of State at the Air Ministry:-

I have the honour to refer to my recent conversation with the Secretary of State for Air and my meeting with the Deputy Chief of the Air Staff on the 14th instant, and to request that the following considerations may be brought to the notice of the Air Council.

2.   The Air Council's estimate of the number of Fighter Squadrons necessary for the defence of this country is 52. This estimate has been endorsed by the committee of Imperial Defence.

3.   On September 3rd, 1939, I had 25 Regular Squadrons and 14 Auxiliary Squadrons in various stages of efficiency; say, the equivalent of 34 Squadrons.

4.   This, although much below the Air Council's estimate of requirements for Home Defence, was, in my opinion, sufficient to cause such heavy casualties to an attacker that in a comparatively short space of time his attacks would be brought to a standstill.

5.   In August I was asked to broadcast to the nation and I expressed myself to this effect.

6.   My opinion, however, was based on the assumption that, on the outbreak of war, every nerve would be strained to increase the Defence force up to the strength laid down by the Air Council themselves.

7.   It is true that 4 Squadrons had for years been earmarked for dispatch with the Field Force, but I had been repeatedly told that these Squadrons would never be dispatched until the safety of the Home Base had been assured.

8.   My consternation, then, will be understood when I learned that 4 Hurricane Squadrons were to be dispatched to France within 10 days of the Declaration of War and before any attack had been made on this country.

9.   In addition, I had received orders to put 6 more Hurricane Squadrons on a mobile basis by January 1940; and, although I received assurances that these would never be withdrawn from the Defence unless this could be done with safety, I know how much reliance to place on such assurances.

10.   My next shock was to discover that the Air Ministry contemplated the reduction of my remaining Fighter Squadrons from 36 to 27 in a few months time; (actually the Organisation Staff were wrong in supposing that I had 36 Squadrons. The number is 35 and, therefore, the number to which I am to be reduced is presumably 26).

11.   This is a grim prospect - the number is exactly half that laid down by the Air Council as necessary for the Defence of the country.

12.   A further unpleasant surprise awaited us; that the output of Hurricanes is less than 2 per diem and will not reach 3 per diem until April next year.

13.   I then took my copy of the Wastage Tables, and worked out the monthly wastage for 4 Field Force Squadrons, assuming no "maximum effort", one week's "intensive effort", and three weeks "sustained effort" in this time: also that 3 Squadrons operated by day and 1 by night.

14.   The wastage works out at 60 per month, which is greater than the present total output and leaves nothing for the 21 Home Squadrons which are either equipped with Hurricanes or due for such equipment.

15.   Furthermore, one Group Pool equipped with Hurricanes is in existence, and another is under orders to form.

16.   Counting a Group Pool as two Training Squadrons, and assuming that a second will not form, the number per month required for the Hurricane Units at home is 184 against "Scale 'B' Opposition" and without any "maximum" or "intensive" effort.

17.   It is clear, therefore, that the dispatch of 4 Field Force Squadrons has opened a tap through which will run the total Hurricane output, and that the Hurricane Squadrons at Home would become a diminishing force, doomed to extinction in February 1940 if the figures in S.D. 98 were accepted.

18.   Now, there are not 21 Hurricane Squadrons at Home, and it is clear that there never will be, because there is no source from which they can be formed: there are actually 14. Furthermore, I do not believe that casualties in Home Defence will be nearly so high as is indicated by S.D. 98 - otherwise I should have been criminally dishonest in reassuring the Public in my broadcast. (I do, however, believe that the figures for the Field Force Fighters, which will encounter enemy Fighters in numbers, are by no means exaggerated, and may in fact be considerably understated if Fighter Squadrons are caught by a heavy ground attack).

19.   The fact nevertheless remains that these 14 Squadrons will have no source of Hurricane replacement and must continuously waste until some new source of supply becomes available.

20.   It now remains to extricate ourselves from the very serious predicament in which we are placed. I am handicapped in making definite suggestions because I have access only to the production figures of Hurricanes and Spitfires. I do not know when the Defiants will come out, nor do I know the Blenheim figures; but I have seen enough to believe that it is physically impossible at the moment to adopt my previous suggestion that 12 new Fighter Squadrons should be formed immediately.

21.   The general outline of my scheme would be to have 1 Blenheim Squadron at each Sector Station to do the night work (with the aid of the A.I. R.D.F.), and to liberate the 9-gun Fighters

for day work, thus incidentally reducing wastage. I have 7 Squadrons which either have, or have recently had Blenheims, and I propose that the latter should revert to that type. I should then have 7 Blenheim Squadrons and 15 Sector Stations, so 8 new Blenheim Squadrons must be formed. I would do this even if it meant breaking up the Non-Mobilizable Squadrons of the Bomber Command.

22.   I would re-equip Nos. 610 and 616 Squadrons with Spitfires, and get them into the line at once.

23.   I would re-equip Nos. 610 and 615 Squadrons with Spitfires as soon as possible, thus releasing Gladiators for other purposes.

24.   I should then have: -

15 Blenheim Squadrons - Nos. 23, 25, 29, 64, 600. 601, 604 and 8 new Squadrons.
15 Spitfire Squadrons - Nos. 19, 41, 54, 65, 66, 72, 74, 602, 603, 607, 609, 610, 611, 615 and 616.
13 Hurricane Squadrons - Nos. 3, 17, 32, 43, 46, 56, 79, 111, 151, 213, 501, 504 and 605.

25.   As the Hurricane Squadrons dwindled, I would replace them by Defiants, which are now beginning to come out.

26.   Finally I must entreat with all the force at my command that the Air Council will take this matter seriously. They have laid down a strength of 52 Squadrons as necessary for the defence of this country. They apparently contemplate with equanimity a reduction of the Fighter strength to exactly half this figure, and when on the 14th instant I had explained the situation to the Deputy Chief of the Air Staff, he replied that the Air Council were contemplating the early dispatch of 2 more Squadrons to France.

27.   According to Air Ministry, weekly Intelligence summary No. 1 dated 6th September, 1939, a force of 850 long-range Bombers lay waiting in north-west Germany to attack us at any moment. It was not engaged in the Polish or in the French fighting.

28.   I must also emphasise that the above remarks are written as such from the Offensive as the Defensive aspect. Presumably the time will come sooner or later when we shall wish to take offensive action with our Bomber striking force. Then that time comes it will be necessary to be strong at Home, so that we may not be diverted from our aim by fear of 'reprisals'.

The weight of preserving his limited resources for the crucial battles which he knew lay ahead caused Air Chief Marshal Dowding great concern. On October 24th, 1939, Air Vice-Marshal Leigh-Mallory wrote to his Commander-in-Chief regarding the shortages in 12 Group:-

I feel most uneasy about the number of squadrons at present in 12 Group. I have, up to the present, lost three squadrons to the Field Force; No 616 permanently to 13 Group, and now No 19 sent north to reinforce 13 Group.
In the last Command Battle Order, no less than four of the squadrons shown under No 12 Group are non-effective as far as I am concerned. They are:

19 Squadron - attached to 13 Group.

616 Squadron - now belonging to 13 Group.

229 and 222 Squadrons - neither of which has any aircraft.

In addition, 46 Squadron is standing by to go out to France.

2.　We have recently been faced with a phase, in which the Germans have been attacking coastal objectives. It seems to me from watching the international situation that we may be approaching very near the time when Hitler resorts to entirely different methods and begins to bomb military objectives in Great Britain itself, such as Rolls-Royce at Derby and various shadow factories and aero-engine factories in the Birmingham, Wolverhampton and Coventry areas. If such an attack develops, my position is a most precarious one.

3.　I only have seven day fighter squadrons at the present moment. Of those, 610 and 611 cannot be regarded as more than 50% efficient when compared to the regular squadrons. They are a very different proposition to 602, 603 and 607 Squadrons, which were all in a very much more advanced state of training. That leaves me five reasonably well-trained squadrons with which to meet a really intensive attack on the Midlands. If one counts 610 and 611 together as one squadron, it gives me a total of six.

4.　With the big area I have to defend and the weight of attack which may be delivered against me, I wish to place on record that I think this inadequate.

There can be no doubt that the Commander-in-Chief was already fully aware of the situation *throughout* Fighter Command; Air Vice-Marshal Leigh-Mallory had told him nothing new, and his paragraph '4' was an unashamed 'back-covering' proviso. Keith Park noted, however, that the AOC 12 Group's report was inaccurate: both 264 and 266 Squadrons were at Sutton Bridge, and the Gladiator biplane-equipped 141 Squadron was receiving Blenheims. Also, 19 Squadron was in the process of returning to Duxford, its home station.

In March 1940, after an interview with the Commander-in-Chief, Air Vice-Marshal Leigh-Mallory stopped off at Air Commodore Park's office before leaving Bentley Priory. Park was to recall that 'Leigh-Mallory was very angry and said he would move heaven and earth to get Dowding sacked'. Park was 'greatly annoyed', and later recalled that his 'peacetime friendship for Leigh-Mallory drained very rapidly'.

Prior to Hitler's advance on the Channel ports in May and June 1940, 12 Group was considered to be a most important Fighter Command line of defence, guarding against attacks from the direction of the North Sea. Protecting London, 11 Group was nevertheless considered to be the senior group. In February 1940, Air Marshal Sir William Welsh had succeeded Air Marshal Sir Leslie Gossage as AOC 11 Group. On April 13th, Keith Park received a pleasant surprise: he was to be promoted to Air Vice-Marshal and would take over from Welsh at 11 Group.

For nearly two years Keith Park had been Dowding's SASO at HQ Fighter Command; his hard work and loyalty had paid off. Having taken over 12 Group on promotion to Air-Vice Marshal in December 1937, Trafford Leigh-Mallory was clearly passed over by an officer junior in rank to him when Park was chosen to succeed Welsh. However, in view of Leigh-Mallory's lack of fighter experience, which had been reflected in his performance to date, it was hardly surprising that Dowding, now the country was at war, chose Keith Park, a fighter leader born and bred. Dowding was in fact blissfully unaware of Leigh-Mallory's hostility towards him, which was only revealed by Park in 1968. Had Dowding realised the situation, evidence from post-war interviews suggest that he would have sought Leigh-Mallory's replacement at this early juncture;

had he done so, the need to write this book would probably never have arisen.

Even with our benefit of hindsight, however, Keith Park must have been regarded as the perfect choice to command 11 Group at that time. He had not only spent two years helping to create the System of Air Defence but also fully appreciated its workings. Owing to Dowding's delegation of tactical control to, largely, Group level, the importance of the Group Commanders could not be underestimated. It was fortunate, therefore, that when the aerial assault on Britain came, both Fighter Command and the all-important 11 Group were entrusted to highly experienced and capable officers. By that time, Dowding had handled the strategy; it would largely be up to Park to fight the tactical battle, against the known enemy at least.

On May 10th 1940, the *Blitzkrieg* was launched against the west. In a devastating surprise attack, highly mobile *Panzer* divisions cut through the supposedly 'impassable' Ardennes, and stormed onwards towards the Channel coast. The Allies were shocked, their command system paralysed. Fighter Command casualties in France were enough to cause the Commander-in-Chief great concern, since if they were allowed to continue unchecked for the sake of what now appeared to be a hopeless cause, it would not be possible to guarantee the security of the 'base'. As we have seen, Air Chief Marshal Dowding had an unwavering belief in this purpose, and from it he refused to be swayed. On May 16th, he wrote to the Air Ministry in a desperate bid to preserve his strength, pointing out that although the Air Council considered that the minimum force necessary for Home Defence was 52 squadrons, losses in France had depleted Fighter Command to just 36. As ever, Dowding spoke frankly:-

I must therefore request that as a matter of paramount urgency the Air Ministry will consider and decide what level of strength is to be left to the Fighter Command for the defence of this country, and will assure me that when this level has been reached, not one fighter will be sent across the Channel however urgent and insistent appeals for help may be.
I believe that, if an adequate fighter force is kept in this country, if the fleets remain in being, and if the Home Forces are suitably organised to resist invasion, we should be able to carry on the war single handed for some time, if not indefinitely. But, if the Home Defence Force is drained away in desperate attempts to remedy the situation in France, defeat in France will involve the final, complete and irremediable defeat of this country.

These strong words of wisdom were fortunately heeded, receiving support from Air Marshal Newall, the CAS. Air Chief Marshal Dowding had in any case only sent Hurricane squadrons across the Channel, wisely preserving his precious Spitfires for home defence. However, on May 18th, two days after Dowding's famous letter, Air Vice-Marshal Leigh-Mallory was making every effort not only to send a further 12 Group fighter squadron to France, but a Spitfire unit at that; 19 Squadron ORB:-

AOC, Air Vice-Marshal Trafford Leigh-Mallory visited squadron. Decided that squadron would move to France but German advance put a stop to it.

Whilst Air Vice-Marshal Leigh-Mallory was probably unaware of his Commander-in-Chief's letter, he undoubtedly had knowledge of Fighter Command's policy on sending Hurricane, not Spitfire, squadrons to France; for him to even contemplate sending 19 Squadron to France would certainly have been unacceptable to Dowding, who would ultimately have had to sanction such a move. This appears to be another indication of Leigh-Mallory viewing the fighting in local, rather than Command, terms.

It was just as well that 19 Squadron remained at Duxford, the Allied military situation generally in France being a disaster. An eye-witness was Air Commodore EW 'Teddy' Donaldson, then the commander of 151 Squadron:-

> I have never seen so many people running anywhere, so long as it was west. The poor British soldiers were continuously let down when the Dutch, Belgian and French soldiers surrendered by the division. The British "Tommies" were marvellous, however, and fought their way through to the flat beaches of Dunkirk.

On May 26th, 1940, orders were given for the complete evacuation of all Allied troops in the area of Dunkirk. From that day onwards, the operation of Fighter Command was to be devoted almost exclusively to patrols along the line Calais-Dunkirk, and some 200 sorties were flown on the first day. As the Royal Navy, together with the heroic 'Little Ships', commenced a shuttle-service across the Channel, Fighter Command's task was to maintain continuous patrols during the daylight hours, and this was largely accomplished. Most of these patrols were at squadron strength, but on three occasions lone squadrons were heavily outnumbered in combat. Despite the fact that the RAF pilots *claimed* nearly three times the number of their own losses (38:14), the port of Dunkirk was badly hit.

Being closest to Northern France, it was 11 Group's fighter stations from which most operational flights were conducted, although squadrons involved also included those from 12 Group. All were eager to gain combat experience, especially as during these Dunkirk air battles the Spitfire was to meet the Me 109 for the first time.

On May 26th, 1940, 19 Squadron had been roughly handled by Me 109s near Calais whilst undertaking a textbook attack on a formation of *Stukas*, the Spitfires being throttled right back, matching the dive-bombers' speed, when 'bounced' by the Me 109s. The CO, Squadron Leader Geoffrey Stephenson, was shot down and captured. Wing Commander George Unwin fought in that combat as an NCO pilot; he now reflects that:-

> The tacticians who wrote the book really believed that in the event of war it would be fighter versus bomber only. What they could not foresee was Hitler's modern ground tactics that would take his armies to the Channel ports in an unprecedented advance, thus providing bases for his fighters in the Pas-de-Calais and therefore putting London itself within their limited range. Our tight formations, which we practised extensively before the war, were actually useless in combat, what happened to Geoffrey Stephenson being a perfect example of just how flawed our fighter tactics were. Over Dunkirk, we had tried to put into practice years of peacetime training, based upon unrealistic perceptions, and paid a heavy price. Our formation attacks were perfectly impressive for the Hendon Air Pageant, but useless for modern air fighting which, after all, is for what they were intended.

Already apparent was that the years of 'disarmament' in Great Britain and France had resulted in the Germans now leading the way in both ground and air fighting tactics.

At 0208 hrs on May 28th, the CAS had instructed Air Chief Marshal Dowding to 'ensure the protection of the Dunkirk beaches (three miles on either side) from first light until darkness by continuous fighter patrols in strength.' Thus Fighter Command was forced to meet two conflicting requirements over Dunkirk, namely continuity and strength. To achieve this, after repeated requests to his Commander-in-Chief by Air Vice-Marshal Park, Fighter Command patrols were operated at an *average* strength of two squadrons, as opposed to an average of only one the previous day. Twelve patrols were flown that day, involving 30 squadron sorties and 321 aircraft sorties. Consequently, there were only short intervals when the area was not being covered. Owing in part to the continuous fighter patrols, the troop loading that day was the fastest so far achieved. Orders were therefore issued for the continuation of such patrols. As a result of the odds encountered by the RAF fighters on May 28th, Fighter Command was given permission during the evening to organise its patrols as it thought best.

The rapid change in tactics was largely a result of Air Vice-Marshal Park's perception of the events unfolding from, so far as it concerned the RAF commanders of the time, a unique vantage point: the cockpit of his personal Hurricane, 'OK1'. To his great credit, the AOC 11 Group had not only maintained flying practice, but had also learned to fly the new monoplane fighters with which his pilots were equipped. Over Dunkirk, he was able to observe the situation first-hand, and that experience, together with intelligence gleaned from personal debriefs with his pilots, convinced him that stronger offensive patrols would both reduce fighter losses and the effect of enemy attacks.

Fighter Leader: Air Vice-Marshal Park poses with his personal Hurricane, 'OK1'.
(Author via Mr Keith Park)

From May 29th 1940, protection was arranged so that up to four squadrons, though often in two separate formations, were on the patrol line at the same time. This meant, however, that there was an absence of fighter cover for periods of over an hour-and-a-half at a time. Even so, Fighter Command was finding difficulty in maintaining such strength, four-squadron formations frequently consisting of less than 30 aircraft, rather than 44. Nevertheless, these new methods of patrolling enjoyed success, and only on June 1st were really damaging attacks made on Allied shipping. Owing to both the availability of patrols and increased shelling, the embarkation of troops then continued only at night, which helped Fighter Command as strong fighter cover was only thereafter required at dusk and dawn, when shipping was approaching and leaving Dunkirk.

The fighters of both sides continued to clash fiercely over the French coast. On June 2nd, 1940, 12 Group's 611 Squadron, operating from Martlesham Heath and flying in a five-squadron Wing, was bounced by II/JG26, an experienced and extremely professional unit. The Me 109 pilots claimed six British fighters destroyed without loss.

Over Dunkirk, it must be appreciated that a 'Wing' was no more than a *convoy* of fighter aircraft travelling together and arriving en masse in the combat area. This enabled the RAF pilots to meet the 109s on equal numerical terms, but there was no cohesion after the 'Tally Ho' because radio contact between different squadrons was impossible owing to the use of different radio frequencies. The squadrons were also out of radio range with their bases and radar, so ground controllers were of no use. In any case, the provisions of the System, which were designed for *defensive* fighting, had no place in this *offensive* context. Having no help from the System was a great disadvantage, however, as in the absence of radar, Park's fighters had to mount exhausting standing patrols, at least until the practice of nocturnal embarkation commenced. As has been seen, although 12 Group's squadrons were involved, the tactical issues pertaining to Dunkirk were dealt with by the Commander-in-Chief and AOC 11 Group. Air Vice-Marshal Leigh-Mallory made no personal *operational* contribution.

Many of the RAF pilots blooded over Dunkirk, it should be remembered, actually had very little experience of flying their relatively new monoplane fighters, and were meeting the enemy fighters for the first time. Park himself was responding to a situation for which there were no precedents; he had done so rapidly and effectively. His personal reputation emerged from the situation enhanced, and as a result of his Dunkirk experiences Air Vice-Marshal Park formulated the sound principle with which he was soon to fight the Battle of Britain: that it was better to spoil the aim of many, rather than to shoot down a few.

Fighter Command had lost 25% of its strength during the Battle of France. As the Prime Minister, Winston Churchill, said:-

What General Weygand called the Battle of France is over ..... the Battle of Britain is about to begin.

CHAPTER TWO

Bader

A mongst the Spitfire pilots who saw action for the first time during the Dunkirk evacuation was a certain 30-year-old Flight Lieutenant; what made this officer particularly remarkable was that he was severely disabled, having two artificial legs. His name was of course Douglas Bader.

Douglas Robert Steuart Bader was born in St John's Wood, London, on February 21st, 1910. For the first two years of his life, the infant Bader was cared for by relatives on the Isle of Man, as his parents returned to India, where his father, Frederick, was a Civil Servant. In 1913, Douglas was escorted to join his parents in India, where they`planned to remain indefinitely. Shortly afterwards, however, the family returned to England for Mr Bader to study law, and set up home at Kew, in Surrey. Allegedly, Mrs Jessie Bader much favoured Derick, her elder son, which led to a certain amount of unhappiness for young Douglas. The following year the Great War broke out and Frederick Bader was commissioned into the Royal Engineers, subsequently serving in France. After the war, by which time his marriage had failed, Major Bader remained in France, initially assisting with re-building but then with the War Graves Commission. Sadly, in 1922, Major Bader eventually succumbed, to a head wound received in 1917. Contrary to the claim in 'Reach for the Sky' he did not expire in St Omer, a French town with which his younger son would later become dramatically connected, but in Brussels where he was buried.

After this bereavement, the Baders found themselves in reduced circumstances which led to a crisis affecting the younger son's education. Derick was already a boarder, but funds were insufficient to provide for Douglas' private education. His only option was to win a scholarship, not an easy task for a pupil more at home on the sports field than in the classroom. That same year he was captain of cricket, rugby and football, won every senior race in the school's sports day, and set a record for throwing the cricket ball. To his great credit, despite these exertions on the games field, Douglas Bader also won a scholarship to St Edward's School, Oxford. At this time, his mother was remarried, to the Reverend Ernest Hobbs, a vicar in Yorkshire, so the family moved home to the large rectory at Sprotborough.

Before his father's death, Douglas Bader's aunt, Hazel, had married a Flight Lieutenant in the Royal Air Force, Cyril Burge, who had flown throughout most of the Great War with the Royal Flying Corps. Not surprisingly, Master Bader was captivated by Burge's tales of war in the air. In 1923, Bader stayed with his aunt and uncle at Cranwell, where Burge was the RAF College's first adjutant. There Bader joined in games with the cadets and sat in the cockpit of an Avro 504 biplane elementary training aircraft. At the end of this visit, the youngster's mind was made up and he determined to eventually return to Cranwell as a Flight Cadet himself. Five years later Douglas Bader was to do just that when he won one of six King's Cadetships to Cranwell, commencing his course in September 1928.

The RAF College at Cranwell was, in many ways, a cross between a Civil Service staff college, a university, a technical college and a flying school; entrants were actually charged a fee. The site, near Sleaford in Lincolnshire, was formerly a naval air station, and the College's first two commandants were both ex-Royal Navy officers. Naval traditions were therefore evident in a regime intended to create professional officers. To ensure that these officers were of only the highest possible standard, and would become educated, cultured and self-assured men destined to become the staff officers and high commanders of the RAF, the Flight Cadet's course was of two years duration and embraced a variety of subjects. Appendix III of Air Publication No 121 describes the syllabus of instruction:-

1st Year

1.   The subjects that will form the course of studies are the following:-
   (i)   **English Language and literature**.- To be studied from the standpoint of enabling flight cadets to express themselves clearly and concisely in speech and in writing, of creating an interest in reading, and of developing the capacity to use books intelligently for the purposes of general culture and research.
   (ii)   **General ethnology**.- To create an interest as an incentive to voluntary study of the subject and to introduce the flight cadet to a general knowledge of the chief races of mankind, their division into nations, their origin, and the general lines of their development.
   (iii) **The British Empire**.- Its history, social and industrial development, and relations with other States.
   (iv)   **Applied mathematics, including mechanics and draughtsmanship**.- To be studied as a subject of practical utility in relation to an officer's professional career and as a means of developing the power of clear and accurate reasoning. A knowledge of elementary mathematics, algebra, geometry, and trigonometry will be assumed, and the work will be closely correlated with that in the technical subjects of study. Special attention will be given to applied mathematics, to graphics, and to practical work in the laboratory.
   (v)   **Elementary physics**.- The fundamental principles in special relation to aeronautics.
   (vi)   **History of the Royal Air Force**.- The part played by it in the Great War (1914-1918) and its present organisation.
   (vii) **Theory of flight and rigging**.
   (viii) **Air pilotage. Map reading**.
   (ix)   **Drill and physical training**.
   (x)   **Air Force Law and administration**.
   (xi)   **Hygiene and sanitation**.
   (xii) **Workshops and engines, including practical work in workshops, with instruction in metal and woodwork**.
   (xiii) **Wireless telegraphy, radio telephony and signal procedure**.
   (xiv) **Practical flying**.

2nd Year.

   (i)   **Theoretical and practical instruction in internal combustion engines, including magnetos and their management**.
   (ii)   **Aerodynamics**.
   (iii) **Practical instruction in rigging**.
   (iv)   **More advanced work in the wood and metal workshops**.
   (v)   **Outline of wireless telegraphy and telephony**.
   (vi)   **Armament**.
   (vii) **Practical flying**.
   (viii) **Air pilotage and airmanship**.

(ix) **Meteorology**.

(x) **Outline of the organisation of the Navy and Army, with characteristics of the various arms and types of ships**.

(xi) **War, strategy and tactics**.

In the *Journal of the Royal Air Force College*, 1930, 'AHE' described Cranwell and its traditions, concluding that:-

The life of the College is resumed with alacrity and care at the beginning of a term. One day the place will be wearing a wan and neglected air; whilst on the next everything will be bustle and confusion. The night seems to bring forth cadets in the same way as a conjuror produces rabbits from a hat. But, as they come, so they depart, yielding place for others in a never ending stream: each one, however, leaves his impression for good or bad on the College. Some may be forgotten; others will be talked of by terms of the distant future. Yet one and all will retain indelible memories of their sojourn at Cranwell, and will regard the College with an esteem and affection which is of more value than the cosmopolitan *camaraderie* of greater seats of learning. For the associations of Cranwell are enjoyed only by a privileged few, who are closely bound together throughout their careers.

Flight Cadet DRS Bader was undoubtedly captivated by Cranwell; the ethos of both camaraderie and prestige perfectly suited his personality and background. From the outset he was destined to become one of 'AHE's' students to be 'talked of by terms of the distant future'. Bader once more excelled at sport, representing Cranwell at rugby, boxing, cricket and hockey, in addition to playing golf against the College staff, which included the Assistant Commandant, Wing Commander Douglas Evill who later becomes an important character in this book.

A College Journal report on a boxing match indicates Bader's enthusiasm and aggressive spirit:-

Light Heavyweights.- F./Officer D. Maclean *v.* F./Cadet D.R.S. Bader. Bader was originally down to box at middle-weight, but his opponent having met with an accident, he went up a weight. He went for all he was worth against his opponent, who was as cool and collected as anyone could wish to be in the boxing ring. Several strong punches were exchanged; then Maclean, stepping back from a rush, shot out a short right to the chin, which, I imagine, half of the audience did not see, and Bader went down and out for the count.

In 1928, Cranwell's Flight Cadets flew the Avro 504N biplane, which had a top speed of about 100 mph. These were the aircraft flown by the First Year students, the Second Year flying the Armstrong Whitworth Atlas, a real Service type. There were also a few of the fast Fairey Foxes, and, for those chosen to become fighter pilots, Armstrong Whitworth Siskin IIIs. Drill, an excellent means of forging team spirit and formation, and flying were the two most important features of the cadets' daily routine. Flight Cadet Bader was a member of the College's 'A' Flight, commanded by Flight Lieutenant Douglas MacFadyen, his instructor being Flying Officer Wilfred Pearson. Bader's flying log books are now preserved at the RAF Museum, Hendon, and from their pages we know that his first flight, 'Air experience', was made in an Avro 504 piloted by Pearson, on September 13th, 1928. Five months later he had flown 25 times, and had logged 11 hours and 15 minutes in the air; on February 12th, 1929, Flight Cadet Bader flew solo for the first time, in Avro 504 J8534.

The exuberance of youth, however, was to land Flight Cadet Bader in trouble. He came 19th out of 21 in the end of First Year exams, and that, coupled with a brush with the law regarding a traffic offence, a misdemeanour also involving Cadets Stephenson, Chance and Field, led to him being carpeted, first by Flight Lieutenant MacFadyen, then, much worse, by the College Commandant, Air Vice-Marshal Halahan. The latter told him in no uncertain terms that the Air Force required *men*, not boys. From that moment on, Bader was forced to transform his attitude and outlook at Cranwell in order to justify his place there.

In his Second Year, Bader commenced flying Siskins, and his ambition was to become a fighter pilot. Although he continued with his sporting interests, Bader's groundwork improved. At that time, Squadron Leader Rupert Leigh was a First Year student:-

To us Bader was a sort of god who played every conceivable game and was the best player in every team.

Air Vice-Marshal Wilfred Oulton was one of Leigh's fellow students, but he describes Flight Cadet Bader as 'an exhibitionist, not a team player.'

The ultimate prize for Cranwell Cadets was the Sword of Honour, awarded to the best all-round cadet. Flight Cadet Under Officer Patric Coote narrowly beat Bader into second place. The flying trophy went to Flight Cadet Sergeant Geoffrey Stephenson. On July 25th, 1930, Squadron Leader Thomas, for the Officer Commanding, RAF College, assessed Bader's flying ability as 'above average'. The final Cranwellian signature in his log book is that of Wing Commander Evill; the service had accepted Douglas Bader, who was commissioned as a Pilot Officer. Although he then left the RAF College, on posting to a fighter squadron, as 'AHE' stated in his article, Pilot Officer Bader could later rely upon the fact that:-

.... the associations of Cranwell are enjoyed only by a privileged few, who are closely bound together throughout their careers.

On August 25th, 1930, Pilot Officers DRS Bader and GD Stephenson reported for duty to fly Gloster Gamecock biplane fighters with 23 Squadron at Kenley. Bader's log book records that at this time his solo flying time amounted to 56.10 hours. On the day he joined 23 Squadron's 'C' Flight, Pilot Officer Bader was checked out by Flight Lieutenant Staniforth in Siskin J9210. The following day, Bader made his first flight proper as a fighter pilot, in Gamecock J8084: 'Landings, take-offs, local flying. First solo.' He flew twice more that day, both sorties described in his log book as 'landings, take-offs and aerobatics'; it was at aerobatics that Bader was to excel. Throughout this time, his flying was predominantly formation and aerobatics practice, often in company with his Cranwell friend Stephenson. On August 23rd, 1930, Bader wrote in his log book: 'Landed (on nose!) at Sidcup owing to mist and rain.' Fortunately, Gamecock J7904 was undamaged, and Pilot Officer Bader was able to take-off again and successfully complete the remaining 10 minutes of flight required to safely make his base at Kenley.

The aerobatic abilities of Pilot Officers Bader and Stephenson, the former a dare-devil exponent of the slow roll at low altitude, was recognised at Kenley, and from April in 1931 onwards, Bader's log book records numerous flights practising for the Hendon Air Pageant. In June, Flight Lieutenant Harry Day, the 'C' Flight Commander, selected Pilot Officer Bader as his No 2 in Hendon's pairs aerobatics competition. 23 Squadron's pair, with Pilot Officer Stephenson as the reserve pilot, won the competition, described by the *Times* as 'the event of the day'. On August 20th, 1931 - one year after Pilot Officer Bader had reported for duty with 23 Squadron - Flight Lieutenant Day led the aerobatic team on a flight from Kenley to Cramlington, near Newcastle, stopping to refuel at Cranwell and Catterick. The following day the Gamecock pilots practised 'synchronised aerobatics' and participated in Cramlington's air display on August 22nd. En route to Cramlington, however, Bader had dropped out of formation and hedge-hopped for an hour, well below the regulation height for low flying. This act incurred the wrath of Flight Lieutenant Day. Bader had been warned; as Air Commodore HW 'Tubby' Mermagen, himself an aerobatics pilot of repute during the latter half of the 1930s, said to me in 1993, 'Douglas was getting cocky.'

Acting Air Commodore HW 'Tubby' Mermagen (centre),at RAF Gatow, 1945.
(Author via Air Commodore HW Mermagen)

In 1931, Bader also pursued his sporting ambitions with great zeal, playing both cricket and rugby for the RAF, and the latter also for the Harlequins, Surrey, and the Combined Services Team. Bader's place as fly-half in the England team looked assured.

Low aerobatics continued to be a problem for 23 Squadron. One pilot was killed in such circumstances, followed soon after by another. Harry Day, temporarily commanding the squadron (during which time Flying Officer Stephenson signed Bader's log book as 'Officer Commanding "C" Flight'), called his pilots together and lectured them on low aerobatics in the Bristol Bulldog, 23 Squadron's new mount. Referring to the height of 2,000' for aerobatics stipulated by Fighting Area regulations, Day indicated that he was prepared to allow *some* latitude; Day's job was to turn out pilots who had courage and judgement for war, and his advice was sound. Pilot Officer Bader ignored this further warning, however, and in November was reported for 'beating up' the aerodrome. Day rightly considered that the 20-year-old Bader, in the wake of his Hendon and sporting successes, was becoming overconfident. Air Commodore Mermagen comments that 'he was a real show off, he could do everything brilliantly, but did it very low.'

On December 14th, 1931, Pilot Officer Bader's Bristol Bulldog biplane joined two other 23 Squadron aircraft on a social flight to Woodley airfield, near Reading. Not surprisingly Bader, the Hendon star, was the subject of much attention in the clubhouse. Pilot Officer Bader took off and commenced a series of very low rolls over the airfield. Suddenly his left wing brushed the ground and within seconds the Bulldog became a bent and twisted mass of wreckage. Within the cockpit, Douglas Bader lay terribly injured. His right leg was consequently amputated above the knee and the left below. In his log book, he later wrote:-

X Country Reading. Crashed slow-rolling near ground. Bad show.

A 'bad show' it certainly was, although, as Lady Bader recounted in 1996, 'he knew that it was his own bloody silly fault and that was that.' Air Vice-Marshal Oulton summed up what was probably the service's reaction as a whole: 'I was very sorry, but not surprised.'

Forever Douglas Bader will be condemned for his disregard of flying regulations on that day at Woodley, but the price he, an outstanding sportsman, paid was the loss of both legs. Make no mistake, a lesser man, without Douglas Bader's incredible toughness, resolve and indomitable spirit would probably have died. For Bader, characteristically, to live was not enough: he had to somehow compete with able-bodied men on equal terms.

Incredibly, Bader mastered mobility on 'tin' legs, and remarkably on September 29th, 1937, just nine months after the crash which left him legless, he flew as a passenger for 25 minutes in an Avro 504, flown by a Flight Lieutenant Leach, at CFS. In direct contrast to the heady days of aerobatics with 23 Squadron, in his log book Bader recorded the occasion as 'Normal flying.' Between that date and October 24th, Bader flew as a passenger in a variety of Avro, Hart and Siskin aircraft, but did not fly solo. These hours in the air brought his total flying time to 440.10. No assessment of his flying ability was recorded at this time, the last, in fact, having been upon leaving Cranwell in 1930.

Not surprisingly, King's Regulations contained nothing regarding pilots without legs, so the service ultimately refused to allow Bader to continue flying. On April 30th, 1933, Flying Officer DRS Bader was retired 'on the grounds of ill health'. Benumbed, having been forced to quit the service he loved so much, Bader started work in the office of the Asiatic Petroleum Company's aviation department, hardly a fair exchange for the cockpit of a Bulldog. Denied of aerobatics, he found his thrills behind the wheel of a fast sports car which he apparently often drove with little regard for other road users: two accidents resulted. Without the RAF, which he had clearly loved so much, the misery of his childhood returned. During this period of virtually wandering in the wilderness he married, at the age of 23, Thelma Edwards, a cousin of the Donaldson brothers who were all to later achieve fame in the wartime RAF.

On September 29th, 1938, Britain's Prime Minister, Neville Chamberlain, attended a conference in Munich with Hitler and the Prime Ministers of both France and Italy. The other leaders conceded to Hitler's demands, and agreed to sign a treaty guaranteeing the remainder of Czechoslovakia against unprovoked aggression. In Britain, France and even Germany the Munich Agreement was well received: many people believed that it had saved Europe from war. Indeed, Mr Chamberlain returned home to the waiting press at Heston airport, clutching his piece of paper, signed by Herr Hitler and himself, supposedly a guarantee of 'Peace for our time'.

If Neville Chamberlain thought that he had preserved peace indefinitely, Douglas Bader was amongst those who disagreed. Although his wife was, to say the least, less enthusiastic, Bader welcomed every aggressive move made by Germany. Immediately, realising that trained service pilots would be in demand and seeing this as his chance, Bader wrote to the Air Ministry offering his services and requested a refresher flying course. The answer was negative but tempered with the offer of a commission in the administrative branch, which he flatly refused.

In April 1939, when, in contravention of the Munich Agreement, Hitler's troops marched into the guaranteed portion of Czechoslovakia, Bader tried again. On August 31st, 1939, Air Vice-Marshal Charles Portal, the Air Member for Personnel, replied to Bader confirming that, provided the doctors agreed, in the event of war he would be used in a flying capacity. War broke out just three days later. Air Vice-Marshal Halahan, Cranwell's Commandant in Bader's day, paved the way for his former Flight Cadet to rejoin the service by sending the doctors at Bader's medical board a note explaining that he had known him at Cranwell and could confirm that Bader was just the sort of officer the service now required. Found to be fit, Bader's next stop was the CFS at Upavon.

When Douglas Bader arrived at the CFS on October 18th, 1939, he was delighted to find that the commander of the Refresher Squadron's 'A' Flight, who was to undertake his flying assessment, was none other than Rupert Leigh, now a Squadron Leader but previously his junior at Cranwell.

Leigh, by his own admission, considered Bader a 'god'. Bader undoubtedly realised that if he did not make some awful error, which was in any case unlikely, the outcome was a foregone conclusion in his favour. The aircraft in which the test was conducted was a Harvard trainer, an American two-seater, radial-engined monoplane. This American design was to cause problems for Bader, however, as Squadron Leader Colin Hodgkinson, himself a legless wartime Spitfire pilot, explained:-

The problem with American aeroplanes, such as the Harvard and Mustang for example, was that the wheel brakes were operated by means of foot pedals which required the flexing of the ankles. Whilst British aircraft posed no problems, because the brakes were operated by hand, it was impossible to operate the brakes on these American machines without legs.

Fortunately for Douglas Bader, his sympathetic examiner operated the foot brakes on his behalf, and so the flying test was completed successfully: 'AHE's' prophecy was being fulfilled.

On November 27th, 1939, Flying Officer Douglas Bader arrived at the CFS and reported for duty to the Refresher Squadron. In his new log book, Bader carried over 'Approximately 500 hours solo'. Later that day he made his first flight, following his return to the service, as a passenger in an Avro Tutor flown by an instructor, Flight Lieutenant Clarkson. The next flight was a solo on the same type, during which he flew an *inverted* circuit of the aerodrome. On December 2nd, Squadron Leader Leigh was again the '1st Pilot' in Harvard N7184, Flying Officer Bader being his passenger. Although the latter could never solo on this type, because of the foot brakes, it remained imperative that he accumulated experience on the Harvard due to its comparatively high performance and prior to flying one of the new, fast monoplane fighters which were completely new to him. On December 4th, Bader flew Fairey Battle N2254, a monoplane light bomber powered by a Rolls-Royce Merlin engine, and on the 10th, Squadron Leader Leigh again flew with him in the Harvard. On December 20th, 1939, Flying Officer DRS Bader soloed in Hawker Hurricane L1873, undertaking 'Circuits and landings and *low-flying*'. I doubt whether he could have had a better Christmas present.

By the end of his Refresher Course Flying Officer Bader had flown a total of 5.20 Hurricane hours. Having been away from the service for eight years, and having *no* experience of air fighting relevant to the monoplane, it is a little surprising that his assessment as a fighter pilot at that early stage was 'Exceptional'. The rating was awarded by the Officer Commanding Refresher Squadron, Wing Commander GH Stainforth who had never, in fact, flown with the pilot concerned. One can only assume, therefore, that the assessment resulted from Squadron Leader Leigh's report.

At this time, Group Captain Alfred B Woodhall was 'Squadron Leader Flying Ops.' at the Duxford Sector Station in 12 Group. 'Woody' remembered:-

One day, Douglas Bader flew over from the CFS in a Hurricane. I was delighted and amazed to see him, as I had not done so since his crash. He was in terrific form, and as it happened the AOC also came to visit us. I introduced Douglas to the AOC, and over lunch Douglas used all his considerable charm in persuading Leigh-Mallory to take him into one of his operational squadrons. After lunch, with the AOC watching, Douglas put on a most finished display of aerobatics, and this finally decided 'L-M'. Douglas was posted almost at once to No 19 Squadron, at Duxford, commanded by his old friend and term-mate from Cranwell, Geoffrey Stephenson. Douglas impressed us all with his terrific personality and his amazing keenness and drive. I have never known his equal. Flying was his supreme passion and his enthusiasm infected us all.

As a spectator, I was intrigued to see the impact that Douglas Bader had on the AOC - and vice-versa. Air Vice-Marshal and Flying Officer, rank did not enter into it. They were two of a kind - born leaders. They were both men who were respected by all, and were affectionately esteemed by most. Their attraction for each other was immediate, and their friendship was, I am sure, established at that first meeting.

With Squadron Leader Stephenson a squadron commander at Duxford, I very much doubt whether the visits of both the AOC and Flying Officer Bader were coincidental!

On February 7th, 1940, Flying Officer DRS Bader left the CFS upon posting to 19(F) Squadron at Duxford: he was home again. At this time, Bader was two ranks behind his former Cranwell contemporaries: Stephenson was now his Commanding Officer, and Rupert Leigh was also a Squadron Leader. He determined to recover lost ground without delay.

19 Squadron had been the first to receive the Spitfire when Supermarine test pilot Jeffrey Quill delivered K9789 to Duxford on August 4th, 1938. By the outbreak of war just over a year later, the squadron was therefore the most experienced Spitfire unit in the RAF. Flying Officer Douglas Bader became a member of 'A' Flight, commanded by Flight Lieutenant Brian Lane. Bader first flew a Spitfire, K9853, on February 12th, 1940. Wing Commander Frank Brinsden was a Pilot Officer in 19 Squadron's 'A' Flight:-

Flying Officer Frank Brinsden pictured at Fowlmere, September 1940.
(Author)

When Douglas Bader rejoined the RAF, junior officers were beneath contempt, his circle being squadron commanders and above; anyone less was to be seen but not heard. An example of this appears in his own book, 'Fight for the Sky', in which he states, regarding his first Spitfire flight:-

I sat in the cockpit whilst a young Pilot Officer, with little experience, showed me the knobs. He omitted to tell me one important thing about the undercarriage operation which embarrassed me in due course, fortunately without damage.

I feel free to elaborate on this since he raised the matter and I was there. It must have been galling to Douglas when Geoffrey Stephenson detailed a mere Pilot Officer to give the great Douglas Bader his first pre-first solo cockpit controls briefing. The result was Douglas's silly comment published in his book. Any 'young Pilot Officer with little experience' on 19 Squadron assigned to brief Douglas Bader would actually have been flying Spitfires since October 1938; by early February 1940, when Flying Officer Bader came on the scene, that Pilot Officer would have been qualified to fly operationally by both day and night. Is such a Pilot Officer therefore likely to have omitted from the briefing the rather important matter of raising the undercarriage? In any case the crew room had an ample supply of Pilot's Handling Notes and anyone who embarked upon his first solo in such a (for that time) radical aircraft without fully understanding its controls was a complete B.F.! It must be remembered that the biplanes with which Douglas Bader had previously been familiar had a fixed undercarriage; although he had flown a handful of hours in a Hurricane, retractable undercarts remained relatively new to him.

Ernest French was a member of 'A' Flight's groundcrew and has only the fondest recollections of Flying Officer Bader:-

Ernest French poses with recovered parts from Spitfire X4231.
(Author)

When Douglas Bader came to Duxford, straight from the Central Flying School at Upavon, there was no publicity at that time, he just simply joined our squadron as an ordinary pilot. My first view of him was arriving in his old MG. He had digs over at March, not far from Duxford. An engine fitter, I was allocated to his aircraft, so I was with him on the airfield whenever 19 Squadron was available. At Readiness, he'd come to the aircraft out at dispersal and remain in the cockpit, so I gradually got to know him and realised that he was someone out of the ordinary. I looked after his aircraft for several months, we would sometimes fly from Fowlmere, or Horsham St Faith, and I was with him throughout this time. You got to know little things about him, like he'd never take his plane off without one of his wife's silk stockings tied around the gunsight! Another little thing I remember was one day when we were Available, he just said to me 'French, I want you to get hold of some webbing, I want it strung across the cockpit, my side of the gunsight, fairly tight'. I couldn't think why, but he was trying out steadying his body during firing by using his chin, as he could not brace himself on the rudder pedals with his legs! Prior to trying this out, he had found that when firing his guns, he was thrown slightly forward due to the recoil. The webbing idea worked perfectly! I always found him to be a perfect officer and gentleman. He often took me and other airmen flying in the station Magister, and made me sit in the front cockpit, but always joked and said 'French, make sure you start her up before you get in!' These were cross-country flights and he would point out his digs in March and other landmarks. I recall the brief time we were together with enormous pride.

Fred Roberts was a 19 Squadron armourer:-

Bader's first flight with us was in the station Magister, and he beat up the aerodrome in every way. He will also be remembered for taking the roof off the old peacetime cricket pavilion on landing a Spitfire, removing his tailwheel in the process!

On February 21st, 1940, 12 Group's AOC, Air Vice-Marshal Leigh-Mallory, visited Duxford and inspected 19 Squadron. To impress the AOC, Stephenson's squadron undertook a 'quick re-arm performed in 16 minutes and 25 seconds'

The ORB summarised 19 Squadron's February of 1940 thus:-

In this month squadron quite active, carrying out a number of convoy and lightship patrols during which several interceptions of friendly aircraft took place, but no enemy aircraft were observed.

Air Vice-Marshal Michael Lyne:-

By March the weather was better, but we now had Flying Officer Douglas Bader to contend with. He was very brave and determined but was having a hard time coming to grips with the Spitfire, a far more advanced machine than the biplanes he had flown when previously an RAF fighter pilot. He particularly experienced problems in cloud. More than once my friend Watson and I, both Pilot Officers, were lent to Bader as a formation by the CO but emerged from cloud faithfully following our leader only to find ourselves in a steep diving turn!

By the time of Flying Officer Bader's arrival at Duxford, the Spitfire's original, fixed-pitch propeller, to which Michael Lyne referred, had been replaced by the de Havilland two-pitch airscrew. The pitch, or angle, of a propeller blade controls its 'bite' into the air and hence the engine speed, and the effect of changing pitch is best likened to that of changing gear in a car. The biplanes flown by Douglas before the war had fixed-pitch propellers similar to those of the original Spitfire, whereas the two-pitch development was to cause him problems.

Throughout March 1940, 19 Squadron deployed a section of three aircraft to Horsham St Faith, in Norfolk, on a daily basis to provide convoy protection patrols. Michael Lyne recalls the events of March 31st:-

On this occasion, Douglas Bader was leading our section, which also included Pilot Officer Watson, and we went off downwind on the shortest run at Horsham. Douglas, however, forgot to put the airscrew into fine pitch for take-off, and cartwheeled across the main road and into a ploughed field. Watson and I stuck with him until the last minute but then pulled up and away on emergency power. I remember only just clearing the hedge and seeing clods of earth flying high overhead from my leader's Spitfire. Bader broke a pair of artificial legs in the accident, in fact, and had to send away for a new pair.

Flying Officer Bader's Spitfire, K9858, was written off. Surprisingly, on the same day, Squadron Leader Stephenson wrote in Bader's log book 'Ability as a Spitfire pilot Exceptional'. Nevertheless, Bader was unhappy in 19 Squadron, particularly with his status as a Flying Officer. Duxford's other Spitfire squadron, 222, was commanded by Squadron Leader Mermagen, who, as Bader himself later wrote, 'was an exact contemporary of mine. We used to play rugby together'; Air

Commodore Mermagen remembers:-

> When I was commanding 222 Squadron at RAF Duxford during 1939/40, Douglas Bader, a personal friend, was serving alongside us in 19 Squadron. However, he was finding it difficult to serve under Squadron Leader Geoffrey Stephenson, with whom he had once shared equal rank at Kenley before his accident. Bader knew that I had a flight commander who was suspected of being lacking in moral fibre whom I wished to get rid of. Bader therefore asked me if I would approach the AOC, Leigh-Mallory, regarding the possibility of him being transferred to 222 as a flight commander. The AOC agreed.

On April 16th, 1940, Douglas Bader was promoted to Acting Flight Lieutenant and assumed command of 222 Squadron's 'A' Flight. On May 28th, 1940, the squadron arrived at Hornchurch to assist with air operations covering the Dunkirk evacuation: 222 Squadron flew as part of a four-squadron Wing formation which also included 19, 41 and 616 Squadrons. On June 1st, Flight Lieutenant Bader scored his first victory when he destroyed an Me109 and damaged an Me 110 over Dunkirk. Air Commodore Mermagen recalls that sortie:-

> When we landed, Douglas stomped over to me and enthused, 'I got five for certain, Tubby, old boy!' Now this was the first time we had met Me 109s, which were damn good aeroplanes, and everything happened very quickly indeed. To be certain of having destroyed five enemy aircraft in such circumstances was impossible. I said 'You're a bloody liar, Bader!' We credited him with one destroyed. Nevertheless, Bader was generally easy to keep in order, as it were, and he had already proved to be an excellent flight commander. He carried out several operational sorties under my command and displayed exceptional leadership qualities; he was a fine Spitfire pilot. He used to come stomping into dispersal saying 'Come on chaps, get out of the way, I want a cup of coffee', barging everyone else aside, but the chaps loved him for it, he was a real morale booster.

The squadron flew over Dunkirk again on June 1st, and Flying Officer Bader returned safely to write in his log book: 'Attacked two Heinkel 111s. Killed one rear gunner and damaged machine'.

Back at Duxford, on June 12th, Flight Lieutenant Bader flew an 'R/T test for AOC' when Air Vice-Marshal Leigh-Mallory visited the Sector Operations Room. The following day, Bader crashed on landing after a night patrol in Spitfire 'ZD-D'. Air Commodore Mermagen:-

> On that occasion Douglas came in far too high and far too fast. He went through a hedge. I drove over to pick him up and he was ranting, shouting that the flarepath was incorrectly laid out. I thought, 'Well look at that, what a total lack of humility, he's blaming someone else now!'

That Spitfire was badly damaged.

Despite this further accident, on June 23rd Squadron Leader Mermagen wrote in Bader's log book: 'Assessment as a fighter pilot on Spitfires Exceptional'. The following day, Douglas Bader was promoted to Acting Squadron Leader. Having returned as a fighter pilot for just four months, he had risen from lowly Flying Officer to Squadron Leader and had therefore caught up with Rupert Leigh and Geoffrey Stephenson (although the latter had been a prisoner of war since May 26th).

This promotion was, of course, despite several blameworthy crashes; even Bader, concerned about this spate of flying accidents, was surprised himself.

By this time, 'Woody' Woodhall was a Wing Commander and the Station Commander at Duxford:-

*Group Captain AB 'Woody' Woodhall
pictured in September 1955.*
(Author via Mr Martin Woodhall)

Soon after the fall of France, Leigh-Mallory rang me to say that No 242 Squadron (Canadian) were reporting to Coltishall and would be under the operational control of the Duxford Sector. He told me that the squadron had had a tough time in France, and that the groundcrews had just been evacuated via Cherbourg, thanks to the resources of their adjutant, Flight Lieutenant Peter Macdonald MP. Their own CO had left them to their own devices after the pilots had landed in England, and the squadron, led by Flying Officer Stan Turner, had landed at Coltishall with nothing but the uniforms they were wearing. Tools, spares, kit, baggage - the lot had had to be abandoned.

LM said 'I've got to find them a new squadron commander but he's got to be good because these chaps are Canadians and they've had a rough time - they are browned off with authority and need a good leader - any suggestions?'

At once, I said 'What about Douglas Bader?'

LM replied 'I thought you'd say that. I think you are right.'

Air Commodore Mermagen:-

By the time Bader was promoted to command 242 Squadron, a Canadian unit suffering from poor morale, he was known personally to the AOC, Air Vice-Marshal Leigh-Mallory, who knew of his record and had particular respect for the way in which he had dealt with both the crash and amputations. I had spoken to Leigh-Mallory on several occasions, confirming that Bader was an 'above average' Spitfire pilot, a most mature character and quite an outstanding personality in Fighter Command. I feel certain that my high opinion of Douglas Bader helped him achieve such rapid promotion which he rightly deserved and as proven by his later service record.

There were certainly other officers in 12 Group awaiting promotion who, although younger, had more current operational experience than Bader. Nevertheless, such fine young officers, without a Cranwell background, Douglas Bader's service connections and personal friendship with the

AOC, were not even in the same race when it came to competing against him for promotion.

Previous accounts claim that on June 23rd, 1940, Air Vice-Marshal Leigh-Mallory sent for Bader and discussed with him his new command. If so, it is surprising that the latter did not fly the considerable distance from Duxford to Group HQ at Hucknall. However, his log book details only a 'Cloud flying' sortie on that day. The following day, he arrived at Coltishall; the interview with Leigh-Mallory actually took place on July 2nd, when Squadron Leader Bader flew from his new base at Coltishall to Hucknall, returning later the same day.

Squadron Leader Douglas Bader (centre) and pilots of 242 Squadron, amongst whom are his two flight commanders, Flight Lieutenants Stan Turner (Canadian, third from left) and Eric Ball (third from right).
(Author via Douglas Bader Foundation)

At Coltishall, Squadron Leader Bader was again reunited with his Cranwell contemporary Rupert Leigh, who had been posted from the CFS in April 1940 to command 66 (Spitfire) Squadron which shared the airfield with the Hurricanes of 242. The latter squadron's new CO immediately commenced leading by both example and deed. Upon arrival at Coltishall, Squadron Leader Bader took off in Hurricane P2967, later describing the sortie of 1 hour 10 minutes as 'Practice on type'. In fact, Squadron Leader Bader executed a breathtaking display of aerobatics, proving the point that he was as good a flyer as anyone with legs. He then rapidly gathered his men about him, having his friend, Flight Lieutenant Eric Ball, posted from 19 Squadron to command 'A' Flight in 242, and Flight Lieutenant George Powell-Sheddon, also an Old Cranwellian, to command 'B' Flight.

At the time, Air Marshal Sir Denis Crowley-Milling was a junior and impressionable RAFVR Pilot Officer who had survived the holocaust of France:-

*Tomfoolery: 'That's where he went!',
this snapshot being one of those captioned
in the album of the late Air Marshal Sir
Denis Crowley-Milling*

*Old Malvernian: Pilot Officer Denis 'Crow'
Crowley-Milling,*

'Poses by 242 Pursuit Squadron', and indicative of the unit's restored morale after Bader's arrival.
(All: Author via Douglas Bader Foundation)

41

BADER

When he received command of 242 Squadron, Douglas Bader was approaching 30 whilst the rest of us were around 20 or 21. After France we were in a bad state, but less than a month after he took command the squadron was fully operational and our morale was high. Fear was always there, of course, but Bader was afraid of nothing and through example and constant encouragement he helped us all conquer our own anxieties. You always felt perfectly safe when flying with Douglas Bader. For me, his arrival at Coltishall was the start of 18 exciting months of operational flying together, an unforgettable experience which helped shape my subsequent career.

Group Captain Woodhall:-

242 Squadron soon became an enthusiastic team led by their single-minded and swashbuckling CO, Douglas Bader.

David Evans was a member of 242 Squadron's groundcrew:-

When Douglas Bader arrived at Coltishall, there was a little resentment and the feeling generally was 'Who the hell is this newly promoted squadron leader without legs, who has seen little action, coming to tell us how to do it after we have been in the Battle of France?' By example, however, Squadron Leader Bader gained our respect, but he was undoubtedly an autocrat. Warrant Officer Bernard West was our Engineering Officer and I always felt that Squadron Leader Bader bullied him a bit to keep the aircraft serviceable. I also recall that our adjutant, a Great War pilot, Flight Lieutenant Peter Macdonald was the Conservative MP for the Isle of Wight.

At the time, Coltishall was a grass airfield, and the squadron was flying endless convoy protection patrols together with 66 Squadron, with whom we shared the airfield. I was a flight mechanic and keeping the Hurricanes serviceable in view of this constant flying was an exhausting undertaking. We used to work a pattern of shifts, from 0800 hrs until noon on the first day, 1630 until 0800 hrs the following day, then 1430 - 1630. We had the use of a Nissen hut at dispersal, but it was such a lovely summer that more often than not we would just kip down under the mainplanes. There was no formal defence set up on the aerodrome, so a couple of chaps who had been in France dug a couple of gun pits and received authorisation to arm them with a couple of Browning machine-guns!

Many of the ground crews were Canadians who had enlisted in the RAF with a view to going on flying duties, an ambition many later achieved through Bader's encouragement and help in recommending their applications.

One incident I recall from this period concerns a Pilot Officer Brown who reported on the R/T that his throttle control was jammed in the fully open position. He was consequently 'talked down' by Squadron Leader Bader. Brown came in low, just clearing the perimeter fence and using the whole length of the airfield before coming into dispersal where 'Chiefy' Mason was waiting and was heard to say 'Your feet won't touch the ground when the CO hears who serviced Brown's kite today'. However, a hole in the engine cowling was the clue, a bullet having hit the outer sheath of the throttle control thus jamming the inner cable against it. 'Chiefy' Mason's remark was consistent with what the CO thought about possible poor work, and his attitude; he wanted as many serviceable aircraft as possible. Nothing wrong with that, the country faced a crisis and could therefore ill afford incompetence. I recall that we once complained regarding the standard of food being served in the Airmens' Mess; our CO intervened personally, leading to an immediate improvement. He could not tolerate inefficiency or incompetence and made this very plain to all and sundry. I wonder whether this is why he fast gained a reputation of being rather bloody minded and arrogant? I would prefer to think that it was more a case of having a single-minded attitude as his priority was clearly to beat the Germans - this was, after all, the object of the exercise.

I will always recall Squadron Leader Bader working his way backwards on his backside along the port mainplane until reaching the cockpit when he then went into a practised routine of swinging his right leg up into it. In conclusion, my personal recollections of my old CO are all happy ones. He was a very brave man, make no mistake.

Squadron Leader Bader initially commenced an intensive regime of training flying, but on July 4th, 1940, he signalled 12 Group, with a copy to Fighter Command, to the effect that 242 Squadron was operational in terms of pilots trained for day flying, but 'non-operational as regards equipment'. It was not 'done' for a newly promoted *Acting* Squadron Leader to send such a signal to HQ Fighter Command, but by having done so Bader had cleverly engineered a situation that required resolution. Squadron Leader Bader consequently argued with an HQ equipment officer of equal rank, as a result of which Air Chief Marshal Dowding requested Bader's presence at Bentley Priory. After the forthright CO of 242 Squadron stated his case, Dowding moved swiftly, sacking the equipment officer and ordering forthwith Squadron Leader Bader's requirements. Needless to say, the incident earned Bader great respect amongst 242 Squadron personnel, but this early indication of his eagerness to misuse official channels was to set a dangerous precedent.

Squadron Leader Bader (centre) with two of his Canadian pilots at Coltishall.
(Author via Douglas Bader Foundation)

Back where he belongs: a very happy Squadron Leader Bader, CO of 242 Squadron
(Author via Douglas Bader Foundation)

*Camaraderie: a snapshot interesting not only because of the Hurricane's heraldry,
but also as it epitomises the close relationship which existed between the essential, but less
glamorous, groundcrews and the pilot who flew 'their' aeroplane. Sadly, this 242 Squadron
pilot, Doug Edmunds, was killed in a mid-air collision with Squadron Leader 'Treacle'
Tracey in April 1941.*
(Author via Douglas Bader Foundation)

Group Captain Woodhall:-

Douglas was very apt to cut corners and ignore regulations or interpret them his own way in
order to get on with the war. On one occasion when he had offended against some rule, I was
given orders from a higher authority to reprove him. He was ordered to report to me office, and
when he stumped in and saluted with his usual cheerful grin he noticed that I was wearing my
cap, and did not tell him to sit down which indicated an official interview. Douglas stood to
attention and said with an impish grin, 'Woody, you're not going to be rotten to me are you?'
What could I do but laugh, then tell him to sit down? Needless to say the reproof was more or
less passed to him as a joke - but the fact that it <u>was</u> passed on proved quite effective.

The administrative and operational tasks and problems increased daily, and hampered as
we were by a set of peacetime rules and regulations designed as they were in the main to
prevent petty pilfering, it is not surprising that everyone trying to do his job had to cut the 'red
tape' in order to get on with the war.

In this Douglas Bader and I saw eye-to-eye, and I can state that we backed each other up
loyally in this matter of tape-cutting. LM, as our AOC, was always on our side too, which was
very comforting!

On July 9th, 1940, just *one* day before the Battle of Britain officially commenced, 242 Squadron
became fully operational.

CHAPTER THREE

Gunsmoke in the sky

After the fall of France, Britain stood alone. If ever Dowding needed any justification for his commitment to ensuring security of the 'base', this was it. The success or failure of Britain's air defences, which alone could prevent the enemy from gaining the air supremacy so essential for an invasion, was to be the decisive factor.

The Battle of Britain is officially deemed to have started on July 10th, 1940, although, in fact, the two air forces had frequently clashed over the Channel since Dunkirk. The conflict was later considered to have gone through specific phases, and the first, between the start-date and August 7th, largely involved attacks on British convoys. Great dogfights took place overhead, often involving up to 100 fighters, but combats over the Channel meant that many Fighter Command pilots were reported 'missing', there being no formal air-sea rescue arrangements at that time. As the Strait of Dover was the focus of these events, the adjacent area of south-east England became known as 'Hellfire Corner'.

The 12 Group squadrons, located further north, had little action, however. Amongst those units was 611 'West Lancashire' Squadron. This was an Auxiliary Air Force (AAF) unit formed at Hendon in February 1936, receiving Spitfires in May 1939. From October 1939 the squadron had been resident at 12 Group's Digby Sector Station in Lincolnshire. The CO, Squadron Leader James McComb, was a 31-year-old former solicitor who had joined the AAF in 1934, transferring to 611 Squadron, his local unit, upon its formation in 1936. He received command of the Lancashire squadron on September 3rd, 1939. Over Dunkirk he had claimed an Me 109 destroyed and an He 111 'probable'.

Squadron Leader James McComb (fourth from right) with his pilots of 611 Squadron, pictured at Digby after Dunkirk.
(Author's Collection)

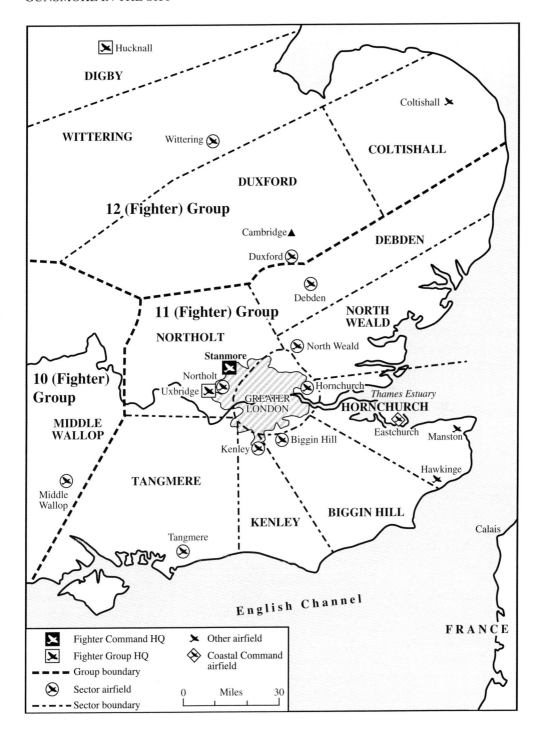

Relevant Fighter Command Group and Sector boundaries.

Mr WA Ellams was a member of 611 Squadron's ground staff:-

Early in 1939, I was employed in Liverpool as an insurance clerk and after the events of 1938, realised that a conflict was on the way. I loved aircraft and as I had heard of the City of Liverpool squadron, the 'weekenders', I decided to join up. I knew that they flew Hawker Harts and Hinds and although I didn't want to be a pilot, I fancied myself as a rear gunner. Having matriculated at school, I was accepted as an Aircraft Hand (ACH). Every Saturday and Sunday I went to Speke, marched up and down, stripped machine-guns and re-assembled them, listened to general lectures until I could do it all with my eyes closed. No flying yet, in fact I hardly saw any aircraft close at hand. Then in August 1939 we went to Duxford for 14 days annual camp - I was full of hope that at last I would fly and get some target practice. During annual camp, war was declared; the crisis had come. I spent days and nights belting .303" ammo and we were equipped with Spitfires - gone, therefore, were my hopes of flying. However, as compensation I was given a Lewis ground machine-gun post. The first air raid came and we were all so keen, we fought to get into the gun emplacement but in our excitement forgot to collect the gun from the armoury! Next I was put to work in the 611 Orderly Room because of my 'civvy' clerical experience - I was well cheesed off! However, one lunchtime when I was alone in the office I noticed a half-typed list of 'Aircraft Hands (Group 5)' being recommended for fitter course training. I typed my name and number, S11223, on the list and said nothing about it to anyone else. Some weeks later I was posted with others to St Athan on a flight rigger course. I took to aerodynamics like a duck to water and, after some weeks, passed out an AC1. I was posted back to 611 Squadron at Digby where I was put in 'B' Flight and given a Spitfire to look after. God I was thrilled!

We slept in dug-outs on dispersal near the aircraft - bunkers well on the edge of the 'drome. We were up every morning at dawn to run up and check everything. Despite it being summer, whilst the flight mechanic revved up, we riggers were straddled over the tailplane, frozen in the slipstream! Once a Spitfire overrode the chocks and started moving forwards despite the brakes being applied! I was so cold and numb that I didn't give a damn. Incidentally, the Dunlop air brakes were the weak part of the Spitfire. I must have spent hours of my time upside down in the cockpit adjusting the air valves to synchronise the pressure with the rudder bar!

Whilst on Standby during the day we would clean the Spitfires with wax dissolved in a petrol mixture, let it dry then polish it like hell to get a shine. The crew undertaking this often included the pilot who also 'mucked in'. By doing this we could get an extra 5 mph in flight. I have since been told by Hans 'Peter' Wulff, a *Luftwaffe* pilot who has previously contributed to Dilip's books, that the Germans did the same! At Digby we very much regarded ourselves as a team, including the pilot, who was more or less considered a friend. We would discuss with him things like the 'hands off' technique. I would place a bit of string doped on the control surfaces or trimming tabs to get perfection - amazing what a little knowledge of aerodynamics can do!

To get the Spitfire back up into the sky as quickly as possible was very important to the rigger, mechanic and armourer. This team would practise the routine over and over again. We could all check control surfaces, refuel and rearm in just four minutes. We made short-handled screwdrivers to undo and fasten the 'Dzus' buttons which secured the panels. Believe me, they were exciting times! During one of these 'panic' turnarounds, I was passing along the leading edge of the mainplane, the armourer was rearming and reloading the Browning guns when as he was pulling back the striking pin with his toggle, it slipped and there was a round up the spout - the bullet passed by my face but I didn't even stop - when the 'kite' had taken off I said a prayer and broke out into a sweat!

Another nasty bit of work was on take-off. The rigger stood by the starter trolley whilst the pilot primed the engine. When the engine fired I had to pass along the leading edge of the main plane and take out the 'plug' just behind the airscrew, fasten up the little panel with the 'Dzus' fastener, run back and pull the chocks away. That airscrew so near one's arm and shoulder was not at all nice, especially as the pilot was anxious to get moving forward to take-off in formation! Many was the time I had to duck and let the mainplane pass over my head.

I remember our Sergeant Levenson taking -off very early one morning in his pyjamas with flying helmet, jacket, one boot and no trousers - panic stations! He was a shade of blue on his return but it was no funk. A particular officer pilot used to spray the inside of his cockpit with lavender water but he was not a pansy. Other pilots had lucky charms but I never once saw a frightened face. The comradeship between pilots and groundcrews was wonderful.

Whilst on duty we were never allowed away from the aircraft, meals were brought out to dispersal. Whilst 'stood down' we had hobbies: I made model aircraft, Gilly Potter grew vegetables, Len Carter made paper knives out of old salvaged flying wire and put perspex handles on them. Some made a poker and pontoon gang and played with matches, others tried to filter the green dye out of the 100 octane petrol to sell to the pilots who often had cars but no fuel. I bought an old bicycle and did it up like new. Whilst off duty I would cycle to Lincoln and have egg and chips at the Salvation Army Canteen, price one shilling (five new pence).

Throughout the morning of July 11th, 1940, German reconnaissance aircraft constantly monitored British coastal waters: over 80 such sorties were plotted by RDF stations from the north of Scotland to Land's End. One of these flights was undertaken at dawn by a Do 17 of *Wettererkundungsstaffel 261*, briefed to report on weather conditions off the Norfolk and Suffolk coasts. Off Yarmouth at 0600 hrs Squadron Leader Rupert Leigh and Sergeant Reg Hyde of 66 Squadron intercepted the intruder. Having damaged the oil tank of Leigh's Spitfire, the Do 17 escaped into cloud. In 'Reach for the Sky', Paul Brickhill claims that the Group Controller had virtually pleaded with Squadron Leader Douglas Bader to scramble a section of 242 Squadron Hurricanes against this 'Bogey'; according to Brickhill, Bader declined, due to the bad weather conditions, but under pressure ultimately agreed to go alone. The account failed to make any mention of the fact that two Spitfires from Coltishall's other squadron were already airborne, and indeed engaged the raider. Furthermore, in view of Douglas Bader's apparently unquenchable thirst for action, it is hard to believe that any persuasion would be necessary to get him airborne in such circumstances; in view of the various romantic embellishments in 'Reach for the Sky' discovered during the preparation of 'Bader's Tangmere Spitfires' (also by the author, PSL, 1996), I have to wonder whether this could be another example of Brickhill 'twisting the tale' (as Wing Commander PB 'Laddie' Lucas, Bader's brother-in-law and another biographer, once said to me of a similar scenario). Nevertheless, shortly after 66 Squadron's inconclusive contact, the Dornier concerned was intercepted off Cromer by Squadron Leader Bader; between clouds, he managed a long burst at the enemy aircraft, which silenced the rear gunner, but was frustrated to lose the bomber in another cloud. At 0610 hrs, the Dornier crashed into the sea, and 242 Squadron thus chalked up its first kill: the new CO had proved himself in combat.

The media made much of this victory scored by the heroic legless squadron commander. The story inspired the nation. Even the comparatively lowly *Malvern Gazette* included the following reference to the incident in an article entitled 'The Extra Bit', aimed at encouraging donations to the town's 'Spitfire Fund':-

Remember the story of the young pilot who lost his legs in a crash? Fitted with artificial legs he argued his way back into the RAF; argued his way through the medical boards; argued his way into a squadron, and one day, quite recently, he went up alone and shot a Dornier down into the sea. Did he say 'I've given the country my legs; why should I now be expected to give them my neck?' Not a bit! Like all those gallant lads he was ready to give the extra. God bless them for it.

Already the facts had become distorted, but such a version understandably made just the kind of morale-boosting story so urgently required by the propagandists; Douglas Bader had become a war hero.

Such lone raiders as Bader's July 11th victim frequently prowled around the Norfolk coast; on July 13th, Squadron Leader Bader wrote in his log book, 'Attempted Interception of Heinkel, never saw it'.

On July 21st, 1940, Squadron Leader Bader led 242 Squadron on a 'Wing Drill'. On July 24th, 242 and 66 Squadrons combined to create a practice 'Wing formation' (two further such practice sorties were later flown on August 6th and 7th). Previous accounts have claimed that these flights give an early indication of the subsequent 'Big Wing' idea supported by both Air Vice-Marshal Leigh-Mallory and Squadron Leader Bader. As there is no *evidence* to support this, however, I feel certain that these sorties were no more than basic practice in flying a 'convoy' formation. As we have seen, Wings had already been used during the Dunkirk fighting, so squadrons obviously had to have some experience of such formations in the event of their use being required again. During the training sorties concerned, there were, in any case, no practice interceptions, as it was just simply a case of two fighter squadrons, commanded by close friends, flying together.

On July 24th, 1940, 19 Squadron had moved from Duxford to take up residence at the nearby satellite airfield at Fowlmere, codenamed 'G1'. John Milne had arrived at Duxford on March 11th, 1940, as a Halton-trained Flight Rigger LAC; he remembers Fowlmere Farm:-

LAC John Milne.
(Author via Mr John Milne)

When we first moved to Fowlmere there was no permanent accommodation. We slept in bell tents, feet to the central pole. A mobile cookhouse accompanied us - one day it caught fire! We dug latrine trenches and spent most of our time out of doors. Nobody seemed to mind. Fowlmere later had Nissen huts, never popular, as condensation dripped down from the underside of the cold steel roof onto both one's bedding and oneself.

A snapshot taken by Pilot Officer Peter Howard-Williams and 'discovered' by the author in the log book of Pilot Officer Arthur Vokes, where captioned 'Just before the Blitz'. 19 Squadron at Fowlmere Farm, left to right: Squadron Leader Brian Lane, Sergeants Jack Potter and Bernard Jennings, Pilot Officer Ray Aeberhardt, Flight Sergeants George Unwin and Harry Steere, Flying Officer Frank Brinsden, Flight Lieutenant Walter Lawson, Flying Officer Alan Haynes, Pilot Officer Arthur Vokes, Flight Lieutenant Wilf Clouston and Flying Officer Eric Thomas. Of interest are the army-style battledress blouses worn by several of the pilots, and the German life-jacket sported by Clouston, the commander of 'B' Flight.

19 Squadron's primitive facilities at Fowlmere Farm.

(Both: Author's Collection)

Flying from Fowlmere must have been fun! The airfield was far from level and dipped down considerably in the corner nearest to Duxford. Part of it was laid with metal mesh decking to improve the surface. There were certain features of both Duxford and Fowlmere which must remain forever recalled by everyone who served there: the sound of Merlin engines starting, taxying and flying low over the airfield; the smell of glycol coolant leaking on hot metal; the smell of 100 octane petrol, and straining the green dye from it.

On July 27th, 1940, 19 Squadron began daily journeys from Fowlmere to operate out of Coltishall, the purpose being 'part of a new policy to give cannon-armed Spitfires a chance to operate from the coast and to relieve 66 Squadron of certain tasks.' 19 Squadron, which was the only operational squadron equipped at the time with the experimental Spitfire Mk IB (armed with two 20 mm Hispano-Suiza cannon), thereafter commenced assisting the Coltishall-based squadrons with the monotonous routine of providing convoy protection patrols. On July 29th, the 19 Squadron Operations Record Book (ORB) recorded:-

The whole of 'B' Flight in three sections of two aircraft sent off in big alarm at Coltishall, when all available squadrons left the ground. 'B' Flight ordered to attack approaching enemy bombers. No enemy aircraft were sighted. 66 Squadron got two He 111s, but 'B' Flight returned after vain search lasting 1 hour and 15 minutes.

The 12 Group Controller was responding to an attack against a convoy off Harwich. Although 66 Squadron, for no loss, certainly did destroy two He 111s of I/KG53, by also scrambling both 19 Squadron's 'B' Flight and 242 Squadron, Air Vice-Marshal Leigh-Mallory had left Coltishall airfield protected by just the former unit's 'B' Flight. What was the purpose of committing some 30 fighters to such an interception? An early indication of Leigh-Mallory's tactical attitude is provided by Wing Commander David Cox:-

I remember in June 1940, we were visited at Duxford by Air Vice-Marshal Leigh-Mallory who, stabbing his finger at a map on the wall, exclaimed 'My fighters will be here, here and here!', from which I now deduce that he always had in mind to intercept the enemy in numbers, as opposed to what later went on down south.

On July 31st, 1940, 19 Squadron was celebrating; Brian Lane had been awarded the DFC. Flight Lieutenant Wallace 'Jock' Cunningham remembers:-

Pilot Officer Wallace 'Jock' Cunningham. (Author via Flight Lieutenant Wallace Cunningham)

We were lying in the sun at Coltishall along with Douglas Bader and other 242 Squadron pilots. It was before our involvement in the Battle of Britain proper but Brian Lane had already received a 'gong' for his good leadership of the squadron and general activities at Dunkirk. There was some banter going on and Douglas asked Brian 'What's that?', in his usual cocky fashion, thrusting his pipe at Brian's DFC ribbon. '*I* must get one of those', said Bader. There was no antipathy between Brian Lane and Douglas Bader, however, they were good friends.

On July 29th, 1940, the DCAS, Air Vice-Marshal Sholto Douglas, ordered Fighter, Bomber and Coastal Commands to undertake strong attacks against E-boast bases, *Luftwaffe* coastal airfields, and gun batteries. Such attacks should be timed, instructed Douglas, to hit enemy airfields immediately after German aircraft had landed following their own raids on England. Although E-boats could certainly be attacked when their presence was known, airfields, on the other hand, were notoriously well defended and therefore attacks were unlikely to be successful. The constant enemy air activity over the Pas-de-Calais made it impossible to identify when a raid was actually in progress until it commenced moving out across the Channel. Due to the speeds of the aircraft involved, the Germans were only five minutes from Dover when thus identified (an observation which puts the problem of interception for 11 Group generally into perspective). The time from the identification of such a raid to it re-crossing the French coast was usually no more than 30 minutes. To strike when the German bombers had just landed, RAF bombers would have to be brought to a state of Readiness whenever such a *Luftwaffe* raid appeared possible. Furthermore, immediately after meeting a raid, 11 Group would clearly experience difficulty in supplying enough fighters to protect such a counter-attack. Dowding's SASO, Air Vice-Marshal Douglas Evill, who had previously served as Bomber Command's SASO, recognised these difficulties. After consultation with his opposite number at Bomber Command, and Air Vice-Marshal Park, the SASO considered that such a venture would be unwise; far better to make a counter-attack in strength, following extensive reconnaissance and study of the targets. Fortunately, therefore, Douglas's potentially suicidal orders came to nought.

Squadron Leader Philip Pinkham
(Author: via Mr Jim Pinkham)

Significantly, on August 12th, 1940, 19 Squadron's 'B' Flight arrived at Eastchurch airfield, near Sheerness, in 11 Group. The Flight was led there by the Squadron Commander, Squadron Leader Philip Pinkham AFC. A career officer, Pinkham had joined the RAF in 1935. He first served as a fighter pilot, flying biplanes with 17 Squadron, and then flew Gauntlets with the

Meteorological Flight. In January 1940, Pinkham took command of the Air Fighting School at St Athan. There he was responsible for training pilots to fly Hurricanes. The unit later became No 6 Operational Training Unit (OTU), based at Sutton Bridge; there, on March 27th, 1940, Squadron Leader Pinkham received a letter from 12 Group HQ informing him that Air Vice-Marshal Leigh-Mallory was greatly pleased with the standard of training achieved by 6 OTU in respect of their Finnish pilots. On June 10th, Pinkham succeeded Squadron Leader Stephenson as CO of 19 Squadron; one month later Pinkham received the Air Force Cross for his flying training work. At that time, the policy was for fighter squadrons to be given to pre-war career officers who, like Pinkham, were former flying instructors without combat experience. A more practical route, perhaps, might have been to promote senior flight commanders from within Fighter Command where they had already gained invaluable combat experience. For example, after Stephenson's capture, Flight Lieutenant Lane assumed command of 19 Squadron until Squadron Leader Pinkham's arrival; thereafter, in any case, Lane largely continued to lead the squadron into action as the CO was preoccupied with the cannon problems and tactics.

At Eastchurch, Pinkham's Spitfires rendezvoused with those of Squadron Leader Rodney Wilkinson's 266 Squadron, which had been sent down from Wittering. These detachments represented an expression of support by the 12 Group AOC for the DCAS's proposed counter-attack. Briefed to strafe E-Boats with the troublesome 20 mm cannon, Pinkham wrote in his log book that the Spitfires were also to 'escort the Battle boys on a beat up of the other side'. Fortunately the sortie was never undertaken, but it was incredible that the DCAS and AOC 12 Group could have contemplated such a plan; the Fairey Battle light-bomber losses in France should have been sufficient to convince anyone of such folly. Due to Air Vice-Marshal Leigh-Mallory's apparent lack of fighter ability, it is doubtful whether he considered, as Evill did, the impracticality of the idea. Whilst it is arguable that if any fighters were to have been used in such a counter-attack they should come not from 11 Group but from one of its reinforcing neighbours, this idea remains an early indication of just how closely Air Vice-Marshals Leigh-Mallory and Douglas were already working.

The following day, the 12 Group Spitfires remained at Eastchurch. According to the 19 Squadron ORB, the airfield was 'most thoroughly bombed' by 15 Do 17s of KG2. Although many bombs fell on the airfield, which was also strafed, there were no casualties to either personnel or aircraft belonging to 19 Squadron. 266 Squadron lost one Spitfire destroyed on the ground, and Coastal Command's 35 Squadron lost five Blenheims. Much damage to airfield buildings was caused and 16 airmen were killed. The raid indicated how weak German Intelligence was in certain respects: the presence of Spitfires at Eastchurch was little more than coincidental to the raid, the airfield not having been otherwise home to fighters for over 10 years.

On August 14th, Squadron Leader Pinkham led his Spitfires back to Fowlmere, but Squadron Leader Wilkinson's 266 Squadron did not return to Wittering, instead flying to Hornchurch for its period of service in the front line. Two days later Wilkinson was dead, and after just one week at Hornchurch the squadron was pulled out and returned to Wittering: by that time, 266 had lost four more pilots killed and two wounded.

Throughout the latter half of August 1940, the tempo of battle increased when the *Adler Angriff* offensive was launched with the specific objective of achieving aerial supremacy prior to the launching of the proposed invasion, Operation *Seelowe*. Extensive aerial reconnaissance of southern England was followed by heavy attacks on shipping, ports and installations, radar stations, and, towards the end, by strikes along the south coast and, in particular, Fighter Command's airfields. 11 Group continued to bear the brunt of the fighting, those Squadrons in 12 Group still largely occupied with chasing lone raiders or, much more mundanely, providing endless protection patrols for convoys travelling around the coasts of eastern England.

At Coltishall, Acting Squadron Leader Douglas Bader was not content to while away his time playing games of patience. He sulked and stormed, unable to accept that his was a lesser part in what was clearly a critical aerial conflict. Together with his pilots of 242 Squadron, he sat restlessly at readiness, eagerly awaiting the scramble call that never seemed to come. For a man with such an irrepressible spirit as Douglas Bader, and a *constant* thirst for action, being kept out of the battle was utterly intolerable. Directly, and contrarily to the provisions of the System, Bader frequently pressured his friends, Wing Commander Woodhall and the AOC directly, imploring that his squadron be sent into action over 11 Group's area. Under the provisions of the System such a move was impossible until 11 Group called for assistance. Air Marshal Sir Denis Crowley-Milling:-

Naturally Douglas wanted to get us of 242 Squadron into the action. He used to say 'Why don't they get us airborne when the Germans were building up over the Pas-de-Calais?' He felt that we could then proceed south and meet the enemy formation on its way in.

Waiting, frustration mounting; pilots of 242 Squadron: Pilot Officer WL McKnight,
Flight Lieutenant GE Ball, Squadron Leader DRS Bader, Pilot Officer NN Campbell
and Pilot Officer D Crowley-Milling.
(Author via Douglas Bader Foundation)

This theory actually had little merit, since RDF was rarely able to tell when a raid was 'building up', owing to the constant enemy air activity over the French coast. The only indication that a raid was impending was when it started moving out across the Channel, by which time it was too late to act as Squadron Leader Bader suggested. Even on occasions when RDF worked sufficiently well to detect a 'build up', the timescale remained insufficient to operate, with all due respect, as Squadron Leader Bader suggested. This is an early indication of the relatively inexperienced Douglas Bader failing to appreciate the technicalities of RDF and indeed his Commander-in-Chief's System.

What 12 Group's pilots generally failed to appreciate was that they were there as a part of Dowding's overall defence, with the Group having its own area of geographical responsibility in addition to the task of reinforcing 11 Group if so required. Although the Commander-in-Chief had delegated the tactical initiative to his Group Commanders, he retained the broad perspective concerning Fighter Command as a whole (as indeed he had pointed out to Air Vice-Marshal Leigh-Mallory in correspondence dated October 1st, 1939, see Chapter One). A heavy attack could have developed at any time on the Midlands or north of England, in which case 12 Group's pilots would have quenched their thirst for action.

On Thursday, 15th August, 1940, all three *Luftflotten* on the Western Front made concerted attacks on targets from Northumberland to Dorset. The *Luftwaffe* planners wrongly believed that their attacks in the north would meet with little opposition owing to the British having been forced to make good losses suffered in the south by reinforcing with squadrons from northern England. The most northerly part of the raiding force, consisting of 63 He 111s of I & II *Gruppen* KG26, escorted by 21 Me 110s of I/ZG76, was intercepted by RAF fighters east of the Farne Islands. Five RAF fighter squadrons were involved, from bases between Catterick in Yorkshire to Drem on the Firth of Forth. It was this 'Valhalla' that gave 607 Squadron's Pilot Officer Harry Welford his first glimpse of a massed enemy formation:-

At 1230 pm we were going off duty for 24 hours leave when the whole squadron was called to Readiness. We heard from the Group Operations Room that there was a big 'flap' on, that is a warning of imminent enemy action along the NE coast. We waited out at dispersal points, at 'Flights', for half an hour, then scrambled in squadron formation. I was in a feverish state of excitement and quickly took off and climbed up to our operational height of 20,000' ready to patrol the coast. We kept receiving messages over the R/T of 40 or 50 plus 'Bogeys' approaching Newcastle from the north. Although we patrolled for over half an hour, we never saw a thing. Just as I was expecting the order to 'Pancake', I heard the senior flight commander shout 'Tally Ho!', and 'Tally Ho' it was! There, on our port side at 9,000' must have been 120 bombers, all with swastikas and German crosses as large as life, having the gross impertinence to cruise down Northumberland and Durham's NE coast. These were the people who were going to bomb Newcastle and Sunderland where our families and friends lived, 607 Squadron being an Auxiliary unit raised from the local area.

I'd never seen anything like it. They were in two groups, one of about 70 and the other about 40, like two swarms of bees. There was no time to wait and we took up position and delivered No 3 attacks in sections. As only three machines at a time, in formation, attacked a line of 20 bombers, I just couldn't see how their gunners could miss us. We executed our attack, however, and despite the fact that I thought it was me being hit all over the place, it was their machines which started dropping out of the sky. In my excitement, during the next attack I only narrowly missed one of our own machines whilst doing a 'split arse' breakaway - there couldn't have been more than two feet between us! Eventually, spotting most of the enemy aircraft dropping down with only their undercarriages damaged, I chased a Heinkel and filled that poor devil with lead until first one, then the other engine stopped. I then enjoyed the sadistic satisfaction of watching the bomber crash into the sea. With the one I reckoned to have damaged during our first attack, these were my first bloods, and so I was naturally elated. The squadron suffered no losses, but claimed six He 111s and two Do 17s destroyed, five He 111s and one Do 17 probably destroyed, and four He 111s and one Do 17 damaged, although we now know that in fact, there were no Do 17s amongst the German formation.

The southerly part of the raid was directed against the airfield at Driffield, in Yorkshire, and comprised 50 unescorted Ju 88s of KG30. This attack was intercepted by the Spitfires of 616 Squadron, from Leconfield, and the Hurricane's of 73 Squadron's 'B' Flight, based at Church Fenton, both 12 Group units. For no loss, those RAF fighter squadrons claimed eight unescorted Ju 88s destroyed. For the enemy, the raid was disastrous; having expected to encounter little opposition, seven Fighter Command squadrons, including three of Spitfires, had mauled the raiders without loss. It is curious, however, that against such a heavy attack, Air Vice-Marshal Leigh-Mallory only responded with some 18 aircraft, especially in view of his over-reaction to the minor threat on July 27th when he scrambled all of Coltishall's 30 fighters. This hardly represents any planned philosophy for dealing with enemy attacks. For Squadron Leader Bader, the day could only be described as yet another frustrating one, with 242 Squadron being, ironically, located too far south to assist. On that day, Squadron Leader Bader dejectedly wrote in his log book, 'Interception. No contact'.

The northerly action on August 15th, was a total justification of Air Chief Marshal Dowding's policy of retaining strength in both 12 and 13 Groups. Also, throughout the rest of the Battle of Britain, Dowding could not be certain that such a massed attack would not be repeated; despite the pressures in southern England, therefore, he had also to maintain a strong force in the north.

So heavy were the attacks on southern England on August 15th, that 11 Group had to call on 12 Group for assistance, the object of the exercise being for the 12 Group squadrons to protect Park's airfields north of the Thames whilst his fighters were engaged further forward. Wing Commander David Cox remembers:-

No 19 Squadron was scrambled to intercept a raid on Martlesham Heath airfield, near Ipswich. The attack was carried out by some 25 Me 110s of *Erprobungsgruppe 210*, led by their brilliant *Kommodore*, Erich Rubensdorfer. The enemy's approach went completely undetected until they were only a few minutes from their target. Only three Hurricanes of 17 Squadron managed to get up from Martlesham before the 110s arrived. Our chances of intercepting the raid, however, were nil, taking into account that the distance from our airfield at Fowlmere to Martlesham was 60 air miles. Taking an *optimistic* speed for our Spitfires of 300 mph, it would take 12 minutes from take-off to reach Martlesham Heath. I doubt that at our altitude, 2,000', our cannon-armed Spitfires were capable of that speed, as its maximum speed was not reached until 19,000'. I would suggest that 280 mph was the maximum possible for height, but even at 300 mph the squadron could not achieve the impossible.

Sergeant David Cox
(Author via Wing Commander DGSR Cox)

The failure of 12 Group's squadrons to protect Martlesham Heath infuriated Air Vice-Marshal Park, although 19 Squadron could not be blamed on this occasion for the reasons outlined by Wing Commander Cox. Nor could the 11 Group Controller be blamed, the cause being the minimal warning of Rubensdorfer's surprise low-level attack on a *coastal* airfield.

Having waited around at Coltishall for action all day, during the early evening of August 16th, a coin was flipped to determine which flight of 19 Squadron was to have tea first; the coin favoured 'B' Flight. Shortly afterwards, 'A' Flight, which had remained at Readiness, was recalled to Duxford immediately. Shortly after take-off, 'A' Flight, led by Flight Lieutenant Brian Lane, were told that there might be some 'trade' further south, an 'X-Raid' having appeared on the radar screen. No doubt anticipating the plot to be nothing more than a friendly aircraft, as so often happened, 'A' Flight were stunned when, 30 miles east of Harwich, the plot transpired to be, in Lane's words, 'about 150 Huns!!' The enemy formation was moving southwards and consisted of bombers protected by 40-50 Me 110s, and a number of Me 109s. 'A' Flight, which on this occasion comprised seven pilots, attacked the Me 110s in two sections of three and four aircraft. Surprisingly, the Spitfire pilots were to report that the 110s appeared not to have rear-gunners. Nevertheless, Lane's formation was to suffer great frustration, to due the experimental cannon, and six of the seven pilots suffered stoppages. 'Jock' Cunningham:-

Sergeant Bernard 'Jimmy' Jennings.
(Author via Wing Commander
B Jennings)

I remember mainly Sergeant 'Jimmy' Jennings on the R/T bemoaning his jammed 20 mm cannon, full of indignation at the unfairness of life in general!

'A' Flight claimed three Me 110s destroyed, and a probable. Their claims were remarkably accurate, in fact, as ZG26 lost two destroyed and one damaged. Had no stoppages been encountered, 'A' Flight's score would undoubtedly have been higher, and had the fight been prolonged, perhaps further 12 Group squadrons could have been vectored. Regarding the acceptance of combat claims relating to this action, Flight Lieutenant Lane later wrote:-

Sergeant Potter had the laugh when he was told by the Intelligence Officer that his seemed a certainty all right. 'Well', said Potter, 'I knocked the port engine out of the wings, and the nose as far as the windscreen fell out as well, but he might have got home with a hell of a draught in his face!'.

19 Squadron's 'B' Flight were unimpressed at their bad luck; again, Brian Lane later wrote:-

Several of 'B' Flight, including the CO and Wilf Clouston, the Flight's Commander, were asking questions and cursing their luck. Wilf shook his head sadly, 'Dammit, it isn't fair!' We all laughed, at least 'A' Flight did!

Having missed the great battles of the previous day, Squadron Leader Bader and 242 Squadron must have also thought 'not fair', to say the least, the luck of 19 Squadron's 'A' Flight on August 16th. That day, Squadron Leader Bader had been vectored to intercept two X-Raids himself, but both, as so often happened in what was, after all, Bomber Command country, transpired to be friendly aircraft. We can only wonder at his mounting frustration. Not only was the battle raging in southern England, but what action was to be enjoyed over 12 Group was largely being had by other squadrons, and 19 Squadron was by now easily the most experienced fighter squadron based in the area.

When later reporting to HQ Fighter Command, Air Vice-Marshal Park was to consider that from August 8th - August 18th, 1940, there had been another distinct phase in enemy attacks. These were, he stated, delivered against the following targets:-

(a) Shipping and ports on the South-East and South coast, between North Foreland and Portland.

(b) Massed attacks against Portland and Portsmouth.

(c) Attacks on fighter aerodromes on the coast, followed by Bomber Command and Coastal Command aerodromes on the coast.

(d) Towards the end of this period, comparatively light attacks were pressed inland by day to various objectives.

The RAF fighters, he reported, had been thus employed:-

The main problem was to know which was the diversionary attack and to hold sufficient fighter squadrons in readiness to meet the main attack when this could be discerned from the very unreliable information received from the RDF, after they had been heavily bombed. To meet these attacks on coastal objectives, it was essential to keep nearly all Readiness squadrons at forward aerodromes, such as Lympne, Hawkinge, Manston, Rochford. The greatest vigilance had to be observed by Group Controller not to have these squadrons bombed or machine-gunned on the ground at forward aerodromes. On only one occasion was any squadron at a forward aerodrome attacked while on the ground refuelling, and this was because the squadron failed to maintain a protective patrol over the base during refuelling.

A very high state of preparedness has to be maintained in order to engage the enemy before he reached his coastal objectives. The general plan in employing the fighters was to detail about half the available squadrons, including the Spitfires, to engage the enemy fighters, and the remainder to attack the enemy bombers, which normally flew at between 11,000 and 13,000 feet, and carried out their attack frequently from 7,000 to 8,000 feet.

During this phase our fighters were mainly employing the Fighter Command attacks from astern. These gave good results against the enemy fighters, which were unarmoured, but were not so effective against the bombers. Our fighters were therefore advised to practise deflection shots from quarter astern, also from above and from below against twin-engined bombers.

During this phase, fighter squadrons not infrequently flew over fifty hours in one day with twelve aircraft in commission.

The casualties to pilots and aircraft were about equal in numbers for any given engagement. Owing to the lack of trained formation and section leaders, also to the fitting of armour to enemy bombers, our casualties were relatively higher than during May and June, when operating over France and Belgium.

Results (of air combat) were satisfactory, the proportion of enemy shot down to our own losses being about four to one, slightly below the average when fighting over France. As much of this fighting took place over the sea, casualties were higher than they would have been if the fighting had been over land. The results of air combat were good because the enemy fighters were frequently too high to protect their bombers. Moreover, the Ju 87 proved an easy prey to both Hurricanes and Spitfires.

It would appear (in conclusion) that our fighter defences proved too good for the enemy, because on August 18th the Germans withdrew their dive bombers, Ju 87s, and there was a break of five days in intensive operations.

On August 17th, another fighter squadron became operational in 12 Group, this being 310 Squadron, based at Duxford and equipped with Hurricanes. The squadron's personnel were largely Czechs who had escaped their homeland prior to flying with the L'Armée d'Air until the fall of France. Thereafter they had escaped to England and offered their services to the RAF, determined to continue the fight. No 310 Squadron was consequently formed on July 10th, 1940.

Group Captain Woodhall:-

Most of the Czech pilots reported in French uniform. On arrival in England they spoke little English, and had to be converted onto Hurricanes. They were therefore provided with with an English squadron commander, Squadron Leader Douglas Blackwood, and English flight commanders, Flight Lieutenants Sinclair and Jefferies, in addition to both an English flying instructor and interpreter.

The Czech CO was Squadron Leader Sacha Hess who was quite famous in Czech Air Force circles. Much older than the rest, at 45, he was a first-class pilot and a dedicated fighter.

Our first problem was to overcome the language difficulty, so I rang the BBC with the result that the interpreter and I spent a day at Broadcasting House where we recorded a series of orders, first in English followed by Czech, covering every order from 'Scramble' to 'Pancake'. The BBC quickly sent us several copies of these records, and in a very short time the Czechs were conversant with orders in English alone.

310 Squadron had a spare Hurricane (needless to say it was the oldest and slowest) which was always at my disposal, and as a result, on the few occasions when I could spare the time from my other duties as Station Commander and Sector Controller, I flew on operations with this squadron as rear-end Charlie.

310 Squadron shortly after formation at Duxford, the Czech pilots still wearing their own air force's uniforms. Amongst the seated Czech officers is the CO, Squadron Leader Sacha Hess (fourth from right). The British Officers include, from left to right: Flying Officer Boulton, Squadron Leader Blackwood, Wing Commander Woodhall and Flight Lieutenant Sinclair. Of interest is Pilot Officer Sterbacek (centre, middle row), the first Czech to die in the Battle of Britain and who remains 'missing' to this day.
(Author via Mr WA Kirk)

Wing Commander Douglas Blackwood:-

I cannot speak highly enough of the Czechs' fighting qualities, although I must admit that they did not always do what was expected of them; they were very keen on attacking enemy aircraft whenever they saw them, no matter what the circumstances. At first we had a great deal of difficulty with the lack of a common language as only a few of them understood even basic English. We overcame this difficulty by various means, however.

Wing Commander Gordon Sinclair:-

I have nothing but praise for my fellow Czech pilots. They were a wonderful bunch of people totally determined to kill Germans. They went about this task with great enthusiasm and courage. I personally found it tremendously comforting in battle to have such pilots around me!

Bill Kirk was an Orderley Clerk attached to 310 Squadron:-

Bill Kirk, in 1940 an Orderly Clerk serving with 310 Squadron. He is pictured in the author's office, posing with a Hurricane control column top discovered by Dilip Sarkar at a local scrap dealer's in 1986.
(Author)

The Czechs were first-class and were anxious to have a go, but it was some time before they were considered to be operationally equal to the other squadrons because they just hadn't had the RAF's training. Once they got into the swim though I think they did very well. It became a tradition for us all to have a Czech top button on our RAF tunics. I was amongst the party sent to form 310 Squadron, at which time I was a Corporal. In the Orderly Room we did everything, all the admin from combat reports to leave passes and Air Ministry Orders. Even now I remember that the Form 1623 was airframes and engines! Working hours were non-existent, you just went on until the job was finished. I lived in the barrack block at Duxford and we got on very well with the Czechs. They were always keeping fit, playing volley ball, and were very keen generally. For us on the ground it was tremendously exciting knowing that the aircraft were going into action, and when they returned we all looked anxiously for those with blown gunport patches, indicating that the guns had been fired. It could also be distressing, talking to a chap in the Mess one night only for him to be a 'gonner' the next day. My office was almost on the airfield itself, so we were very close to the pilots and aircraft. I never heard anyone complain about not being in the action, however, so far as I was aware we were being used as much as was either possible or appropriate.

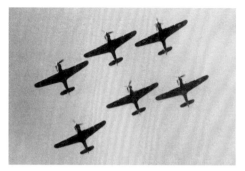

310 Squadron practising close-formation flying, but indicating the tight 'vics' in which RAF fighters once sallied forth into battle.

(Both: Author via Mr WA Kirk)

310 Squadron's dispersal, Duxford, circa 1940; note that the flowerbeds are arranged as a Czech pilot's flying badge and Czechoslovakia itself!

Duxford, near Cambridge, was amongst the earliest RAF stations. Even before construction was complete, 200 members of the United States Aero Squadrons commenced training at Duxford. In 1924, Duxford became a fighter station, home to 19, 29 and 111 Squadrons; it was to undertake this role with distinction for 37 years. As previously explained, the Duxford Station Commander

A 310 Squadron Hurricane, P3146, dispersed at Duxford, summer 1940.
Note the dug-out shelter constructed for the use of groundcrews, a British
member of which poses for the camera.
(Author via Mr WA Kirk)

and Sector Fighter Controller during the Battle of Britain was Wing Commander Alfred Woodhall. A key character in this book, previous accounts have again frequently reported inaccurate biographical details. The following was provided by his son, Martin, and so can be considered authoritative:-

Wing Commander 'Woody' Woodhall, Duxford's Station Commander and 'Boss Controller'. (Author via Mr Martin Woodhall)

My father was born at Kirkby-in-Furness on January 9th, 1897. As a child he moved with his parents to Johannesburg, South Africa, and when war broke out in 1914 he was a volunteer in the South African Defence Force. He worked his passage to England and joined the Manchester University OTC before gaining a commission in the Royal Marine Light Infantry. He served as a subaltern and sniper at Vimy Ridge and was severely wounded on November 13th at Beaumont Hamel during the Battle of the Somme. Early in 1917 he was back on light duties at Gosport and it was here that he first found his love of flying when he was given unofficial lessons in a B.E.2c by Vernon Castle (he of dance fame). Posted as Marine Gunnery Officer on HMS Agincourt in early 1918, he then served on HMS Hawkins in the Middle East, Singapore and China. He then spent a brief period in Ireland in 1921, then went to Bermuda and the Caribbean on HMS Constance.

He volunteered for flying training with the newly formed Fleet Air Arm in 1925, training at Netheravon and Gosport, and undertaking deck landings in a Blackburn Dart. His first active posting was on HMS Furious. He served on a number of the early carriers and saw some action in the Palestine 'troubles' whilst on HMS Courageous. It was whilst flying off carriers that he first wished for accurate and reliable controlling as it was very easy in the pre-radiotelephone and radar days to 'lose' your carrier. In 1936, while a Captain of Marines, he was told that he was being posted to Gosport for shore duties, it being considered that at the age of 33 he had done enough of the frivolous business of flying and should return to duties better suiting a Royal Marine Officer. He promptly asked for and soon received a transfer to the RAF (although he dropped in rank to Flight Lieutenant) and was posted to 111 Squadron, flying Siskins, then to 54 Squadron (Bulldogs) at Hornchurch. Two years later he went to Martlesham Heath as a test pilot where he tested, amongst other aircraft, the Fairey Swordfish. He survived unscathed when the engine failed on the Blackburn M130 with a torpedo and he was forced to go birds' nesting. In 1937 he led the RAF Guard of Honour for the Coronation of George VI. Coinciding with Mussolini's invasion of Abyssinia, he was posted to 41 Squadron at Northolt and the squadron was sent to Aden. Invalided home with a torn cartilage six months later, he then went to Leuchars where he commanded the Advance Training Flight (Deck Landings & Catapult Take-Offs). He was promoted to Squadron Leader on New Year's Day, 1937, and given command of 824 Squadron on HMS Eagle. The carrier was almost immediately sent on China station and while off Malaya was ordered to make a dummy attack on Singapore to test the efficiency of the newly completed fortress. Squadron Leader Woodhall's flight was disqualified for attacking in the wrong direction by coming in from the Malay peninsula, as opposed to seawards, from which direction the defenders anticipated attack.

In 1938, Squadron Leader Woodhall was posted to the Air Ministry where he and a Major Tony Powers submitted a paper suggesting the Royal Marines should be trained as paratroopers with the RAF - this was returned with the comment that the parachute was not considered either 'practical or economic'! The DCAS, Air Vice-Marshal Sholto Douglas, reported that 'Woodhall has worked hard and conscientiously but due to lack of staff training is apt to take short cuts. I think therefore that he will be more suitably employed on an operational station'. Consequently 'Woody' was then posted to Duxford in March 1939 as Squadron Leader Flying (Operations). He was later promoted to Wing Commander and became the Station Commander and Group Sector Controller.

Flight Lieutenant HE 'Teddy' Morten remembers meeting the Duxford Station Commander:-

Pilot Officer 'Teddy' Morten.
(Author via Flight Lieutenant HE Morten)

I received my commission in late June 1940, and was posted to RAF Duxford for supernumerary duties in Operations; the 'VR' letters on my lapel shone brightly on my tunic. There were several of us who arrived at the same time, including an elderly Pilot Officer who was a retired solicitor. We were all introduced to the Station Commander, Wing Commander AB Woodhall. The old solicitor was wearing a Boer War ribbon on his tunic, but 'Woody' asked him where his 1914-18 ribbons were; 'I was too old for the Great War', he replied, and so the Wing Commander decided that, due to his general experience of life, he should become assistant adjutant to 19 Squadron, to help the CO write his casualty letters.

At that time, the Sector Controllers were, first and foremost, Wing Commander Woodhall, Squadron Leader KC Horn, who had commanded a squadron of Strutters (his brother was a successful Sopwith Camel commander), Squadron Leader Marsden, Squadron Leader Stanley Cooper, and Squadron Leader Livivosk.

As dawn broke each day that summer, if on duty at Ops 'B', the Controller would be resting (i.e. asleep only to be disturbed if necessary). Straight after dawn, I would telephone Wing Commander Woodhall on his direct line and inform him of the situation over southern England. There was dire trouble if ever 'Woody' was not told first!

As an embryonic Controller, a 'Wingless Wonder' or 'Penguin', I always made it my business to get to know as many pilots as possible, so as to gain their trust and understand the problems they faced in the air. All of us on the ground, of course, wanted to help them as much as possible.

Group Captain Woodhall:-

When I first arrived at Duxford, it was as 'Squadron Leader Flying Ops.' and second in command to Wing Commander 'Pingo' Lester. In addition to being administrative officer I was made responsible for the development of the Fighter Control System and the training of operations room crews. It was at Sector level that fighter control became a personal affair. From the Sector Station the Controller was in direct communication with the fighter pilots by R/T. With the introduction of VHF R/T, the distances at which one could communicate was increased tremendously.

When I arrived at Duxford there was only a skeleton operations room crew. The priority was to train sufficient personnel to man the operations room on a 24 hour basis. When the WAAF came into being, we were delighted to get female plotters. These girls were a credit to the Air Force, and were so good looking that an officer from Group HQ christened them as 'Woody's Beauty Chorus'!

Mrs Jill Nielsen (née Pepper, commonly known as 'Half Pint'!) was a plotter amongst 'Woody's Beauty Chorus':-

In 1939 and part of 1940, the Duxford Operations Room was situated on the station. Later it was moved some way outside and rebuilt in a sort of shed in a copse. A bus took us there to go on watch. The Operations Room has since been reconstructed at the IWM Duxford Airfield and is very authentic.

In 12 Group we did not get much action. The atmosphere was quiet and we had plenty of time to chat with the Observer Corps on the other end of our headphones. Voices can be very misleading and we sometimes got quite a shock when we met the blokes in person!

After Dunkirk things got more lively and we were kept busy on our watches - concentration and calmness were essential to get the plotting right. The planes went up and it was always exciting when we heard 'Tally Ho!' over the intercom. We felt then that we were doing our bit to help stop the 'bloody Huns'. It was sad, though, when some of our aircraft failed to return, even if we did not know the pilots personally.

There were often dances too in the big hangar and whenever I hear 'In the Mood' I'm back there again and can see the Station Commander, Wing Commander Woodhall, complete with monocle, playing his clarinet with great enthusiasm!

Jill Pepper in 1940

'Woody' 'In the Mood'!

(Left: Author via Mrs Jill Nielsen, right, author via Mr Martin Woodhall)

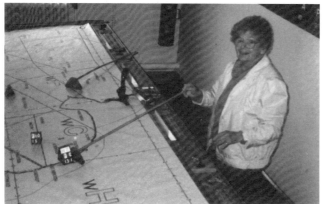

Mrs Jill Nielsen (née Pepper) back in the Duxford Ops Room, April 1995.
(Author via Mrs Jill Nielsen)

On August 18th, the *Luftwaffe* hammered 11 Group's fighter airfields in a bitterly contested day described by eminent historian Dr Alfred Price as 'The Hardest Day' (see Bibliography). For our purposes the date is significant, as it represented the first time that Air Vice-Marshal Park requested reinforcements in numbers from both 10 and 12 Groups; 19 Squadron's Pilot Officer Arthur Vokes recorded in his log book:-

Interception Patrol. S. London, 20,000'. Kenley and Biggin Hill bombed.

A new phase in the aerial conflict began on August 19th, 1940, and lasted until September 5th. During this time, the emphasis of enemy attacks concentrated on inland aerodromes and aircraft factories, industrial targets and, according to Air Vice-Marshal Park, 'areas which could only be classified as residential'. Responding immediately to the changing conditions, on the very day on which the new phase started Air Vice-Marshal Park sent a memorandum to his 11 Group Controllers:-

The following instructions are issued to meet the changing conditions:-

a) Despatch fighters to engage large enemy formations over land or within gliding distance of the coast. During the next two or three weeks, we cannot afford to lose pilots through forced landings in the sea;

b) Avoid sending fighters out over the sea to chase reconnaissance aircraft or small formations of enemy fighters;

c) Despatch a pair of fighters to intercept single reconnaissance aircraft that come inland. If clouds are favourable, put a patrol of one or two fighters over an aerodrome which enemy aircraft are approaching in clouds;

d) Against mass attacks coming inland, despatch a minimum number of squadrons to engage enemy fighters. Our main object is to engage enemy bombers, particularly those approaching under the lowest cloud layer;

e) If all our squadrons around London are off the ground engaging mass attacks, ask No 12 Group or Command Controller to provide squadrons to patrol aerodromes Debden, North Weald, Hornchurch;

f) If heavy attacks have crossed the coast and are proceeding towards aerodromes, put a squadron, or even the Sector Training Flight, to patrol under clouds over every Sector aerodrome;

g)   No 303 (Polish) Squadron can provide two sections for patrol of inland aerodromes, especially while the older squadrons are on the ground refuelling, when enemy formations are flying over land;

h)   No 1 (Canadian) Squadron can be used in the same manner by day as other fighter squadrons.

Note: Protection of all convoys and shipping in the Thames Estuary are excluded from this instruction (Paragraph (a)).

Several conclusions can be drawn from Air Vice-Marshal Park's report. Firstly he was obviously concerned about losing pilots in the Channel, and his instructions were sensibly geared towards preventing such wastage. Secondly he was determined to carefully preserve his force by responding using small formations; in so doing his fighters would not be drawn into battle and possibly destroyed en masse. Thirdly, and just as significantly, the Air Vice-Marshal did *not* consider 11 Group to be fighting its own private war, paragraph 'e' indicating the necessity of receiving reinforcements from 12 Group, particularly in the event of his own forces being committed. The idea was essentially one of forward interception, whereby 11 Group's fighters met the enemy as far forward as possible, whilst the bombers were en route to their target; in the event of all of Park's forces being engaged, 12 Group was to supply squadrons to patrol over and protect the 11 Group airfields north of the Thames.

At 1415 hrs on August 19th, five bombs were dropped on Coltishall's new hangar, causing slight damage and killing two men. Although no more than a nuisance raid, compared with the heavy attacks against 11 Group airfields, the raid nevertheless emphasised the need to protect even such northerly aerodromes.

On August 21st, the poor weather over England prevented massed raids, but so as not to offer the RAF even the briefest respite, both *Luftflotten* 2 and 3 conducted scattered raids over a wide front, each undertaken by small formations of bombers. One such sortie was flown by five Do 17s of II/KG3, striking inland across Norfolk so far as the airfield at Horsham St Faith before being detected. Two sections of 611 Squadron were scrambled to intercept from Digby, but owing to the raiders' apparently aimless track, the Controller experienced difficulty in accurately vectoring the Spitfires. Consequently it took over an hour to find and engage the bombers. Red Section of 'A' Flight, comprising Pilot Officers Watkins, Brown and Lund, destroyed one, of a formation of three, near Burnham Market at 1235 hrs, the Do 17Z of KG3 diving into the North Sea off Skegness. Despite a search by the Skegness lifeboat, two crew members, *Feldwebel* Zimmerman and *Unteroffizier* Wiegand, remain missing. The remaining crew, *Unteroffizier* Skibitski and *Gefreiter* Schlafer, baled out but were both killed. Five minutes later, Red Section despatched a second Dornier into the North Sea, off Scolt Head. Pilot Officer Brown's original combat report states:-

After sighting the enemy aircraft firing for a second time, I attacked with leader in echelon port. The enemy aircraft were rather close and Red Three was not quite in position. I attacked No 3 of the enemy formation. After firing for some seconds, black smoke came from the port engines. I saw my ammunition entering the enemy aircraft and consider that a number of hits were made. After breaking away, I saw the enemy aircraft diving towards the sea, two of the crew baled out.

The third raider escaped from Red Section's attack.

Squadron Leader McComb's Yellow Section dealt with another pair of raiders which eventually collided and crashed near Alford.

On the day in question, whilst leading 242 Squadron home from a practice flight, Bader heard over the R/T Squadron Leader Rupert Leigh's 66 Squadron being vectored onto a 'Bogey' over Yarmouth at 7,000'. Despite the fact that the Ground Controller had given him no instructions, Bader abandoned his squadron and sped the 15 miles to Yarmouth. In his log book, he wrote:-

Intercepted Do 17 above cloud whilst flying alone. Hit it but saw no result as he dived into cloud.

Although Squadron Leader Bader made no claim after the inconclusive combat, he later added:-

Subsequently confirmed crashed in sea. Crew killed.

When the remains of the German airmen killed on August 21st were recovered from the sea, Squadron Leader Bader was credited with having destroyed the Dornier. Even at the time, this conclusion was highly questionable. From the foregoing accounts, it appears that the Do 17 engaged by Bader was the bomber which had escaped from 611 Squadron's Red Section; the *Luftwaffe* Quartermaster General's Loss Returns, which were not for propaganda purposes but for internal audit (and copies of which are now available for anyone to inspect at the Imperial War Museum) indicate that in fact this fleeing raider, engaged by Bader, was neither destroyed nor damaged. It seems strange that it was decided to award the victory to Squadron Leader Bader despite the overwhelming evidence in support of the claim by the three pilots of 611 Squadron's Red Section. Over half a century later, however, the record is now straight.

By this time, squadrons in 11 Group were suffering such heavy casualties that certain of their number required replacing. To effect such relief, squadrons from the northern groups took their place in the line, and there then began a cycle of units to and from the battle area. It is the subject of such relief that indicates Air Vice-Marshal Leigh-Mallory's attitude to the effect of the battle on Fighter Command as a whole; on August 26th, 1940, Air Vice-Marshal Park thus reported to HQ Fighter Command:-

In paragraph 39 of my report, 11G/533, dated 8th July, 1940, attention was drawn to the fact that the heaviest casualties to pilots and aircraft were experienced among reinforcing squadrons that had been formed in the North since the outbreak of war. During the past two months' fighting over our own territory, our former experience has been confirmed, as will be seen from the figures given below.

2.   In order to keep our casualties in pilots and fighter aircraft to a minimum, especially during the next critical month, it is strongly recommended that only highly trained and experienced eight-gun fighter squadrons be sent from Northern Groups to exchange with depleted squadrons in the South of England, because of the German practice of employing fighter screens and close escorts to mass formations of bombers in this part of the country.

3.   The marked difference in results shown in the table below can hardly be due to the difference in standard of fighting efficiency of Northern Groups. It is thought probably to be due to the fact that No 13 Group have always made a practice of selecting squadrons for temporary duty in the south from among their most experienced squadrons, because of the appreciation of the heavy fighting up to date in the south of England:-

Squadron	Period under No.11 Group	Enemy Casualties Destroyed	Own Casualties Kld.	Msg.	Wnd.	Total
41	26/7 to 8/8	13	-	1	-	1 (13 Group)
152	12/7 to 4/8	4	-	-	1	1 (13 Group)
602	17/8 to date	26	-	1	1	2 (13 Group)
266	12/8 to 21/8	9	2	4	-	6 (12 Group)
616	19/8 to date	8	-	6	1	7 (12 Group)

4.   Sector Commanders have commented favourably on the high standard of flying and fighting efficiency of the several squadrons of No 13 Group that have been sent south on exchange or for temporary duty during the past four months.

Air Vice-Marshal Park also pointed out that during the Dunkirk fighting, the Northern Groups had considered 11 Group:-

..... a good training ground in air fighting for less experienced squadrons ..... the practice proved expensive in pilots and aircraft in the instance of newly formed squadrons.

With the Battle of Britain approaching its zenith the situation had changed, however, and survival required experience.
    On the subject of the losses of RAF squadrons, post-war research can offer updated statistics concerning the squadrons under review by Air Vice-Marshal Park:-

Squadron	Period under No.11 Group	Own Casualties Kld.	Msg.	Wnd.	POW
41	26/7 to 8/8	-	1	1	-
152	12/7 to 4/8	-	1	1	-
602	17/8 to 26/8	-	-	4	-
266	12/8 to 21/8	4	2	2	-
616	19/8 to 26/8	2	1	4	1

It is also interesting to note when these squadrons were both formed and received their Spitfires:-

Squadron	Date formed or re-formed	Date Spitfires received
41	RF 1/4/23	1/39
152	RF 2/10/39	12/39
602 (Aux)	F 12/9/25	5/39
266	RF 30/10/39	1/40
616 (Aux)	F 1/11/38	10/39

Air Vice-Marshal Park's report was undoubtedly prompted by the catastrophes suffered that day by 616 Squadron, which had arrived at 11 Group's Kenley Sector Station just one week previously: seven Spitfires lost, four pilots wounded and four killed; the squadron's clerk, clearly a master of the understatement, had recorded the action as 'a very unfortunate engagement.' One of those pilots wounded was Pilot Officer William Walker, probably shot down by the great *experte* Major Werner Mölders, *Kommodore* of JG51; the following day, whilst in transit between Ramsgate Hospital and RAF Hospital Halton, Walker stopped off at Kenley to collect his belongings:-

Whilst there I asked my driver to take me to dispersal so that I could say farewell to any remaining pilots. It proved a sad occasion, however, as the squadron had suffered severe losses and very few pilots actually remained operational.

A week later, 616 Squadron, by that time comprising just eight of its original members, was relieved by 64 Squadron and thankfully flew north to Coltishall.

Regarding the 13 Group squadrons mentioned in Air Vice-Marshal Park's report, it is worth mentioning that recently accurate cross-referencing of RAF combat *claims* against *actual* German losses during the Battle of Britain has revised the formerly accepted list of top-scoring fighter squadrons. In this new and far more accurate list, 41 Squadron is placed third with 45.33 victories against 32 aircraft lost, and 602 ninth with 37 for 15. 266 Squadron is credited with eight victories but 11 aircraft lost, and 616 Squadron 12.75 victories to 14 lost. Therefore, Air Vice-Marshal Park's interpretation of the situation as it affected reinforcing squadrons during August 1940 remains correct.

An examination of the Fighter Command Order of Battle on August 8th, 1940, reveals the following squadrons in 12 Group; a further statistical analysis:-

Squadron	Date formed or re-formed	Received monoplane fighters	Length of monoplane time up to and including August 1940
73	RF 15/3/37	7/38	2 years & 1 month
19	RF 1/4/23	8/38	2 years
46	RF 3/3/36	3/39	1 year & 6 months
611 (Aux)	F 10/2/36	5/39	1 year & 3 months
616 (Aux)	F 1/11/38	10/39	10 months
66	RF 20/7/36	10/39	10 months
266	RF 30/10/39	1/40	8 months
242	RF 30/10/39	2/40	6 months
229	RF 4/10/39	3/40	5 months
222	RF 4/10/39	3/40	5 months

From the above statistics, it can be seen that up to the time of Air Vice-Marshal Park's report on August 26th, 1940, Air Vice-Marshal Leigh-Mallory, in first sending 266 Squadron, followed by 616, had committed to the crucible of battle over southern England not his most experienced squadrons, in terms of monoplane experience at least, but actually his sixth and joint fifth respectively.

Before leaving our analysis, detailed below are the dates when all 12 Group squadrons were sent south:-

Squadron	Date to 11 Group	Aircraft Lost	Days of combat
266	12/8/40	11	8
616	19/8/40	13	16
222	1/9/40	15	25
46	3/9/40	24	13
66	3/9/40	25	27
73	9/9/40	17	10
229	9/9/40	12	11

When considering losses it should of course be borne in mind that direct comparison of squadrons is difficult as those committed to battle in September 1940 were engaged far more than those in August. For the record, 249 Squadron went to 10 Group on August 14th, 1940, so when sent to 11 Group on September 1st, had already ceased to 'belong' to 12 Group and is not, therefore, included in the above table. Significantly, apart from when 'B' Flight of 19 Squadron operated from Eastchurch for two days in mid-August in anticipation of the DCAS's counterattack measures, Air Vice-Marshal Leigh-Mallory was never to send 19, 242, and 611 Squadrons to 11 Group. Not surprisingly, neither of the two foreign squadrons, 302 (Polish) and 310 (Czech), which became operational in 12 Group during August 1940, were sent. All of the squadrons which remained in 12 Group throughout the Battle of Britain were to eventually comprise the 12 Group Wing with which this book will shortly become principally concerned.

This subject of reinforcement again indicates Air Vice-Marshal Leigh-Mallory's reluctance to properly assist 11 Group; he appears to have considered the fighter squadrons in 12 Group very much as 'his', having clearly forgotten that *all* units in Fighter Command were actually those of the Commander-in-Chief. As already discussed, Dowding had anticipated the need for his squadrons to be moved freely about the line; he had every reason to expect only the fullest obedience to his orders, and that both supporting groups would give only their best to assist 11 Group. During this early stage of the Battle of Britain, Leigh-Mallory seemed unable to perceive the conflict in broad Fighter Command terms, only observing unfolding events from a local viewpoint. This was to be a crucial factor in the coming weeks of battle.

An interesting question arising in relation to the movements of squadrons, is why, as Squadron Leader Bader was so obviously thirsting for action, Air Vice-Marshal Leigh-Mallory did not send him and 242 Squadron south to 11 Group in August 1940? In the absence of any other logical reason, their friendship, possibly allied with the fact that the newsworthy Bader had started attracting publicity for 12 Group, has to be the answer.

During what Air Vice-Marshal Park described as the 'Second Phase', taking place from August 19th - September 5th, 1940, he considered enemy fighter tactics to have been as follows:-

Some formations of long-range bombers have been boxed in by close fighter escorts, some of which flew slightly above to the flank or in rear, others slightly above and ahead, with a lot of fighters weaving between the sub-formations of bombers. On several occasions, raids of this type barged through our first and second screen of fighters and reached their objectives by sheer weight of numbers, even after having suffered numerous casualties to stragglers and flank sub-formations. On several occasions, smallish formations of long range bombers deliberately left their fighter escort immediately it was engaged by our fighters, and, losing height, proceeded towards objectives in the South or South-West of London without any close fighter escort. Most of these raids were engaged by our rear rank of fighters, either when about to bomb or when retreating, and suffered heavy casualties.

Regarding the employment of his own fighters, Park reported:-

As the enemy penetrated further inland, we adopted the tactics of meeting the enemy formations in pairs of squadrons, while calling on Nos 10 and 12 Groups to provide close cover for our aerodromes near London and for suburban aircraft factories West of London. This arrangement enabled us to meet the enemy further forward in greater strength while giving a measure of close protection against enemy raids which might elude us at various heights. On some occasions it therefore became practicable to detail a Wing of two Spitfire squadrons to engage escorting enemy fighters while a Wing of Hurricanes engaged the bombers.

Losses and claims remained of primary concern:-

The heavy fighting much depleted many squadrons, and a number were withdrawn (and sometimes their ground personnel as well), for rest and training of new pilots, their places being taken by fresh squadrons from Northern Groups which had been comparatively inactive. It was again very noticeable that the heaviest casualties were experienced in the newly arrived squadrons, in spite of their being stronger in numbers.

Results of combats were numerically satisfactory, although the enemy escort fighters engaged more closely and so reduced the number of enemy bombers turned back or shot down. Moreover, the latter were increasingly heavily armoured and in greater strength, also better handled than previously. The employment of more heavily armoured and armed bombers resulted in our casualties to pilots being high, and the wastage in aircraft being very heavy.

The incredible difference between the fighting in 11 Group and the northern Groups was caused by one thing: the Me 109. Due to their limited range, no 109s operated over either the 12 or 13 Group areas. Me 109s did operate over the 10 Group area, although the long flight from Cherbourg rarely allowed them to them to venture far inland.

Air Vice-Marshal Park also reported on the effect enemy bombing was having on his airfields:-

Contrary to general belief and official reports, the enemy's bombing attacks by day did extensive damage to five of our forward aerodromes, and to six of our seven Sector Stations. The damage to forward aerodromes was so severe that Manston and Lympne were on several occasions for days quite unfit for operating fighters.

Biggin Hill was so severely damaged that only one squadron could operate from there, and the remaining two squadrons had to be placed under the control of adjacent Sectors for over a week. Had the enemy continued his heavy attacks against the adjacent Sectors and knocked out their Operations Rooms or telephone communications, the fighter defences of London would have been in a parlous state during the last critical phase when heavy attacks have been directed against the capital.

The Sector Operations Rooms have on three occasions been put out of action, either by direct hits or by damage to GPO cables, and all Sectors took into use their Emergency Operations Rooms, which were not only too small to house the essential personnel, but had never been provided with the proper scale of GPO landlines to enable normal operations of three squadrons per Sector. In view of this grave deficiency, arrangements were made to establish alternative

Sector Operations Rooms within five miles of each aerodrome, and this work is now proceeding on the highest priority.

At several important aerodromes and Sectors, enemy bombing put out of action the Station's organisation by destroying telephone communications, buildings, etc. Fortunately the enemy switched his raids from aerodromes onto industrial and other objectives, and gave a short respite during which the Station organisation at bombed aerodromes was completely reorganised.

The attacks on our fighter aerodromes soon proved that the Air Ministry's arrangements for labour and equipment quickly to repair aerodrome surfaces were absolutely inadequate, and this has been made the subject of numerous signals and letters during the past four weeks.

Critical of the Air Ministry, Park's report did not endear him to the Air Staff. On the contrary, it further convinced the DCAS, Air Vice-Marshal Douglas, that he should be replaced. In being so honest, Park had put his future at risk in the hallowed corridors of Whitehall. Air Chief Marshal Dowding's covering report added, however:-

That although the scale of attack certainly exceeded the capacity of the works organisation existing at the outset, this was rapidly strengthened, and I do not wish to express any dissatisfaction with the measures taken to effect this improvement.

Strangely, not mentioned were the further problems being experienced between the 11 and 12 Group AOCs. During the last week of August 1940, the intensity of the fighting led, as both Dowding and Park had anticipated, to the latter calling upon 12 Group for assistance. In accordance with Dowding's strategy, and Park's various instructions issued to his Group Controllers, the plan was for 12 Group to protect 11 Group's airfields whilst the latter's squadrons were engaged further forward in an attempt to inflict losses on the enemy bombers before they reached their targets.

On August 24th, virtually all of 11 Group's squadrons were engaged shortly before 1600 hrs. Consequently, 12 Group was asked to assist by again providing aircraft to protect Park's airfields north of the Thames. 19 Squadron ORB:-

Squadron in 'panic' take-off at 1545 hrs. Vectored onto formation of approaching 50 enemy bombers, Me 110s and Me 109s. Bombers thought to be Do 215s.

The pilots of 19 Squadron perfectly understood their role, as Flight Lieutenant Lane wrote in 1942:-

..... after lunch we were ordered off to the London area as a covering patrol whilst other squadrons down there were refuelling after battling with the Boche.

At least one previous account claims that on this date, Air Vice-Marshal Leigh-Mallory attempted to form his squadrons up into a Wing over Duxford prior to their heading south, but as these orders were misunderstood, no such 'Balbo' materialised. Having been unable to find *any evidence whatsoever* to support this claim, I would suggest that this is unfounded. At this time, the Duxford Sector squadrons were still acting under individual orders. Referring back to the 19 Squadron ORB, that unit had gone off alone in a 'panic', there being absolutely no reference to, or apparent intention to operate with, another unit. In the event, the only 12 Group fighters to engage the raiders were, once again, Flight Lieutenant Brian Lane's 'A' Flight of 19 Squadron which caught the enemy heading east over the Thames Estuary having bombed North Weald Sector Station in

Essex. Lane's Red Section took on the Me 110 fighter escort whilst his Green Section kept the Me 109s at bay. Although three 110s were later claimed destroyed, Lane's pilots again experienced infuriating cannon stoppages.

At North Weald, bombs had hit various station buildings but fortunately the operational capability of the airfield was unaffected. Air Vice-Marshal Park was unimpressed, to say the least, since just as in the case of Debden on August 15th, 12 Group's fighters had failed to protect this vitally important Sector Station. In fairness, however, the 19 Squadron ORB's use of the phrase 'Squadron in "panic" take-off' gives some corroboration to the claim that reinforcements were called for too late, for whatever reason, by 11 Group.

On August 26th, Duxford's 19 Squadron was ordered to patrol Debden at 10,000'; David Cox remembers:-

The actual raid came in at 1,000'. As 19 Squadron were at 10,000' and above 10/10ths cloud (a complete covering), we saw nothing of what was going on below. It appears that the Observer Corps had reported a raid coming in at 1,000', but the 11 Group controllers thought this must be a mistake and consequently asked 19 Squadron to patrol at 10,000', which of course we did. The subsequent intelligence report stated that the 'Spitfires from Fowlmere were slow in getting off the ground', which was certainly not the case.

The raid concerned comprised 40 Dorniers from both KG2 and KG3, briefed to bomb Debden and Hornchurch. The fighter escort of 80 Me 109s and 110s proved of limited worth owing to the former not only operating at the limit of their fuel capacity, but also having to protect the 110 *Zestörers*! As a result, only about six unescorted bombers attacked Debden: three airmen were killed, one aircraft was severely damaged, and the Sergeants' Mess, transport yard and stores were all hit. This was the last straw for Air Vice-Marshal Park, although, again, from Wing Commander Cox's account, we can have sympathy with 19 Squadron which was clearly given incorrect information by 11 Group. Flight Lieutenant 'Teddy' Morten:-

The 11 Group Controllers definitely called for 12 Group too late. By the end of August there was a certain amount of hostility between the respective Operations Rooms. 11 Group accused us of always being too late, we said that they called for us too late. Whenever 12 Group squadrons arrived after the action, we would have to suffer sarcastic remarks from the 11 Group Controller, so the situation was not good.

Group Captain Woodhall:-

In those early days, the RDF information was not very accurate, particularly regarding height and numbers of aircraft, and of course there was a time lag of several minutes before the information reached the Sector Operations Room. The Sector Controller therefore had to use intelligent guesswork to direct his fighters on an intercepting course and also to position them up-sun, above the enemy. To begin with, the operations table in No 12 Group only extended to the North bank of the Thames, and enemy plots were only passed to us when they reached this point. In No 11 Group however, enemy plots were received whilst the enemy was still over France. Command Operations Room had the whole picture, of course, but in my opinion there was never enough liaison between 11 and 12 Groups.
Luckily, Wing Commander Victor Beamish, the Sector Commander at North Weald, was a good friend of mine, so I extended our operations table to the south as far into France as St

Omer, and as soon as North Weald were informed of enemy activity, we kept the tie-line telephone open, and the plots were passed from North Weald to Duxford. In that way we obtained earlier warning, but in spite of this, we were frequently scrambled too late because we were not allowed to fly over 11 Group territory unless asked for by them. I was frustrating to see an enemy raid plotted on our board, obviously going for a target in 11 Group, then to wait on the ground, with the pilots in their cockpits for 15 or 20 minutes, and finally to be scrambled too late to get into the fight.

To be fair to 11 Group, Air Vice-Marshal Park was not expected to call for assistance until he had exhausted his own resources. That having been said, at this stage of the Battle of Britain, it is clear that 12 Group was undoubtedly responding to his calls. The reinforcing squadrons were certainly patrolling where vectored, and had no intention of doing otherwise; Wing Commander Frank Brinsden:-

During late August 1940, I always felt a bit cheated as we always seemed to be late off the ground and therefore too late to intercept; we often arrived over the battle zone only to find that all had gone home.

The following day, August 27th, Air Vice-Marshal Park wrote to Fighter Command's SASO, Air Vice-Marshal Douglas Evill, complaining about the problems being experienced, so far as he saw them, with 12 Group's fighters always arriving too late to protect his northerly airfields. It can be considered that on this date any previously existing liaison between the two Groups finally broke down, as Park instructed his Controllers that, in the event of reinforcements being required, they were to be requested only via HQ Fighter Command, and not directly from 12 Group itself.

The role of the SASO was to deal with such problems, so it is therefore surprising that Air Vice-Marshal Evill, who was senior to both Park and Leigh-Mallory, did not tactfully arrange a meeting between the commanders concerned to analyse and rectify the obvious breakdown in communication. Air Vice-Marshal Park had quite rightly placed the matter in Air Vice-Marshal Evill's hands; an intervention at that early stage by the Commander-in-Chief would have been inappropriate and could only have exacerbated the already unhappy relationship between the two Group commanders. In not taking appropriate action after Park's complaint, Evill, perhaps unwittingly, had made a significant contribution to the serious problems which lay ahead.

On August 28th, Squadron Leader McComb led 611 Squadron on the 30 minute flight from Digby to Duxford where the unit thereafter remained at Readiness throughout the day (returning to Digby in the evening). This move made three squadrons available in the Duxford Sector and therefore in a position to assist 11 Group if requested. At this time, however, the squadrons concerned, 19, 310 and 611, were still under individual orders. Both 66 and 242 Squadrons remained relatively inactive at Coltishall.

The same day also saw a significant development occurring across the Channel. Following heavy bomber losses, Goering had ordered that from mid-August onwards his fighters would provide an inflexible close escort service. Consequently, on August 28th, virtually all of *Luftlotte* 3's Me 109s were transferred north from the Cherbourg area to the Pas-de-Calais, in *Luftlotte* 2's area. This gave *Generalfeldmarscall* Kesselring an almost overwhelming provision of escort fighters for the great daylight battles which lay ahead.

The crescendo of the Battle of Britain was fast approaching.

CHAPTER FOUR

Tally Ho!

B y August 30th, 1940, the *Luftwaffe's* attacks against Great Britain had grown in ferocity. 11 Group's airfields increasingly became the German bombardiers' targets: the Battle of Britain was entering its most critical phase.

On the morning of August 30th, Squadron Leader James McComb led his 611 Squadron south from Digby on the 30 minute flight to Duxford, continuing 12 Group's policy of having squadrons available at its most southerly Sector Station. The Hurricanes of 310 Squadron were also on duty at Duxford, and the Spitfires of 19 Squadron at nearby Fowlmere.

At around 1100 hrs that morning, after the enemy had made a forward fighter sweep in strength, the Observer Corps reported waves, consisting of over 100 'bandits' coming in over the south-east coast, and which split up over Kent and Surrey to attack the airfields at Biggin Hill and Eastchurch. As the high explosives cascaded down on Air Vice-Marshal Park's airfields, another wave of enemy bombers crossed the Sussex coast, fighting its way north. No 19 and 310 Squadrons patrolled over Duxford itself but without event.

The scale of fighting was such that Air Vice-Marshal Leigh-Mallory decided that one of Coltishall's squadrons was also required to be at Readiness in the Duxford Sector; however, it was not Squadron Leader Rupert Leigh's Spitfire-equipped 66 Squadron which received the call, but Squadron Leader Douglas Bader's 242 Squadron: this was it, at last! To Bader's great chagrin, whilst en route to Duxford 242 Squadron was recalled to Coltishall. Fuming, 242's CO, according to Brickhill, 'harangued Ops over the phone'. Later Bader got his chance when 242 Squadron was ordered off again and arrived at Duxford without further incident.

About 1600 hrs, 300 plus enemy aircraft were reported over Kent and the Thames Estuary. The raiders split up to attack the airfields at Kenley, North Weald, Hornchurch, Debden, Lympne, Detling and Biggin Hill. At 1620 hrs, 60 He 111s of I/KG1 and II/KG53, escorted by Me 110s, crossed the coast north of the Thames. No doubt expecting the enemy to attack those airfields in that vicinity, the 11 Group Controller, via HQ Fighter Command, immediately requested assistance from 12 Group.

At 1623 hrs, Wing Commander Woodhall, the 12 Group Controller, scrambled 242 Squadron. Squadron Leader Bader led 14 Hurricanes off from Duxford with orders to patrol North Weald at 15,000'. In view of previous claims that 12 Group's Wing philosophy had been long-standing, I would suggest that if this was true, the four squadrons at Readiness at Duxford on this occasion would have been scrambled together and sent south, albeit under individual orders, especially considering the size of the enemy formation approaching. Instead, the scramble times and details of the other three squadrons were as follows:-

1640 hrs: 310 Squadron, available contemporary records indicate only that the squadron undertook a 'Patrol' until 1800 hrs; in all probability this was of a local nature.

1645 hrs: 19 Squadron, patrol Duxford at 20,000', landing at 1755 hrs.

1715 hrs: 611 Squadron to patrol Duxford at 5,000'. Later, the Spitfires were vectored to North Weald at 20,000' but did not sight the enemy and landed back at Duxford shortly after 1900 hrs.

The foregoing facts indicate that Wing Commander Woodhall was sensibly looking to defend Duxford itself from a possible attack, rather than reinforcing 11 Group in strength (although 611 Squadron were also vectored to North Weald, there was around an hour between that order and 242's original scramble). This has to be further evidence against previous claims that the 'Big Wing' philosophy existed in 12 Group prior to events involving 242 Squadron during this sortie.

At about the time of 242 Squadron's scramble, the incoming enemy formation split in two, I/KG1 heading for the Vauxhall Motor Works and aerodrome at Luton, whilst II/KG53, now the larger of the two formations, commenced fighting its way to the Handley Page factory at Radlett.

As the Radlett-bound raiders forged westwards, north of the Thames, the 11 Group Controller scrambled 56 Squadron, from North Weald, at 1625 hrs, by which time the enemy aircraft were approaching that aerodrome. Six minutes later, 11 Hurricanes of 1 Squadron were ordered off from Northolt. At 1655 hrs, just two Spitfires of 222 Squadron were also scrambled from Hornchurch. 501 Squadron had already taken off from Gravesend at 1600 hrs, and at 1650, whilst flying east over Chatham, Squadron Leader Harry Hogan's pilots sighted a large force of He 111s sub-divided into *Staffel* formations, each in an arrowhead pattern. According to 501's combat report:-

> The bombers were at 15,000' and flying west, south of the Thames Estuary towards London. 'Stepped up' behind them were formations of Me 109s and Me 110s. The enemy aircraft turned north over Southend, and the Squadron circled round them, attacking the second 'vic' head-on. This broke up, and one He 111 turned SE and jettisoned its bombs. Another was pursued by two of our fighters and landed on the water near the 'Girdler' lightship; another crashed in Southend. Our aircraft were not attacked by the fighters, who were some distance behind.

At 1724 hrs, back at Gravesend, 501 Squadron claimed two He 111s destroyed and three damaged; certainly one He 111 had crashed in Lifstan Way, Southend.

Shortly after take-off at 1631 hrs, 1 Squadron sighted six enemy aircraft 'north of London' which it prepared to attack but fortunately recognised as Blenheims before anyone pressed the gun button. Unbelievably, an affiliation exercise was underway in the combat area! Upon breaking away, Squadron Leader Pemberton's pilots saw the enemy formation: '30-40 bombers protected by a similar number of fighters in no standard formation from 12,000 - 25,000'. 1 Squadron's subsequent attack was carried out with each pilot acting independently; Sergeant Merchant:-

> I was No 2 of Red Section and upon sighting the enemy followed my Section Leader in line astern. After attacking a Do 17 which was in company with another E/A, an Me 110 dived on me from astern. Breaking away, I shook him off, and then saw ahead a single He 111K. Climbing and going ahead, I attacked from the beam. On the second attack the port engine stopped. At this moment a Hurricane from another squadron dived from the rear of the He 111 and got in a burst. Again attacking from the front I got in a long burst, and a man jumped by 'chute. A further two parachutists jumped after about one minute as I put in another burst. The aircraft dived down and crashed in the middle of a road near a cemetery to the east of Southend.

In his identification of the 'Do 17', Sergeant Merchant was mistaken, and in fact the aircraft was probably another Me 110. At least one previous account claims that the enemy formation consisted of He 111s 'and a few Dornier 17s'. This is completely untrue, however, and reflects a lack of research into German records. The He 111 claimed by Sergeant Merchant as crashed in Southend was the 3/KG53 raider also reported by 501 Squadron; so far two squadrons had got it.

1 Squadron's Pilot Officer Pat Hancock (now a retired Wing Commander and the apparently tireless Honorary Secretary of the Battle of Britain Fighter Association):-

I pursued the main body of enemy aircraft. One He 111 was lagging behind. I gained height and prepared to attack it. Before doing so, however, a Spitfire did an astern attack of about 5 seconds duration. I then went in and fired several long bursts at each engine in turn. I observed smoke, oil and flames coming from each engine. I did not follow the aircraft to the ground as a Vic of Me 110s appeared to be attacking me. I evaded them and returned to base.

Pilot Officer Hancock's He 111 was claimed as a probable, although it is now believed likely that this was yet again the 3/KG53 machine which crashed in Southend. The Spitfire mentioned in the foregoing combat report is believed to have been one of the two 222 Squadron fighters which had also intercepted: both Flying Officer Cutts and Sergeant Davis claimed a He 111 'probable' in similar circumstances over Billericay, Essex.

1 Squadron's Sergeant Clowes continues:-

I sighted the enemy and reported to Garter (Control). 15 leading bombers fairly close at 11,000' with 20 - 30 stragglers up to 15,000' and a larger number of Me 110s (50-60) up to 15 - 25,000' in no standard formation. I looped up to one Me 110 and gave him a short burst which caused the starboard engine to emit a strong streak of white smoke. I then made an astern attack on three He 111s at 12,000'. The first He 111 emitted smoke and some flames. On the second its perspex nose exploded and I made a head-on attack on a Do 17 at 10,000' with no apparent results. My range in each attack was about 250 yards and bursts were of about two seconds each.

The Me 110 attacked by Sergeant Clowes was certainly in trouble as it was streaming coolant, but as he did not report seeing the aircraft crash, we cannot be certain as to whether this was amongst the Me 110s which did not return to France, or one of those which managed to return to the Pas-de-Calais in a damaged state. Again, in Clowes' combat report it is interesting to see reference to a 'Do 17' which was no doubt also in reality an Me 110. It is quite possible that the He 111 which 'emitted smoke and some flames' was also the aircraft which crashed in Southend.

After breaking away from the Blenheims with the CO, Pilot Officer Matthews, also of 1 Squadron, was attacked by Me 110s at 12,000'. His assailants, however:-

... were attacked by Hurricanes. I saw a straggling He 111 and fired all my ammunition into it from astern. Starboard engine packed up. I broke away when I had finished my ammunition and a Hurricane of 56 Squadron came in to finish it off. I did not see the result. Rear gunner fired the whole time until I broke off.

The 56 Squadron ORB states that, in addition to claiming the destruction of two Me 110s:-

Also the squadron destroyed together an He 111. Flight Lieutenant Gracie destroyed an He 111 and damaged another. Wing Commander Beamish (North Weald Station Commander) flew with the squadron and claimed an Me 110 probable.

It is believed that the He 111 destroyed by Gracie was of 5/KG53 and crashed at Colne Engaine, near Halstead. It is likely that this bomber was also attacked by many other fighters, possibly including 1 Squadron's Pilot Officer Matthews who reported having seen a 56 Squadron Hurricane during his attack.

The CO of 1 Squadron, Squadron Leader Pemberton, reported that he attacked an 'E/A':-

..... in company with a Hurricane of 'LE' squadron; the rear gunner continued to fire until within a few seconds of hitting the ground. This E/A, which fell near Epping, will be claimed by that Hurricane.

Squadron Leader Pemberton's report is of vital importance to our understanding of this action; 'LE' were the code letters of 242 Squadron. The 'E/A' was an Me 110 and could have been one of either two aircraft, belonging to 5/ZG2 and 4/ZG76, both of which crashed at Ponders End, to the east of Enfield.

Traditional accounts of the day's events claim that Squadron Leader Bader was ordered to patrol North Weald at 15,000', but instead climbed 242 Squadron to 19,000', so as to be above the enemy's reported height of 15,000', before flying 20 miles west of his allotted position so as to have the sun behind him. Consequently, attacking from the sun, 242 Squadron bounced the enemy perfectly. In fact, the official 242 Squadron combat report, submitted on September 1st, offers a slightly different view:-

Squadron 242 were ordered at 1623 hrs from Duxford to patrol North Weald at 15,000' on a vector 190 degrees just north of North Weald. They received a vector of 340 degrees. Three aircraft were noticed to the right of the formation, so the Squadron Leader detached Blue Section to investigate.

These three aircraft were almost certainly some of the Blenheims also reported by 1 Squadron. The changing vector was probably to counter the enemy's westward moving track. The Coltishall Sector Intelligence Officer, Flight Lieutenant Maybaum, continues:-

Green Leader then drew attention to a large enemy formation on their left so the rest of the squadron turned and saw a vast number of aeroplanes flying in an easterly direction. These were recognised to be from 70-100 E/A, twin-engined in tight formation, stepped up at 12,000', after which there was a gap of 1,000', then another swarm of twin-engined machines stepped up from about 15,000 - 20,000'.

From the foregoing, it appears that the enemy bombers were some 3,000' below the height prescribed for 242 Squadron by the Controller. The escorting Me 110s, however, were stepped up to about 20,000'. Nothing suggests that Squadron Leader Bader did anything, in fact, other than patrol and attack from 15,000' as and where instructed. Indeed, Squadron Leader Bader's own report, also dated September 2nd, confirms that:-

242 Squadron was flying in sections line astern at 15,000' when large enemy formation was sighted on the left.

He continues, and in this I rest my case:-

242 Squadron had the height advantage on the lower group and as it was obviously impossible to attack all the enemy it was decided to attack down sun on the lower group.

So, far from having disregarded the Controller's instructions, Squadron Leader Bader had actually observed them to the letter. With no experience whatsoever of meeting massed formations over England, it could be suggested that, contrary to the *romantic* version, 242 Squadron was in no position to do otherwise. Also, the squadron was situated up-sun not because Squadron Leader Bader allegedly knew better than the Controller and had directed his squadron accordingly, but was there due to the vector provided. The sight of so many enemy aircraft must have been incredible for Bader and his pilots, this being reflected by the 242 Squadron combat report which describes the quantity as 'vast'. However, the 11 Group squadrons now also known to have been involved made no comment to indicate that this raid was anything other than the size they were used to encountering.

Maybaum's report continued:-

Green Section were ordered to attack the top of the lower formation; Red and Yellow Sections were ordered to get into line astern. It seemed impossible to order any formation attack. The Squadron Leader dived straight into the middle of the formation closely followed by Red Two and Red Three; the packed formation broke up and a dogfight ensued. Squadron Leader Bader saw three Me 110s do climbing turns to the left and three to the right. Their tactics appeared to be to climb in turns until they were nearly stalling above the tail of Squadron Leader Bader's aircraft. Squadron Leader Bader fired a short burst into the Me 110 at practically point blank range and the E/A burst into flames and disintegrated almost immediately. Squadron Leader Bader continued his zoom and saw another Me 110 below and so turned in behind it and got a very easy shot at about 100 to 150 yards range. After the E/A had received Squadron Leader Bader's first burst of from 2 to 4 seconds, the enemy pilot avoided further action by putting the stick violently backwards and forwards.
Squadron Leader Bader got another burst in and saw pieces of the enemy's starboard wing fly off; then the whole starboard wing went on fire and E/A went down burning in a spiral dive. Squadron Leader Bader then saw in his mirror another Me 110; he did a quick turn and noticed 5 or 6 white streams coming out of forward-firing guns; the E/A immediately put his nose down and was lost but subsequently seen far below.
Squadron Leader Bader saw nothing around him, called Duxford and was told to land.

Red Two Pilot Officer WC McKnight went into attack with Squadron Leader Bader; he got behind an Me 110 and opened fire at 100 yards, the E/A burst into flames and crashed to the ground. Next he attacked an He 111 formation, carrying out a beam attack on nearest one; E/A rolled over on back, port engine caught fire and it finally crashed to the ground. P/O McKnight was then being attacked by an Me 110 but succeeded in getting behind and followed E/A from 10,000' to 1,000'. P/O McKnight opened fire at about 30 yards; E/A's starboard engine stopped; the port engine caught fire and E/A crashed in flames alongside a large reservoir.

As McKnight had seen his victim crash, and from the landmark given, this Me 110 can be identified as being from 4/ZG76, crashing at Enfield Sewage Farm, Ponders End (and therefore might have also been attacked by Squadron Leader Pemberton of 1 Squadron). The 242 Squadron report continues:-

Red 3 P/O Crowley-Milling also went into attack with Red 1 and 2. Seeing an He 111 break away from the formation he made an astern attack giving a five second burst. The enemy did not avoid action, but rear gun fire was experienced. Starboard engine of E/A started to smoke then E/A made dive to the ground. At this particular moment an Me 110 was commencing an attack so did not observe He 111 crash, though P/O Hart confirms seeing this aircraft going down in flames.

Yellow 1 F/Lt GE Ball sighted an He 111 diving and turning and gave him a third of his ammunition.

P/O Stansfield was also attacking this a/c which went down with engines alight and went down on an aerodrome full of cars. F/Lt Ball then attacked an Me 110, making a port attack finishing with a stern attack. One engine stopped dead and no return fire was experienced .... the sun was behind in both attacks.

Yellow 2 Sub/Lt Cork, Royal Navy, saw an Me 110 which he attacked in company with several others and which he saw going down, he broke away and saw another Me 110 flying east, made a beam attack noticing port engine in flames. E/A did a stalled turn and dived to ground.

Yellow 3, Sgt Lonsdale attacked an He 111 which had broken away from its formation. After a prolonged burst of fire from quarter attack, E/A circled and crashed in flames, made no evasive tactics.

Green 1, F/O Christie was with his section attacking a higher formation of E/A when he sighted an He 111 and 3 Me 110s. He carried out a head on attack on 1 Me 110. E/A dived to port. He then attacked from astern, damaging starboard motor, then gave him two quarter attacks. Finally causing E/A to dive from 2,000' crashing into a greenhouse 500 yards west of Welsh Harp Lake. One short burst from rear gunner, but no effect.

Due to the very specific location given, we can identify this last Me 110 as being a machine belonging to 5/ZG2 which crashed amongst greenhouses whilst seeking a forced-landing at Rochford's Nursery, Ponders End; again, however, this may have been the 110 also attacked by Squadron Leader Pemberton.

Green 3, P/O Hart saw 3 He 111s below him and started to dive on them. He saw Yellow 1 attacking the last one and so attacked the second which went into a steep dive. He was about to follow the first E/A which started a right hand turn. He turned inside the E/A and gave him all his ammunition. E/A plunged downwards in flames and crashed in a field.

White 2, Sgt Brimble, was flying at the rear of the sqn and after E/A formation had been broken saw an He 111 which he gave a burst of 3 secs. P/O Stansfeld was also attacking this a/c and followed it to the ground. White 2 then broke away and saw behind him an Me 110 doing a gentle turn to port. He made a quarter attack opening fire for 3 seconds at 250 yards. E/A immediately burst into flames and crashed to the ground. On rejoining his leader he saw another Me 110 commencing an attack on his a/c from the front. He opened fire, finally making a quarter attack, noticing the glass in front of E/A splinter and machine go into a violent dive. He did not see the a/c crash as another 110 was on his tail but feels certain that the pilot was dead.

So far as 242 Squadron was concerned, it could take the credit for all German losses in the action and claimed seven Me 110s destroyed and three probables, and five He 111s destroyed. At the time, 242 Squadron's claims were accepted in their entirety by Air Vice-Marshal Leigh-Mallory. It was just the kind of overwhelming victory he craved for. He sent a signal to the squadron: 'Heartiest congratulations on a first-class show. Well done 242.' The CAS added his congratulations: 'Magnificent fighting. You are well on top of the enemy and obviously the fine Canadian traditions of the last war are safe in your hands.' The Under-Secretary of State for Air also sent a similar message to the squadron. A total of 12 enemy aircraft destroyed in one action, without loss, would certainly have been remarkable if it had been accurate.

Owing to the typical confusion of this battle, which according to the records quoted involved over 50 RAF fighters, and *not* just the 14 of 242 Squadron, it is impossible to substantiate with certainty any of the combat claims made by Bader's pilots except for the two Me 110s referred to in the foregoing text (although the Germans lost nine Me 110s and He 111s during the course of this particular afternoon). That is not to say that 242 Squadron did not destroy more, but without accurate locations, and in view of the number of similar claims by pilots of other squadrons, it is impossible to ascertain exactly who-shot-down-who. It is strange that the involvement of RAF fighters from other squadrons in this action was never mentioned by 242 Squadron, despite at least two pilots from those other units recognising, even in the heat of combat, Hurricanes from both 56 and 242 Squadrons. Apart from just two Spitfires, all of the engaging fighters were Hurricanes; it is certainly odd, therefore, that neither Squadron Leader Bader nor the other 242 Squadron pilots noticed that their 14 Hurricanes had multiplied somewhat! Without wishing to detract at all from the obvious bravery of the pilots concerned, it is clear that 242 Squadron certainly did not execute the great solo victory as claimed by popular romantic legend (and even by certain supposed historical studies). Such overclaiming, however, was a common feature when large numbers of fighters were in action together; this was later to become a crucial factor in the subsequent Big Wing controversy.

Another popular exaggeration is that the raid in question was broken up and turned back; this is also untrue as the majority of intercepting RAF fighters, low on fuel and ammunition, broke off 10 miles before the bombers, then hampered only by anti-aircraft fire, reached the Handley Page factory. Fortunately the damage caused was insignificant so production of the new Halifax bomber was not disrupted. The other part of the raiding force hit the Vauxhall Works hard, however, killing 53 people.

Squadron Leader Bader's report on the action, entitled 'Fighter Tactics v Escort & Bomber Formation', dated September 2nd, 1940, commences thus:-

At the suggestion of the Intelligence Officer, I am writing a report on the tactics employed on August 30th against large formation of enemy bombers and twin-engined escort fighters. It has been suggested that this report might be of interest in view of the warning signal from 11 Group of increased casualties suffered in that Group due to enemy tactics of tight formation with bombers and escort-fighters intermingled, and the good fortune enjoyed by 242 Squadron of complete immunity from damage to aeroplanes or personnel.

1.   In regard to the second point it must be appreciated that luck definitely played a part since any squadron leaving an engagement without any damage cannot claim all credit for cleverness in flying etc.

The Squadron Leader's report went on to describe the combat in similar vein to the squadron combat report already quoted. Thereafter, he continued:-

..... It appears that bombers escorted by twin-engined fighters can be dispersed by shock tactics of the sudden arrival of a Hurricane or Spitfire in their midst, preferably out of the sun.

6.   It is not suggested that these tactics (the head-on attack) can always be employed since from the fighter's point of view risk of collision is likely. But the fact remains that the effect of a near collision on the German pilots causes immediate and violent evasive action which of course immediately breaks up any tight formation and leaves the fighters behind to take their pick.

7.   This report is written by 242 Red Leader and gives his own impressions and the impressions

of the pilots following so far as can be remembered. It will be appreciated that in the heat of the moment pilots' impressions are not necessarily cold and calculating with a view to rendering an intelligence report when they get home *(author's note: or contributing to a history book over 50 years later!)*, but this report is as accurate as can be reasonably expected. It was anticipated (and the fight in question proved it) that if a squadron of Hurricanes and Spitfires met a large enemy bomber and fighter formation (provided that there were no single-engined fighter escorts) the Hurricanes or Spitfires would have the advantage (in spite of numerical inferiority) if the enemy formation could be broken up, and provided the squadron started with the height advantage. In any case, the primary object is achieved if the formation is broken because it ruins the enemy's chance of accurate bombing, and even if one's own squadron's successes in E/A shot down is slight, the E/A are scattered in small groups or singly and other fighters which are certain to be at hand can pounce on them.

8.   In conclusion it is noted that Red Leader did not open fire in the initial dive because it was not possible to attend to his sights and at the same time pass as close to the enemy aeroplanes as was considered necessary to produce the required result; there was no fire from enemy rear guns probably because it is believed the Me 110s were being used as front-gun fighters or because they did not see us coming out of the sun.

9.   It is emphasised that this report is submitted for possible interest to others, and that as far as 242 Squadron is concerned the attacking and fighting conditions were very favourable.

Whilst Squadron Leader Bader's enthusiasm and willingness to get involved cannot be criticised, I wonder how 11 Group squadron pilots received this report which was submitted after just *one* such engagement? The head-on attack, was already in use against bomber formations; the CO of 253 Squadron at Kenley, Squadron Leader (later Group Captain) Gerry Edge, was an enthusiastic exponent of this tactical method:-

They didn't like that head-on attack, you know, but you had to judge the break-away point right. If you left it to the last 100 yards then you were in trouble, due to the fast closing speeds, but once you got the hang of it a head-on attack was a piece of cake. When you opened fire, you'd kill or badly wound the pilot and second pilot. Then you'd rake the whole line as you broke away. On one attack the first Heinkel I hit crashed into the next.

Interestingly, no mention was made in Squadron Leader Bader's report of increasing the number of attacking fighters; indeed that he assumed the interceptors would be outnumbered was emphasised in paragraph 7. Nevertheless, we are led to believe that out of 242 Squadron's action on August 30th arose the 'Big Wing' concept. Evidence regarding the exact sequence of events is scant, but I quote herewith an extract from an interview which my friend Dr Alfred Price taped with Group Captain Sir Douglas Bader shortly before the latter's death (the interview, published here for the first time, is reproduced in its entirety in the concluding chapter of this book):-

DB: ..... What happened was that on August 30th, 1940, I think it was, we got off a squadron, just 12 of us, and we had everything in our favour, height, I knew where they were *(author's note: from information provided by the Controller)* and we had the sun. We shot down a few without any problems whatsoever. When we were writing out our combat reports afterwards, Leigh-Mallory rang me up and said 'Congratulations Bader on the squadron's performance today', and so I said, 'Thank you very much, Sir, but if we'd had more aeroplanes then we would have shot down a whole lot more'. He asked what I meant and I explained that with more fighters our results would have been even better. He said, 'Look, I'd like to talk to you about this', and so I flew over to Hucknall and told him what I thought. He agreed and created the Duxford Wing, under my leadership and comprising 242, 310 (Czech) and 19 Squadrons. Leigh-Mallory said to try the idea and see what we could do.

In contradiction to the foregoing, no evidence can be found to support the claim that Squadron Leader Bader flew to Hucknall to discuss his idea further with the AOC 12 Group prior to any decision being made regarding the so-called Duxford Wing. In fact, Squadron Leader Bader did not make a flight to Hucknall until September 10th, 1940, by which time the Wing had already been in action, as we shall see. The truth of the matter is that the formation of the Duxford Wing was a far more *ad hoc* arrangement which was only made possible by the close personal relationships between Douglas Bader, the AOC and Sector Commander.

In any case, on August 30th, 1940, over 50 RAF fighters, rather than just 242 Squadron, had destroyed approximately nine enemy aircraft. The 'Big Wing' was therefore built upon a *total* misapprehension from the outset. Nevertheless, Air Vice-Marshal Leigh-Mallory and Squadron Leader Bader had tasted success; both parties were anxious for more.

There can be no doubt that whatever the correct sequence of events concerning the birth of the 'Big Wing', the philosophy represented a misunderstanding of the System by all involved. In reality, the massed fighter formation concept represented the opportunity for Douglas Bader to become part of Fighter Command's front line, and for his ambitious AOC to play a prominent part in the Battle of Britain. The question which should be asked is just what credentials or experience were possessed by both Air Vice-Marshal Leigh-Mallory and Squadron Leader Bader to justify them challenging the System established by two of the most experienced fighter commanders in the world at that time?

Jubilant pilots of 242 Squadron, but from our safe peacetime vantage point of over 50 years later, just how accurate were their combat claims in the heat of the battle?
(Author via Douglas Bader Foundation)

CHAPTER FIVE

Big Wing

O n August 31st, 1940, the *Luftwaffe* continued its heavy attacks against Fighter Command's airfields. Both Biggin Hill and Kenley Sector Stations were seriously damaged, but neither was rendered non-operational. The indiscriminate bombing of East Anglia by 250 aircraft in five waves also took place, and later there were raids on the East End of London and Kent by waves of first 100 plus and secondly 200 plus bombers. Attacks were also made on the Duxford and Debden Sectors. 19 Squadron's base at Fowlmere was bombed, as armourer Fred Roberts recalls:-

LAC Fred Roberts. The frame was constructed from a propeller blade of Spitfire K9809 in which Pilot Officer Trenchard was killed as the result of a night flying accident on 29.02.40.
(Dr Dennis Williams)

Amongst the most famous photographs taken during the Battle of Britain, at Fowlmere on September 21st, 1940. Although it is widely known that the pilot concerned was 19 Squadron's Sergeant Jennings, until recently the armourer remained anonymous; he is Fred Roberts!
(Imperial War Museum)

It was between 8-8.30 am when the first bombs were dropped. We, the ground staff, were queuing for breakfast, the squadron's Spitfires being airborne. We heard the noise of what transpired to be Do 17s approaching. I dived into the nearest slit-trench and upon looking up could see the sun shining on little dots high in the sky. I could also see the first stick of bombs falling. Fortunately they were released too late and so only two fell on the airfield, one amongst the bell tents making a crater about four feet deep and five feet across. The earth blown out of the crater collapsed one of the tents. There were two lads asleep inside who were partially buried, but neither was harmed. The second bomb exploded near the boundary fence, but the rest of that stick fell in the orchards and watercress beds beyond the airfield. We had permission to collect as many bombed apples as we wanted. Looking back now it makes me smile to think of myself and others crouching in that trench holding enamel plates over our heads with cutlery and mugs in hand! I also recall that we had Flight Sergeant George 'Grumpy' Unwin's 'A' Flight Spitfire up on trestles in the blister hangar when the scramble came. He came running along with the other pilots, but due to his aircraft being indisposed, was unable to take-off with the others. He was yelling and swearing for his plane, and I reckon that we broke the record for returning a Spitfire to serviceability! George was airborne and after the others just 10 minutes later following a straight take-off from the hangar across wind and with no engine warm-up. It certainly showed the courage of the man and the faith he placed in his groundcrew.

Wing Commander David Cox, then a Sergeant Pilot, recalls that:-

We were caught on the hop! Most of us were still in bed as the squadron was stood down. We got a panic message to scramble immediately. I put on my flying boots and jacket over my pyjamas. We took off at about 0800 hrs and climbed south to 17,000'. It was jolly cold up there as the flying jacket only came down to my waist!

19 Squadron intercepted the raid by II/KG2 Do 17s escorted by ZG26 Me 110s. During the next few minutes, Sergeant Cox destroyed an Me 110, and Flight Lieutenant Clouston together with Pilot Officer Burgoyne shared a second. Two Spitfires were lost, however. Flying Officers Frank Brinsden and James Coward both baled out, as the latter remembers:-

Flight Lieutenant Clouston led us into a copybook Fighter Command No 1 Attack from dead ahead, turning in three sections line astern, to come up in sections echelon port behind the enemy who were in sections of three in vic line astern. Our fourth section, led by Flying Officer Frank Brinsden, was detailed to climb and intercept the fighters. I got a cannon shell through the cockpit which shattered my left leg below the knee, also severing the elevator controls, and I had to bale out. I put a tourniquet around my thigh, using my helmet radio lead, and landed by parachute about four miles north of Duxford on the Royston to Newmarket Road. I was admitted to Addenbrooke's Hospital in Cambridge and was obviously out of the battle from then on.

It is believed that the two 19 Squadron Spitfires were shot down by *Oberleutnant* Hans Barschal, *Gruppenadjutant* of *Stab*. III/ZG26, and *Oberleutnant* Sophus Baagoe of 8/ZG26.

Back at Fowlmere, 19-year-old Pilot Officer Ray Aeberhardt tried to land his damaged Spitfire without flaps, but the aircraft overturned and he was killed in the resulting fire.

Battle of the Airfields: a 222 Squadron Spitfire lies wrecked at Hornchurch (Author via Mr Joe Crawshaw)

Whilst 19 Squadron was in action against the Fowlmere raiders, Squadron Leader Bader's 242 Squadron was brought from Coltishall at 0825 hrs to protect the Duxford Sector but did not see action. Likewise, 310 Squadron went up from Duxford at 0825 but was too late to engage. Both 242 and 310 Squadrons, still acting under individual orders, landed at Duxford an hour later. At lunchtime, 242 Squadron, according to the CO's log book, 'Patrolled London District. Nil'. The Czechs, however, took-off at 1300 hrs to patrol Hornchurch at 15,000' and, with 11 Group units, engaged a raid on Hornchurch in Essex. Between 1315 and 1330, east of Hornchurch, 310 Squadron attacked a formation of Dorniers escorted by Me 110s and Me 109s. This was the squadron's first action, in which four Do 215s and one Me 109 were claimed destroyed, together with two damaged. Two Hurricanes were lost: Pilot Officer Kredba baled out safely but Pilot Officer Sterbacek remains missing to this day; the ORB recorded:-

Pilot Officer Sterbacek's aircraft seen to go down very steeply. Presumed that he went into the Thames. Pilot Officer Sterbacek has the proud distinction of being the first Czech fighter pilot to give his life for England.

Group Captain Woodhall:-

On the first occasion the Czechs got into action, early in the Battle of Britain, they made an excellent showing. I met them on their return to the aerodrome and spoke with Sacha Hess; he had disabled a Dornier over Epping Forest which made a wheels-up forced-landing in a field. He followed it down with the intention of making certain that no-one got out of it alive. He saw three Germans climb out, who, when they realised that Sacha was diving on them, held up their hands. To quote his own words: 'I hesitate, then it was too late, so I go round again to make sure I kill them - they wave something white - again I do not shoot - then (disgustedly) I think it is no use, I am become too bloody British!'

Hess had good cause to hate the Germans; he had recently received notification that both his wife and daughter had been killed by the Nazis.

On August 31st, 611 Squadron had again flown down to Duxford from Digby, but before landing patrolled Feltwell without contact. By the time of 611's return to Digby that evening, McComb's pilots had flown two more patrols, one over Duxford, the other of NE London, but, like 242, made no interception.

During the action on August 31st, 19 Squadron had again suffered problems with the experimental cannon. This being the last straw, Flight Lieutenant Lane made representation on behalf of the pilots to the CO, Squadron Leader Pinkham. On September 1st, the latter wrote to Wing Commander Woodhall requesting that the cannon Spitfires be replaced with standard eight-gun machines.

On September 1st, 611 Squadron's 'A' Flight relieved 46 Squadron's detached flight at Ternhill, in north Shropshire, thus leaving the former squadron's 'B' Flight as the only operational day-fighters at Digby. The move was a major upheaval, groundcrews being ferried to Ternhill in both an Albion lorry and a Ford Tri-Motor aircraft (ORB).

The same day, a move was also in the offing for 310 Squadron, although curiously, considering the apparent eagerness of the 12 Group pilots to get into the more southerly action, the ORB recorded:-

The projected move of the squadron to NORTH WEALD was cancelled much to the delight of everybody.

The 242 Squadron ORB simply notes that:-

The squadron carried out patrols from DUXFORD - No combat.

During this first week of September, Air Vice-Marshal Park was to increasingly call upon Air Vice-Marshal Brand's 10 Group for assistance. During August, Brand's Spitfires and Hurricanes had already protected certain 11 Group airfields; there were no complaints from either Group. Situated inland of Southampton, the Middle Wallop based Spitfire squadrons, 234 and 609, were well positioned to patrol aerodromes and aircraft factories south of London. Further west, at Warmwell near Weymouth, were the Spitfires of Squadron Leader Peter Devitt's 152 Squadron. In the coming month, all would find themselves in action over south-east England. Both Southampton and Portsmouth, in the immediately adjacent 11 Group area, represented important targets to the enemy, and were within range of escort fighters. Brand's squadrons, particularly 609 'West Riding', already had experience of meeting massed formations over those cities, and had frequently clashed with Me 109s and Me 110s above Lyme Bay and the Solent. Early in September, 609 Squadron frequently patrolled the Northolt, Brooklands and Windsor area, west of London, but did not meet the enemy. Had any raids been directed against Northolt, Kenley, Croydon or even Biggin Hill airfields, or the Hawker Aircraft Factory at Brooklands, Brand's fighters would have been in position to attack.

On September 2nd, 242 Squadron, operating over London, also recorded a nil result. Red and Blue Sections of 310 Squadron patrolled Debden, below cloud, but likewise did not encounter the enemy. 19 Squadron undertook four patrols, one over Debden, led by Flight Lieutenant Clouston, and three orbiting Duxford and Debden, all led by Squadron Leader Pinkham. No enemy aircraft were seen. Although Duxford's Station Commander had given his support to Pinkham's request that the cannon-armed Spitfires be replaced, on this day it was decided that the squadron should move out of the battle area to Digby, and its place at Fowlmere be taken by the machine-gun equipped Spitfires of 611 Squadron. Gloom naturally descended over 19 Squadron's personnel who felt that due to the coordination problems experienced between 11 and 12 Groups, and because of their unreliable armament, they had been denied the opportunity to meet the enemy on the same terms as other units.

On this day, September 2nd, 19 Squadron received three replacement pilots, all fresh from 7 OTU, Hawarden: Flying Officer Forshaw, Pilot Officer JE Johnson and Sergeant Ward. During less desperate days, pilots had proceeded directly to their squadrons from Flying Training School

(FTS). The squadron then oversaw conversion to the aircraft type to be flown operationally, and provided such training as was necessary until the new pilot was considered combat ready. In January 1940, however, the Air Ministry agreed in principle that an adequate network of Operational Training Units should be established for Fighter Command. Consequently 5 and 6 OTUs were created, followed by No 7 in June. These decisions were not welcomed, however, by Air Chief Marshal Dowding who was carefully preserving UK-based fighters and considered OTUs as a 'comparative luxury'. He particularly objected to the formation of 7 OTU as his front-line requirements had yet to be met. By August 1940, fighter pilot losses had reached a critical stage, and OTU courses were therefore reduced from four to two weeks. At this time, upon leaving OTU, pilots had generally recorded from 10-20 flying hours on Spitfires. This represented merely a conversion to the type as opposed to the 'operational training' which it had been envisaged OTUs would provide; no air-to-air firing whatsoever was conducted, although some pilots did fire their guns into the sea, and no tactical instruction was given. Unfortunately for the three keen young pilots posted to 19 Squadron, there was no flying to be had at Fowlmere; the squadron was simply too busy to provide the training necessary to make their replacements operational. Experienced replacements were desperately required.

During the morning of September 3rd, Squadron Leader Pinkham led 19 Squadron on a 'Security Patrol over Duxford and Debden'; the Spitfires were vectored to North Weald, which was badly bombed. Arriving after the attack, 19 Squadron, flying in pairs line astern, attacked the enemy formation, reported as 60 bombers and 150 fighters, from above and ahead. The combat was Squadron Leader Pinkham's first, in which he personally suffered the frustration of jammed cannon. Flying Officer Alan Haines and Flight Sergeant Unwin each claimed an Me 110 destroyed.

Flight Sergeant George 'Grumpy' Unwin, probably 19 Squadron's most genuinely successful fighter pilot of 1940, together with his dog, 'Flash'.
(Author via Flight Lieutenant Wallace Cunningham)

310 Squadron had also been ordered to patrol North Weald and attacked from 25,000', out of the sun and in line astern. The ORB records:-

It was unfortunate that the squadron had already been on patrol for just over an hour before the enemy were sighted and consequently the petrol was running short, and three pilots were forced to land and refuel before making base.

The squadron claimed six enemy aircraft destroyed, and one probable (although only two can be confirmed with any certainty), offset against one Hurricane which Sergeant Kopriva safely abandoned. Later, the squadron again patrolled North Weald but without sighting the enemy.

Throughout this day, 242 Squadron remained at Coltishall, from where it flew further fruitless patrols, while Squadron Leader Rupert Leigh took his 66 Squadron south to join 11 Group at Kenley; Bob Morris, a flight mechanic, remembers that the former 12 Group squadron:-

... found Kenley a complete shambles, there was hardly a building left standing. As we drove around the airfield to our assembly point, I saw a car park full of vehicles - all had been riddled by gunfire or shrapnel. Even shelters had been destroyed, buildings flattened.

66 Squadron had relieved 616, which had been virtually annihilated, the survivors flying gratefully north to Coltishall. Again, the transition from 12 Group to 11 Group operational conditions was to be traumatic: on September 4th, 66 Squadron's first full day at Kenley, Leigh lost six Spitfires, four pilots being wounded. By September 10th, when the squadron was moved north of the Thames to Gravesend, two more pilots had been wounded and one killed.

On September 3rd, 'A' Flight of 611 Squadron was recalled from Ternhill and proceeded directly to Fowlmere, arriving at 1120 hrs. En route from Digby, 'B' Flight was vectored towards Bedford, but saw no action and subsequently joined 'A' Flight at Fowlmere.

The 19 Squadron ORB records that:-

Squadron very pleased to hear from the Commander-in-Chief that they were to be equipped with 8 gun machines.

For the rest of the day, 611 covered 19 Squadron's duties whilst the changeover to machine-gun Spitfires took place. At 1425 hrs, 611 Squadron's Red Section patrolled Mildenhall, whilst the other three sections orbited Hornchurch. There was no action, and the Squadron returned to Fowlmere; ORB:-

.... where they found time bombs exploding and the AOC-in-C on a visit to 19 Squadron.

Group Captain Woodhall:-

The failure of 19 Squadron's cannons was unacceptable, so I got on the telephone to LM and urgently requested that the Squadron should have its eight-gun Spitfires back. The following afternoon the C-in-C, 'Stuffy' Dowding himself, landed at Duxford without warning. I greeted him and he gruffly said, 'I want to talk to 19 Squadron', so I drove him over to Fowlmere. There he met Sandy Lane and other pilots. He listened to their complaints almost in silence, then I drove him back to his aircraft, which he was piloting personally. As he climbed into the aeroplane, he merely said 'You'll get your eight-gun Spitfires back'. 'Stuffy' was a man of few words, he listened to all of us, asked a few pertinent questions, then made his decision. As a result of the C-in-C's visit, that same evening the instructors from Hawarden OTU flew their eight-gun Spitfires to Fowlmere and returned with the cannon Spitfires.

This was a significant visit by Air Chief Marshal Dowding. Previous accounts claim that throughout the summer of 1940, the Commander-in-Chief remained at Bentley Priory, aloof and detached from his fighter squadrons. This visit dispels that traditional image. He was not prone to making 'social' visits to stations, like many other officers of Air rank, but when it really mattered, 'Stuffy' was there for his pilots. There is no question that Dowding cared deeply for his men, as had been indicated as early as 1916 when he quarrelled with Trenchard regarding losses on the Somme.

On September 4th, 242 Squadron continued to operate from Coltishall, and 611 Squadron remained at Digby. In the Duxford Sector, 310 Squadron made two patrols over base without result, whilst Squadron Leader Pinkham led 19 Squadron firstly on a patrol of Debden, then secondly of Debden, North Weald and Hornchurch. The ORB recorded that:-

First day with 8-gun machines, and what wrecks. At least the guns will fire!

On this date, 11 Group had called upon 10 Group to patrol the Tangmere Sector Station, near Chichester. The Spitfires of 234 Squadron obliged, and at 1320 hrs attacked Me 110s of III/ZG76 over the West Sussex coast. The squadron claimed three destroyed, and German records indicate that 7, 8 and 9/ZG76 all lost one aircraft each to the guns of 234 Squadron. This particular day was a bad one for the Me 110 generally, as 15 were lost on operations over England.

On September 5th, 242 Squadron again flew locally from Coltishall, as did 611 at Digby. At 0945 hrs Squadron Leader Pinkham led 19 Squadron to patrol Hornchurch at 15,000'. Over the patrol line, Sergeant Bernard 'Jimmy' Jennings sighted an enemy formation, consisting of 40 Do 17s escorted by 40 Me 109s, approaching from the west and crossing the Thames Estuary. As Jennings had sighted the enemy, he directed his comrades until the CO himself could see them and act accordingly. Squadron Leader Pinkham then ordered 'A' Flight to attack the 109s, whilst he led 'B' Flight against the bombers. Having climbed, 'B' Flight then attacked in pairs from the rear. In the bright sun, Flying Officer Walter 'Farmer' Lawson, Pinkham's Blue 2, lost sight of the CO; at that point the 109s cascaded down on 'B' Flight. A real cut-and-thrust combat developed as 19 Squadron became embroiled with the enemy fighter escort. Such was the confusion that only two claims were made: Flying Officer Alan Haines pursued a 1/JG54 Me 109E across Kent at hedgetop height, his victim eventually crashing into No 6 Hardy Street, Maidstone, and the Czech Sergeant Plzak engaged a 109 which he left pouring black smoke. Pilot Officer Lawson's Spitfire was damaged, as was Pilot Officer Eric Burgoyne's. The Squadron was to wait in vain for the return of Squadron Leader Pinkham and Spitfire P9422.

Pilot Officer Eric Burgoyne poses with his 20mm cannon-shell damaged Spitfire, P9391, on September 5th, 1940. Modellers please note the unusual location of the serial number, at the top of the fin, and its strange style.
(Author's Collection)

Again contrary to popular legend, and indeed the 'Battle of Britain' film, a study by British Intelligence indicated that when attacked by fighters, large enemy bomber formations seldom, if ever, broke up, or even adopted evasive tactics. The veteran *Kampfliegern* well appreciated the benefits of mutual fire support achieved by retaining a cohesive formation whilst under attack; any bomber which became detached from such a formation was courting disaster. The mutual fire support of a large bomber formation was withering, and it was into such a hornet's nest that 19 Squadron had sallied forth on September 5th. Later that day, a Spitfire was reported down at Birling in Kent; the pilot, having been wounded, baled out too low and was killed: the body was identified as Squadron Leader Pinkham (who died with 1,240.30 flying hours). As Pinkham had last been seen attacking a vic of bombers, it is likely that he fell victim to their effective cross-fire.

When the news of Squadron Leader Pinkham's death reached 19 Squadron at Fowlmere, the three replacement pilots, Flying Officer Forshaw, Pilot Officer 'Johnnie' Johnson, and Sergeant Ward, were in the adjutant's office. As 19 Squadron was so busy and therefore unable to train them to operational standard, they were to be posted to 616 Squadron at Coltishall, which had been withdrawn from Kenley two days previously and was now rebuilding to strength. Away from the combat zone, 616 was able to provide extra training for pilots fresh from OTU, prior to them being sent to front-line squadrons in the south. This problem of being unable to provide combat experienced replacements was an area of grave concern for Air Chief Marshal Dowding.

'Johnnie' Johnson, of course, was later to become the Wing Leader *par excellence*, and the top-scoring British fighter pilot of WW2. In his book, 'Wing Leader', Air Vice-Marshal Johnson recalled the news of Squadron Leader Pinkham's death:-

The phone rang and the adjutant picked up the receiver.
'They've found the CO. Probably dead when he crashed'.
For a moment he brooded.
'Well, good luck with 616'.

Air Vice-Marshal Leigh-Mallory wrote to Pinkham's mother:-

It is with very great regret that I offer you my sincerest sympathy on the occasion of your son's death.

I always found him so full of enthusiasm over anything connected with his job. He was a fearless leader and a first rate squadron commander beloved by all those under him.

In him I feel that the service has lost an exceptionally promising young officer.

At lunchtime on September 5th, Flight Lieutenant Lane led 19 Squadron on a patrol of North Weald and Hornchurch but no enemy aircraft were seen. The extremely able and popular Brian Lane learned later that day of his promotion to Acting Squadron Leader. He was to succeed Pinkham as CO of 19 Squadron, although, as he himself later wrote, it was a 'sad promotion'. Pilot Officer Lawson was promoted to Acting Flight Lieutenant and succeeded Lane as 'A' Flight commander. Over the coming months, the full potential and exceptional qualities of leadership possessed by Lane would rise to the fore; Wing Commander George Unwin:-

Brian Lane was completely unflappable and instilled great confidence in all who flew with him through his absolute coolness.

Sergeant 'Jimmy' Jennings (from left), Flight Lieutenant 'Farmer' Lawson and Flying Officer Michael Lyne (wounded May 1940), at Fowlmere, early 1941.
(Author's Collection)

Wing Commander David Cox:-

Brian Lane was the finest squadron commander I ever served under, not only as a fighter leader but also as a man; he was always kind and considerate and had time for everyone, no matter how lowly their rank.

Strain of battle: 23-year-old Squadron Leader Brian Lane discusses a combat with Flight Lieutenant 'Farmer' Lawson (left) and Flight Sergeant 'Grumpy' Unwin, Fowlmere, September 1940.
(Imperial War Museum)

Wing Commander Gordon Sinclair:-

He was a very quiet person, rather intellectual, but in his own quiet and calm way he was a compelling leader, particularly as he was an excellent pilot with an 'Exceptional' rating. He had a delightful sense of humour and was quick to laugh.

During the afternoon of September 5th, further large enemy formations intruded over south-east England. Again 10 Group's 234 Squadron responded from Middle Wallop, but intercepted some considerable distance away, over the Isle of Sheppey. The squadron arrived in time to attack seven Me 109s which had pounced on a Hurricane squadron; Pilot Officer Bob Doe reported:-

I dived down and fired at the front E/A but my bullets went behind him. I saw them enter the second 109 and then the third burst into flames and blew up. I went right between the rest.

I was then attacked by the remainder who left the Hurricanes. I did tight turns with three shooting at me and three above me who came down in their turn. I half-rolled down round the edge of the balloons, went through a pall of smoke above burning oil tanks at full boost and at nought feet, weaving up the river.

Not surprisingly short of fuel, Doe landed at Kenley. The Me 109 he destroyed was of 7/JG53, also attacked by Flight Lieutenant Pat Hughes of the same squadron, and probably two 46 Squadron pilots. Hughes and Pilot Officer Zurakowski, also of 234 Squadron, pursued one 9/JG53 Me 109 from Sheppey, south-west across Kent and into East Sussex until forcing it to ditch in the Channel 12 miles off Hastings. Although 10 Group's 609 Squadron was used quite correctly throughout the week to protect the area south-west of London, this interception over the Isle of Sheppey by 234 Squadron begs a question: were the fighters of Air Vice-Marshal Brand, due to the good relations between him and AOC 11 Group, being allowed greater latitude than 12 Group without incurring criticism?

During the evening of September 5th, whilst 19 Squadron mourned Squadron Leader Pinkham's loss but celebrated Brian Lane's promotion, 310 Squadron patrolled Debden between 1744 and 1937 hrs without incident.

At the end of September 6th, 19 Squadron's ORB recorded that:-

In future, 19 Squadron will fly with Wing, Nos 242 and 310 Squadrons. This should prove very much more effective as it was pointless, several machines attacking the formations at present being encountered.

That morning, 242 Squadron flew down from Coltishall to Duxford, for the first time in four days. Regarding the day's first patrol, commencing at 0850 hrs, the 19 Squadron ORB recorded:-

Wing on patrol over Hornchurch and North Weald. S/Ldr Lane and F/Lt Lawson leading in 19 Squadron.

The 310 Squadron ORB merely refers to a 'Wing patrol with 19 Squadron'.

For the next sortie, 19 Squadron recorded:-

Wing on patrol over Hornchurch and North Weald. No E/A seen, but most comforting feeling indeed.

310 Squadron merely duplicated its remark concerning the previous sortie. The third sortie of the day, in which 19 Squadron did not participate, was another patrol of North Weald; 310 Squadron's ORB, however, makes no reference to having operated with another squadron, recording simply:

'Patrol'. The 242 Squadron ORB is unhelpful, the day's entry being 'Squadron Operating from Duxford'. Certainly from Bader's log book we know that he led 242 Squadron on three patrols this day, two of North Weald and one of Northolt, but he makes no reference to the Wing. It is curious why these references are so vague in view of previous claims that the Big Wing was such a carefully planned entity. Surely if that had been the case, mention would have been made of the first time that the squadrons supposedly acted in concert?

Wing Commander Gordon Sinclair, at the time a flight commander in 310 Squadron, remains adamant that the squadrons remained under individual orders:-

310 Squadron's Adjutant, Flying Officer Chesney (centre), listens to tales of derring-do (from left): Flight Lieutenant Gordon Sinclair, Pilot Officer Janouch, Sergeants Puda and Kaucky, and Flight Lieutenant Jerrard Jefferies. (Author via Squadron Leader Vic Bergman).

There was never any possibility of three or more squadrons taking off from Duxford together and receiving battle orders from a Wing Leader whilst airborne. Our R/T sets, TR9s, were not up to it, but in any case such a situation NEVER arose or was even contemplated. Each squadron acted on its own - down to Flight or Section level - and we received information regarding the whereabouts of enemy aircraft from the Duxford Operations Room, based on advice which they had received from the relevant RDF station. Douglas Bader was a natural leader of men, but I never heard of the COs of the other squadrons operating in the Duxford Sector agreeing to his "leadership" in the air.

The available evidence does not entirely support Wing Commander Sinclair, as only 242 and 310 operated from Duxford itself at this time, while 19 Squadron remained at nearby Fowlmere and rendezvoused with the Wing in the air. Furthermore, the contemporary records, such as ORBs and combat reports, do refer to the joint operation of all of the squadrons concerned as a Wing formation from the following day onwards. Nevertheless the Wing Commander is quite correct to point out that there was no Wing Leader as in 1941 when fighter squadrons were formally organised into Wings, each with a dedicated Wing Commander (Flying). Certainly evidence indicates that this patrolling in strength from Duxford was of a less planned nature and was operated on a day-to-day basis with varying squadron strengths and compositions.

Wing Commander Douglas Blackwood was leading 310 Squadron at the time:-

The Big Wing thing was all started by Douglas Bader, who of course had a Cranwell background, and so he naturally became leader. At the time, I was younger than he, and had received command of 310 Squadron shortly after Douglas received 242. Certainly amongst the three squadrons initially involved, Douglas was the senior squadron commander; Brian Lane had only just received command of 19 Squadron so although he had the most combat experience, he was the most junior Squadron Leader in the Sector. When Douglas suggested the Wing, as he was senior, we just automatically assumed that he would lead. He was a *very* forceful character, of course, and so even if we had wanted to, it would have been impossible to argue with him! An example of this occurred when we were together at Duxford during the making of the 'Battle of Britain' film; Douglas was there as a consultant but would not stop interfering with the shoot. In the end the Director said 'I'm making this film, not you' and ordered him off the set. That was Douglas to a 'T'. In 1940, his ideas regarding the Big Wing had the support of the Duxford Station Commander, Wing Commander Woodhall, but even he could not have stood up to Douglas if it had ever come to that, he just said 'I'm doing this', and that was that. There is no doubt, however, that Douglas Bader was a very brave man and it was because of the way he conquered his disabilities caused by the crash in 1931, that he became popular amongst his acquaintances - his 242 Squadron pilots would have followed him anywhere. We are talking, after all, about a man who played squash well and had a low golf handicap despite having no legs!

Another question arising from the foregoing information concerning the period August 30th - September 6th inclusive, must be where is the evidence to support previous claims of Duxford Wing practices? As we have seen, 242 Squadron had not even operated from Duxford between September 2nd and September 6th; it is clear that in relation to patrols over 11 Group on the latter day, the Duxford Sector squadrons just went straight off. There were no practices, and this confirms that contrary to popular legend, little thought was at first put into the Big Wing scheme; in any case there was not time. Nor is there any evidence, at this early juncture, of HQ Fighter Command or 11 Group being informed of these evolving tactics.

Wing Commander Blackwood:-

We never did any practice sorties as a Wing, we just went off on an operational patrol together one day with Douglas leading.

Wing Commander 'Laddie' Lucas claims in his book 'Flying Colours' that during this period 11 Group had deliberately kept 12 Group out of the battle; the evidence now presented proves that this is untrue as Leigh-Mallory's squadrons *were* patrolling 11 Group airfields north of the Thames on a daily basis and as per the System's requirements: had any attacks developed against those targets, then the 12 Group squadrons would have intercepted, as indeed they did on several occasions. Air Vice-Marshal Park could hardly be blamed when no such action arose, but he was clearly using 12 Group's reinforcements in the manner required by the Commander-in-Chief, no matter how frustrating Air Vice-Marshal Leigh-Mallory and Squadron Leader Bader found this situation.

Wing Commander Blackwood:-

I think that we should have been requested earlier as that would have enabled us to climb out to sea and then attack high over the Thames Estuary. But I think that *everyone* was doing their best, we were all learning. 11 Group felt that it was their responsibility to defend London without 12 Group interfering unless requested.

What most pilots do not appear to appreciate, as has been said before, is that Fighter Command was subject to a formal *overall* strategy, despite delegation of tactical control to Group

Commanders. No single Group Commander could 'hog' the Battle of Britain through his own intentions. Again, for example, on the morning of the day now in question, September 6th, 10 Group's 234 Squadron was again in action over 11 Group. Above Beachy Head, the squadron clashed with III/JG26, engaged on an escort sortie to Kenley. The Hughes and Zurakowski duo destroyed one Me 109, a 7th *Staffel* aircraft which crashed at Old Romney, and Sergeant Boddington got another which came down at Hothfield.

On September 7th, 1940, the codename 'CROMWELL' was broadcast: invasion imminent.

At 0735 hrs, 242 Squadron, still making the daily journey down from Coltishall, flew into Duxford. At 1125 hrs the Wing took off to patrol base; in his book 'Spitfire!', Squadron Leader Lane later wrote:-

We were operating in a Wing again of three squadrons led by S/Ldr B.... with his Canadians. The Czech squadron followed them and we were the top covering squadron, our Spitfires having a better performance than the two Hurricane squadrons.

Although Lane's book (written under the pseudonym 'BJ Ellan') was subject to censorship, I think we can assume that the above reference concerns Douglas Bader. This is in fact the first documentary confirmation of his leading the so-called Duxford Wing.

The patrol in question proved fruitless and the Wing returned to Duxford an hour later.

Later that day, Air Chief Marshal Dowding called a meeting at Bentley Priory to decide upon measures to be taken to 'go downhill' in an economical manner which would then permit a rapid climb back. As we have seen his policy at that time concentrated strength in 11 Group, which called upon neighbouring Groups for reinforcement during periods of hectic action. When losses decreed, individual squadrons in 11 Group were replaced by fresher units from the other Groups, but the scale of attack indicated that such a scheme could not be maintained indefinitely. Dowding had quite rightly recognised this, and had convened the meeting to discuss the options should the heavy attacks continue. Through various means enough pilots would be available, but they would be inexperienced and not combat ready; again, as we have seen, *combat experience* was the key to survival. As 609 Squadron's Pilot Officer David Crook wrote:-

Whilst aircraft losses were quickly made good, experienced pilots could never be replaced. You could only train the new ones as best you could, keep them out of trouble as much as possible in the air, and hope that they would live long enough to gain some experience. Sometimes they did.

Both Pilot Officers David Crook and Geoffrey Gaunt, of 609 Squadron, flew frequent patrols reinforcing 11 Group during September 1940; sadly, Gaunt was shot down and killed over South London on September 15th. (Author's Collection)

David Crook was quite correct; it is now accepted that both squadrons and individual pilots were at their most vulnerable during their first five operational patrols in 10 or 11 Groups.

The DCAS, Air Vice-Marshal Douglas, considered that the Commander-in-Chief was being 'pessimistic' about such matters, however. Douglas appeared unable to appreciate the difference between a pilot simply trained to fly and a *combat ready* pilot. Dowding was baffled by this lack of understanding. His SASO, Air Vice-Marshal Evill, provided figures which proved that there were *not* enough pilots: in the four weeks ending September 4th, casualties totalled 338; throughout the same period, the OTUs had only converted 280 pilots. Air Vice-Marshal Park confirmed that there was indeed a shortage of pilots, and in his Group alone casualties were approaching 100 per week. Interrupting, the ever forthright Air Chief Marshal Dowding spoke directly to Air Vice-Marshal Douglas and said 'You must realise that we *are* going downhill.' Douglas suggested opening a fourth OTU, but Evill interjected, pointing out that this was impractical due to the time it would take to organise: the crisis was now. Dowding also observed that such a unit would be a further drain on his already limited resources. The solution, arrived at by Air Chief Marshal Dowding and Air Vice-Marshal Park, was the 'Stabilising Scheme'.

The 'Stabilising Scheme' divided fighter squadrons into 'A', 'B' or 'C' units. 'A' squadrons were those in the front line, maintained with a minimum strength of 16 operational pilots. 'B' squadrons were those being rested, with up to six combat ready pilots amongst the establishment of 16, but which could be called upon if necessary. 'C' squadrons were those unlikely to be called into battle, since they were rebuilding to strength after having suffered losses in the battle area; their quota of operational pilots was a minimum of three. The purpose of the latter units was to provide operational flying experience and tactical training to pilots fresh from OTU, prior to passing them on to 'A' or 'B' squadrons. As we have seen, when Pilot Officer 'Johnnie' Johnson and his colleagues arrived at Fowlmere on September 3rd, 19 Squadron was too busy to consider training them to operational status; two days later they were posted to 616 Squadron which was being rebuilt at Coltishall after suffering heavy losses in 11 Group. 616, which shortly afterwards moved to Kirton-in-Lindsey, received and trained a stream of pilots until it returned to 11 Group on February 26th, 1941.

When the minutes of the 'Going Downhill' conference were provided to the DCAS, Air Vice-Marshal Douglas, he objected. He claimed that the minutes misrepresented him, casting him in the role of 'Mutt', a foolish music-hall comedian who asked stupid questions. The Fighter Command SASO, Air Vice-Marshal Evill, responded that the minutes were, in fact, almost verbatim.

Air Chief Marshal Dowding and Air Vice-Marshal Park stood firm in the belief that their use of resources was sound, but, especially at such a time of crisis, they had no time for Air Ministry politics. Thus they failed to appreciate that their open contempt of Douglas at the September 7th conference had placed them in great danger from the enemy within. Evidence suggests that Air Vice-Marshal Douglas was already working 'hand-in-glove' with Air Vice-Marshal Leigh-Mallory. The former attended no further meetings at Bentley Priory. It may also be significant that the latter was not at the 'Going Downhill' meeting (although the other officers attending were all based in the London area).

September 7th, 1940, was to be a date significant from many viewpoints, however. With a huge force of escorting fighters now available in the Pas-de-Calais, Goering made the *tactical* decision to attack London by day. Many have interpreted this act as a reprisal for Bomber Command's night attacks against Berlin, and so far as the propagandists were concerned that might have been so. The '*Luftwaffe* War Diaries' (see Bibliography) confirms, however, that the true motive was to force Fighter Command into the air for destruction en masse; London was, of course, the only target capable of producing such a reaction.

The *Luftwaffe's* first major daylight attack on London did not come until 1635 hrs on Saturday, September 7th, 1940. During the course of this attack, some 350 enemy aircraft made for the

Thames Estuary, East London and fighter airfields both north and south of the Thames. *Reichsmarschall* Goering, who had taken personal command of the battle, stood with his entourage on the cliffs at Cap Gris-Nez as his aerial armada roared overhead. 11 Group's Controllers anxiously monitored the formation's progress, easily the largest to attack England so far. It was naturally assumed that Sector Stations were the intended target. At 1617 hrs, 11 squadrons were scrambled in 11 Group, and by 1630 hrs all of Park's 21 squadrons were airborne. At this time, assistance was requested from 12 Group, and at 1645 hrs the Duxford Wing took off, heading for Debden and North Weald. 310 Squadron combat report:-

A Wing comprising 19, 242 and 310 Squadrons were ordered to patrol North Weald/Hornchurch at 10,000' under command of S/Ldr Bader of 242 Squadron.

Assistance was also provided by 10 Group; Wing Commander Bob Doe:-

..... after 234 Squadron was scrambled from Middle Wallop, I climbed like mad in an attempt to avoid the trauma of the previous two raids where I had been at a disadvantage from the very start, and managed to reach London at a reasonable altitude where I could have a go at the bombers on my terms.

At the time, Flight Lieutenant Keith Lawrence, a New Zealander, was an experienced and successful fighter pilot also serving with 234 Squadron:-

On the question of 10 Group providing support to 11 Group, I would say that whenever we were vectored to the Brooklands area, we climbed to 20,000' so as to reach the patrol line at a reasonable altitude before action. My recollections of Middle Wallop scrambles in August and September is that they were generally ordered in good time for us to climb to an appropriate height for interception en route.

It has previously been claimed many times that on this occasion the Wing was scrambled too late. However, having taken off at 1645 hrs, heading for North Weald, the enemy was contacted at 1720 hrs and a running battle commenced over the area of North Weald, Chelmsford, Brentwood and the Thames Estuary. North Weald is situated only 26 miles from Duxford, flying time being little more than 10 minutes at climbimg speed, which argues against these previous claims. The problem was therefore one of *height*, not time. The foregoing account by Wing Commander Doe indicates that whilst en route to London, 10 Group 'climbed like mad' so as not to be disadvantaged.

242 Squadron combat report:-

Squadron 242 was ordered off from Duxford at approximately 1645 hrs to patrol North Weald at 10,000'. Arriving at 15,000', the squadron noticed AA fire to the east and saw a number of e/ a at 20,000'. The enemy was about 70 - 90 strong. The bombers were flying in a tight box formation with Me 110s circling round and Me 109s flying 5,000' higher. On sighting the enemy, the Leader, S/Ldr Bader, advised Duxford and obtained permission to engage. The squadron was at an initial height disadvantage, being below the enemy, and had to give full throttle to climb and get level with the enemy formation, thereby eliminating the element of surprise. When climbing up to make astern attack, enemy fire was very heavy but not effective.

Squadron Leader Bader, on his own initiative, had disregarded the Controller's instructions and climbed the Duxford fighters to 15,000'. In view of the fact that most German attacks were made from such a height, I would suggest this was a sensible expedient (although the benefit of hindsight indicates that 20,000' would have been even more so). Had the 12 Group formation arrived in the combat area at 10,000', the height specified by the Controller, it would have been at an even greater disadvantage. Sir Keith Park's biographer, Dr Vincent Orange, in referring to this action, has accused Bader of having interpreted his orders 'broadly' and claims that he went 'in search of action'. This is, I believe, unfair in this instance, particularly in respect of the latter accusation: prior to engaging, Squadron Leader Bader had obtained permission from Duxford Control. In any case, the North Weald and Hornchurch Sectors, with battle having been joined above the latter, were immediately adjacent and both north of the Thames.

242 Squadron combat report:-

During 242's steep climb to attack, the squadron formation straggled out so that full weight could not be pressed home. In this first attack, 242 was supported by 19 and 310 Squadrons. 242 Squadron, now being spread out, started a dogfight with the enemy, picking out individual bombers, at the same time avoiding the Me 109s that came down from their position above.

19 Squadron:-

Whilst they were climbing to attack, an Me 110 dived past and Red Leader (Squadron Leader Lane) led 'A' Flight after it. It was also being attacked by two Hurricanes. All five members of 'A' Flight fired at this machine which crashed about 1 mile east of Hornchurch and south of railway line. The crew of two baled out but one parachute failed to open. The other landed safely in a field and appeared to be taken prisoner by two women from a nearby house. At the end of this attack, Red Leader, Red 2 and Yellow Leader returned to base.

The two Hurricanes which also attacked the Me 110 were those of 1 Squadron's Flying Officer Holderness and 310 Squadron's Pilot Officer Janouch; the enemy aircraft, of Stab II/ZG2, crashed at Park Corner Farm, Hacton Lane, Cranham at 1710 hrs. The ZG2 aircraft were providing close escort for KG53 He 111s attacking the oil storage tanks on Thameshaven.

Meanwhile, 242 Squadron engaged the bombers:-

Red 1 (S/Ldr DRS Bader) on sighting e/a opened full throttle and boost, and climbed and turned left to cut off enemy and arrived with Red 2 (Sub/Lt RJ Cork) only, on the beam slightly in front. S/Ldr Bader gave a very short beam burst at about 100 yards at e/a which were then flying section of 3 line astern in a large rectangle. Then accompanied by Red 2 gave short bursts at the middle of e/a of back section. The e/a started smoking preparatory catching fire. S/Ldr Bader did not notice result which was later confirmed by P/O Turner as diving down in flames from the back of the bomber formation. At the time of S/Ldr Bader's attack on the Me 110 a yellow-nosed Me 109 was noticed reflected in his mirror and he turned to avoid the e/a. Big bang was heard by him in the cockpit of his Hurricane. An explosive bullet came through the right-hand side of fuselage touching map case knocking the corner off the undercarriage selector quadrant and finished up against the petrol priming pump. S/Ldr Bader executed a steep diving turn and found a lone Me 110 below him which he attacked from straight astern and above him and saw e/a go into a steepish straight dive finishing up in flames in a field just north of railway line turning approximately East (West of Wickford due North of Thameshaven).

*Two "nautical types" serving with 242 Squadron,
Sub-Lieutenants Cork and Gardner of the FAA.*
(Author via Douglas Bader Foundation)

Red 2 (Sub/Lt RJ Cork) sighted e/a to East and above. He climbed to meet e/a and carried out a beam attack of the leading section of bombers, firing at a Do 215 on the tail end of the formation. Port engine burst into flames after two short bursts and crashed vertically. Red 2 was then attacked by e/a from rear and hit a starboard mainplane. He broke away downwards and backwards nearly colliding head on with an Me 110. Red 2 gave short burst before pulling away and saw front cabin of 110 break up and machine go into vertical dive. Two of the crew baled out. Whilst Red 2 was following e/a down, e/a was stalling and diving. An Me 109 attacked Red 2 from the rear, one shot from the e/a going through the side of Red 2's hood, hitting bottom of reflector sight and bullet proof windscreen. Red 2 received a number of glass splinters in his eyes so broke away downwards with half roll and lost sight of e/a.

The Me 110 destroyed by Bader and Cork crashed at Downham Hall, near Wickford; both crew members, *Leutnant* Hans Dietrich Abert and *Unteroffizier* Hans Scharf were killed.

*Pilot Officer Denis Crowley-Milling's 242 Squadron Hurricane, 'LE-H' P3715, in which he was shot
down on September 7th, 1940. Note the two-colour spinner cap; oh for colour film!*
(Author via Douglas Bader Foundation)

Pilot Officer Crowley-Milling displays the shattered armoured windscreen of 'H'; it saved his life.
(Author via Douglas Bader Foundation)

The report continued:

Red 3 (P/O Crowley-Milling) flying in vic formation sighted AA fire to east. He climbed to meet e/a and engaged flight of 20 bombers. He fired two second burst at left hand rear bomber and then observed Me 110 just behind last bomber. He fired 4 second burst at Me 110 setting port engine on fire and starboard engine smoking. Red 3 was then attacked by Me 109 receiving cannon shell in radiator, one in left aileron and one behind pilot's seat.

Crowley-Milling fortunately forced-landed Hurricane P3715 at Stow Maries; David Evans, of 242 Squadron's groundcrew, recalls: 'He was lucky: there was a spent 7.9 mm bullet jammed in the space between the front and rear screen.' The Me 110 which Red 3 accounted for, although jointly with Green 4, Sub-Lieutenant RE Gardner, crashed at Little Burstead. The latter reported the impact location as '3 miles NW of Shell Haven'.

Blue 1 (F/Lt D Powell-Sheddon) climbed to 22,000' to engage e/a but did not engage for some 10 minutes. He finally chased an Me 109 which was itself chasing a Hurricane. Both swerved in front of Blue 1 about 100 yards away. Blue 1 gave a quick deflection burst at e/a as it passed. E/a turned left and again crossed Blue 1's path at the same range. Blue 1 gave another burst and hit e/a's tail. Blue 1 then got a third burst from above and behind at a range of 50 yards, bullets hitting e/a from which pieces came off. Blue 1 got into e/a slipstream, ceased fire and got out slightly to one side and fired again at e/a which then hung in the air for a few seconds and then fell forward in a vertical dive, smoke pouring from the starboard wing and fuselage. E/a disappeared into black smoke over Thames Haven.

It is possible that Powell-Sheddon's victim was *Leutnant* Geske, of 1/JG27, who baled out to become a prisoner; his aircraft also crashed at Park Corner Farm, Hacton Lane, Cranham at 1710 hrs.

Pilot Officer Stansfeld, Black 1, reported having attacked a 'Do 215' which consequently 'dived into ground'. As there were no Do 215s amongst the enemy formation, it is likely that this was either the 110 at Cranham, or that down at Wickford.

Although Squadron Leader Lane, Sergeant Jennings and Flight Lieutenant Lawson had returned to base after their successful combat with the Cranham Me 110, the rest of the squadron remained in action. After breaking away from 'A' Flight's pursuit of the 110, Red 3, Pilot Officer Cunningham, blacked out and lost the squadron. When he came to, he joined up with a squadron of Hurricanes travelling south-east. At 1720 hrs the RAF fighters executed a front-quarter attack on 20 He 111s at 15,000'. Red 3 hurtled through the bombers, in an attempt to break their formation, but he then singled out an individual Heinkel which caught fire and lost height. After a further attack, Cunningham last saw the damaged raider 10 miles inland from Deal. He then found another vic of He 111s, but after a short burst his ammunition was expended and he returned to base.

Squadron Leader Lane, Flight Lieutenant Lawson and Sergeant Lloyd make out their reports to the 19 Squadron Intelligence Officer, Flying Officer Cresswell, immediately after landing from an engagement. None of these pilots were to survive the war.
(Imperial War Museum)

'A' Flight's Flight Sergeant Unwin had also found himself alone, at 4,000', after the initial attack against the single Me 110. Climbing to 25,000', he too saw a 'Hurricane squadron going somewhere in a hurry' and followed them. Suddenly three separate enemy formations, comprising 30 bombers each, appeared with their inevitable fighter escort. As the Hurricanes attacked the bombers, 'Grumpy' found himself surrounded by Me 109s; fighting a running battle between Ramsgate and west London, he remembers:-

The usual fight ensued during which I definitely hit at least five of them but only two were shot down, both in flames. I then climbed for a breather and shadowed the third enemy formation when I saw yet a fourth arriving. By this time two of the other three formations had turned north and the other went straight on in a westerly direction. The leading formation turned east and I was at 25,000' and above them. As there did not seem to be any of their escorts left, I dived on the rear vic and gave them the rest of my ammunition, about 50 rounds in each gun, and from 450, closing to 50 yards range. The bomber at which I fired wobbled a bit but otherwise carried on. Without ammunition, I then returned to Fowlmere.

Without crash locations, it is difficult to ascertain which Me 109s were destroyed by Flight Sergeant

Unwin, although two of the three machines lost over England that afternoon by JG51 appear most likely.

Pilot Officer Dolezal had also acted independently of the squadron but later linked up with Hurricanes with which he attacked an He 111; although the Czech reported that this bomber crashed '10 miles inland from Deal or Ramsgate', no supporting evidence can be found.

By the time 'B' Flight of 19 Squadron had climbed to the enemy's height, the raiders were out of range. Consequently Flight Lieutenant Clouston and Flight Sergeant Steere returned to Fowlmere with the fabric covering their gun-ports intact.

When Squadron Leader Bader 'Tally Ho'd', and led 242 Squadron up at the bombers, 310 Squadron's Hurricanes headed for the fighters. The Czechs manoeuvred into sections line astern, but again, after the initial attack, the unit became fragmented and its pilots either fought the 109s alone or *ad hoc* with other units. Sergeant Furst attacked a 1/LG2 machine over Canterbury which ultimately exploded in mid-air; the pilot, *Unteroffizier* Götting, baled out and was captured. Furst then struck against an Me 110 of 6/ZG2 which ditched in the Channel off Birchington.

Sergeant Furst of 310 Squadron displays the parachute harness and to good effect. (Author via Squadron Leader Vic Bergman)

For any aircraft to be attacked whilst climbing is disastrous: flying slowly and therefore with less manoeuvrability, any such fighter would be a 'sitter' for an enemy enjoying the advantages of height and speed, not to mention perhaps sun and surprise. Back at Duxford, Squadron Leader Bader was furious and claimed that his fighters had been caught on the climb owing to having been scrambled too late. However, given the time of the scramble (1645 hrs) and the time and location of the interception (1710 hrs, Hornchurch area), it would appear that there *was* actually sufficient time to have climbed to height en-route before intercepting.

Flight Lieutenant 'Teddy' Morten:-

Squadron Leader Bader would frequently telephone Ops 'B' to get the 'form'. At Mess parties he would button-hole me to discuss tactics, the 'Hun in the sun' and all that, and demanding to know why the Wing wasn't scrambled by 11 Group sooner. Alternatively, he would insist on speaking to 'Woody' to get scrambles effected. It did seem that 11 Group were a law unto themselves.

Feeling that the squadron had been scrambled too late was not a situation peculiar to 12 Group;

BIG WING

Air Commodore Peter Brothers:-

Until September 9th, 1940, I flew with 32 Squadron, and during our time at the coastal aerodromes at Hawkinge and Manston, or even Biggin Hill which was further inland, we were often scrambled late. The Controller obviously had to ensure that it was the real thing and not a 'spoof' to get us airborne and catch us whilst refuelling. This was frustrating as at such forward bases there was so little time anyway.

The claims of the Duxford Wing squadrons during the September 7th action were as follows:-

242 Squadron:	10 destroyed, 2 probables, 3 damaged.
310 Squadron:	5 destroyed, 3 probables, 3 damaged.
19 Squadron:	5 destroyed.

Wing total:	20 destroyed, 5 probables, 6 damaged.

The Wing's own losses were as follows:-

242 Squadron:	One pilot killed, two Hurricanes damaged.
310 Squadron:	One pilot badly burned, Hurricane destroyed, one Hurricane damaged.
19 Squadron:	Nil.

Signals of congratulation were again sent to 242 Squadron from the AOC 12 Group and Secretary of State for Air, Sir Archibald Sinclair.

As the only substantiated combat claims are the six referred to in the text, overclaiming by the Duxford Wing in respect of destroyed aircraft was over 3:1. Again, 242 Squadron's claims were particularly inflated. The *Luftwaffe* lost a total of 40 aircraft on operations throughout this day, 17 of which either crashed in England or close enough to the coast for their crews to be captured or bodies recovered.

Air Vice-Marshal Leigh-Mallory accepted Bader's claim that as the Wing had been disadvantaged from the outset, the idea's perceived potential had yet to be realised. Again, the Wing's combat claims were accepted without question by the AOC 12 Group, although Group Captain Woodhall points out that:-

.... after the war, the Germans produced so-called official records showing that the numbers of their aircraft destroyed were far less than the quantity we claimed. I do not believe it. Bader and the Intelligence Officers checked these figures of our claims very carefully, with me.

The fact remains, however, that the details of crashed enemy aircraft as quoted are not only from *Luftwaffe* records, but also from RAF Intelligence reports. Despite the understandable reluctance of many to accept it, the German records, which were not for propaganda purposes but for internal audit, can be considered as complete and accurate as our own. It is a demonstrable fact, particularly in relation to combat claims, that the *Luftwaffe* records are actually far more precise than our own.

Nevertheless, Air Vice-Marshal Leigh-Mallory readily agreed to further fighter operations from Duxford in Wing strength, firm in the belief that his massed formation was inflicting great losses on the enemy.

Wing Commander Woodhall also supported Squadron Leader Bader's ideas:-

Douglas had made an intimate study of the fighter tactics developed by famous pilots like McCudden, Ball and Bishop in the First War, and was a great believer in the advantages of making the correct use of the sun, and first gaining superior height.

As I saw it, my job as Sector Controller was to vector the Fighter Leader on a course and to a height which would place him above and up-sun of the enemy, and keep him informed of the enemy's position, course and speed as accurately as possible from the information we had on the operations table. As soon as our fighter leader sighted the enemy, it was over to him.

My interviews with many survivors indicate that all, without exception, appreciated the advantages of height and sun. The airborne interception practices being developed by Woodhall and Bader were, of course, contrary to the System, but, as we have seen, both were prone to 'tape-cutting', to enable them to 'get on with the war', as they saw it, and in this endeavour both men had the support of their AOC

As previously indicated, the huge raid against London on September 7th had forced Air Vice-Marshal Park to call also on 10 Group for help. At this time the 10 Group squadrons operated under individual orders. 152 Squadron's Pilot Officer Roger Hall later wrote:-

We saw our own fighters - the 11 Group squadrons, and some from 12 Group in the Midlands - climbing up from the north. There seemed to be quite a number of us. They too were black dots, climbing in groups of 12 or 36 in Wing formation. Most of them were Hurricanes.

152 Squadron soon became embroiled with enemy fighters; 15 minutes later the combat was over and the Spitfires were scattered over western Kent. As London blazed, Roger Hall thought:-

I recalled for an instant Mr Baldwin's prophecy, not a sanguine one, made to the House of Commons some five years before when he said that the bomber would always get through. Now it was doing just that.

From this point onwards, Air Vice-Marshal Brand's squadrons were to be engaged over London frequently. Pilot Officer David Crook, of 609 Squadron, wrote:-

In the next week or two we flew up to London almost every day, sometimes twice a day, in order to give the overworked London squadrons a helping hand. They certainly needed it; the weight and intensity of these raids exceeded anything I'd ever seen before.

On 'Black Saturday', Londoners had witnessed combat on a scale previously unseen throughout the short history of aerial warfare. Through sheer weight of numbers the German force had reached its target, starting huge fires in both the docklands and East End. Vast areas were devastated and nearly 1,800 Londoners were killed. Late that evening Air Vice-Marshal Park was up from Northolt in his personal Hurricane and flew over the blazing capital. It was a sight he was to remember for the rest of his life. He realised immediately that such a significant switch in targets would not be for a day, or even a week; in all probability a new phase had begun, with London the prize, and which would enable Fighter Command to rectify damage to both airfields and communications. Forever this day represented the turning point so far as Air Vice-Marshal Park was concerned.

That night the bombers returned, wave after wave stoking the blazing conflagrations. With Britain's night defences still in their infancy, the bombers were able to make such *Nachtangriff* in comparative safety. For the Londoners, worse lay ahead: the Battle of the Airfields was over, but the Battle of London had begun.

CHAPTER SIX

Battle for London

At 0630 hrs on Sunday, September 8th, 1940, 13 Spitfires of 611 Squadron left Digby and again flew down to join 19 Squadron at Fowlmere in the Duxford Sector. These joined one of McComb's Spitfires which had been left at Duxford overnight, while a 15th aircraft of 611 Squadron arrived at lunchtime. At this time, however, 611 Squadron was not being absorbed into the Wing formation but was used instead to provide a local defensive precaution or extra reinforcement. 242 Squadron, still based at Coltishall, joined 310 Squadron at Duxford itself. In anticipation of protracted future operations from Duxford, 242 Squadron despatched a servicing party by road to remain at the latter Sector Station and maintain the squadron's aircraft. After the action of the previous day, Fighter Command anticipated another heavy assault, but in fact the day became a lull with comparatively little action. No doubt exhausted by its round-the-clock bombing, the enemy sent only two raids, attacking London and the airfields south of London, which were effectively dealt with by 11 Group. No assistance was therefore requested from 12 Group, and so the aircraft awaiting action at Duxford, as the 611 Squadron ORB records, '... remained on the ground all day'. That evening, the Duxford Sector's visiting fighters once more returned to their home bases.

September 9th, dawned a cool day with 9/10ths cloud. Such conditions, which were to become more frequent as the autumn wore on, hampered the Observer Corps' reporting owing to enemy formations flying above the cloud and therefore being screened from the ground. Early that day, 15 Spitfires of 611 Squadron again arrived at Fowlmere, and 242 Squadron once more flew down to Duxford.

During the late afternoon a spate of raids attacked targets in the South London area. Again these were dealt with by 11 Group and combat erupted in the skies high above Kent, Sussex and Surrey. The main attack of the day developed at 1635 hrs when some 300 German aircraft crossed the coast between North Foreland and Dover, heading for London. Amongst these raiders were 26 He 111s of II/KG1, escorted by 20 Me 110s of III/ZG76 and 60 Me 109s of JG3. This formation was briefed to attack the Royal Aircraft Establishment at Farnborough. To reach this target, the enemy had to pass over the Biggin Hill, Kenley, Croydon and Northolt Sectors: running the gauntlet indeed!

At 1650 hrs, 611 Squadron was the first 12 Group unit scrambled when ordered to patrol the familiar North Weald line, firstly below cloud base and then above at 27,000'. Although a distant enemy formation was sighted, there was no contact. Clearly Squadron Leader McComb displayed discipline in not succumbing to the temptation of chasing after Germans, which would have left his allocated patrol line unprotected.

At 1700 hrs the Duxford Wing was scrambled, also to the North Weald line at 20,000'. The squadrons involved, 19, 242 and 310, joined up in the air with 242 Squadron in the van. In his log book, Squadron Leader Bader later wrote: 'Patrolled London with Wing, 242 leading'.

310 Squadron ORB:-

A formation of about 75 Do 215s escorted by about 150 Me 109s, 110 and He 112 were sighted south of the THAMES ESTUARY heading NW. The squadron was ordered to form line astern in preparation for an attack on the main enemy formation. The attack was delivered south of LONDON at 1735 hrs at 22,000', cloud about 4/10 at 7,000'. A collision occurred between two Hurricanes which was seen by other pilots of the squadron who then broke formation to avoid further ones and a series of dogfights ensued. F/Lt SINCLAIR was hit by a cannon shell and forced to bail out.

It must be appreciated that from combat altitude visibility was far-reaching; given favourable weather conditions, from North Weald, north of London, it would easily be possible to see the action over and south of the Capital. Having been ordered to patrol the North Weald line, Squadron Leader Bader, unlike Squadron Leader McComb earlier in the day, clearly rejected his orders and crossed the City, actually intercepting south of the Thames Estuary. What would the consequences have been if another raid, as on August 30th, had attacked north of the Thames? Having been led off south at the first sight of the enemy, such raiders would not have found Bader's fighters barring their way as was intended by the System. The possibility of such an attack could surely not have been discounted?

Flying Officer Boulton with Flight Lieutenants Jefferies and Sinclair, all of 310 Squadron; On September 15th, 1940, Boulton and Sinclair collided during an engagement over the capital; Boulton was killed but Sinclair fortunately baled out safely. (Author via Squadron Leader Bergman)

Flight Lieutenant Gordon Sinclair, of 310 Squadron, had collided with Flying Officer Johnnie Boulton, a 20-year-old who had been attached to the squadron as an instructor almost since its formation; he had specially asked to serve with 310 Squadron on operations. On the way down, Boulton hit a 'Do 215' and the two machines reportedly impacted together. In fact, the enemy aircraft with which Boulton collided was an Me 110C of 9/ZG76 which crashed at Woodmansterne (between Epsom and Coulsdon in Surrey, at least 30 miles SW of North Weald). This southerly location, coupled with the fact that this enemy aircraft was of III/ZG76, suggests that the Duxford Wing had attacked the KG1 formation proceeding to Farnborough. Despite the Duxford Wing combat reports frequently referring to Dorniers during this action, no such German type was involved; again it appears as though in reality the enemy aircraft concerned were Me 110s. It is also interesting to note the reference in 310 Squadron's report to the 'He 112'; such a type did not exist, so the reference probably referred to the He 113, a single-engined monoplane fighter which looked not unlike a Spitfire and despite having been a propaganda ruse only, was often incorrectly reported in British skies by Fighter Command's pilots. The fact that two aircraft of the Duxford Wing had collided was also a pertinent point. As we have seen through his correspondence of August 19th, 1939, Air Chief Marshal Dowding was concerned about the risk of collision if large numbers of monoplane fighters were used together, which is why the squadron, or even flight, was concluded to be the best tactical arrangement.

During the remainder of the combat in question, 310 Squadron's Flying Officer Fejfar and Pilot Officer Bergman destroyed an Me 110 of 15/LG1 which exploded at the Maori Sports Club in Worcester Park. Pilot Officer Zimprich attacked an He 111, which had already been engaged by 607 Squadron's Sergeant Burnell-Phillips; the 3/KG1 machine forced-landed near Sundridge and the crew were captured. Having fought it out with 10 Me 109s, Flight Lieutenant Rypl forced-landed at Oxted, out of fuel.

A 310 Squadron 'briefing' posed for the camera; from the left, standing: Pilot Officer Bergman, Sergeants Furst and Zima, Pilot Officers Fechtner and Zimprich, Sergeant Kaucky, Pilot Officer Maly, unknown, Pilot Officer Goth. Front row: from third left, Flight Lieutenant Gordon Sinclair, Flying Officer Boulton and Flight Lieutenant Jefferies.
(Author via Squadron Leader Vic Bergman)

19 Squadron reported:-

Whilst patrolling North Weald at 20,000' .... sighted large formation of enemy bombers and fighters flying north-west. The bombers were in vic formation, the vics being in line astern. The fighters were above weaving and searching.

It had been arranged that 19 Sqn should attack the fighters, so Blue 1, who was leading them (F/Lt WG Clouston DFC), put them into line astern and climbed to 23,000' preparatory to an attack on six or seven Me 110s who were also climbing in line astern. As they were about to attack, two Me 109s cut across in front and Blue Leader opened fire on them. The first burst into flames and the second glided down in apparent distress.

Still in line astern, the squadron proceeded to attack the main body of Me 110s. Flight Sergeant Harry Steere attacked a 110 with full deflection before chasing another across the Channel but without closing to within firing range. Red Leader, Flight Lieutenant Lawson, attacked an Me 110 from astern, stopping its starboard engine during an 'enjoyable dogfight' which ended in the enemy machine 'crashing in a field five miles east of Biggin Hill'. Despite this specific location, however, no contender from records available can be identified. Red 2, Sub-Lieutenant Blake, followed the main formation out to sea where he attacked a straggling He 111, leaving it

Sub-Lieutenant Arthur 'Admiral' Blake RN.
(Author's Collection)

on fire and descending. The armoured glass windscreen of Blake's Spitfire was pierced by a 7.9 mm machine-gun round which eventually lodged in his self-sealing fuel tank (the damaged windscreen is now preserved at the RAF Battle of Britain Museum, Hendon). Blue 2, Pilot Officer

Vokes, damaged a 'Do 215' but wrote in his log book that he was 'hit by blast from AA fire on breaking away' (in Spitfire R9874). Pilot Officer Cunningham attacked an Me 109 which he left 'enveloped in flames'. This was possibly an 8/JG53 machine which crashed near Ditcham at 1815 hrs, the pilot being killed. Low on fuel and with a bullet through the mainspar, Pilot Officer Cunningham landed at Detling. Flying Officer Brinsden also engaged the Me 109s before joining a Hurricane in attacking an He 111 which he left 'down to 1,000 feet with both engines stopped and his flaps and undercarriage down. He was gliding in an easterly direction with the apparent intention of making a forced-landing a little south of Detling'. Fortune must have smiled upon this German crew, however, as no He 111 made such a landing in this area. Meanwhile, Sergeant Cox had become embroiled in the dogfight with the Me 109s but left one diving vertically in flames. Interestingly, the squadron combat report remarks that 'R/T receipt was poor from ground-to-air owing to interference by other stations'. This was a result of the squadron having progressed so far south in the combat and therefore over several other Sectors.

Having detailed 19 Squadron to deal with the fighter escort, Squadron Leader Bader led 242 Squadron off with 310 Squadron to attack the bombers. Bader himself attacked the leader, which he left 'turning on its back'. Taking evasive action, he managed a few short bursts without conclusive effect before returning home. Pilot Officer McKnight claimed a Dornier in flames, and the destruction of an escort fighter which was attacking a Hurricane. Flight Lieutenant Ball claimed an Me 109 in flames, and Pilot Officer Tamblyn attacked several Me 110s during what was now a free-for-all, one of which he left with a smoking engine; it is possible that this was the same enemy aircraft as attacked by 310 Squadron's Fejfar and Bergman, crashing at Worcester Park. Other claims brought the 242 Squadron total to 10 destroyed. In his log book, Squadron Leader Bader recorded that he had personally 'got the leader in flames'. However, 242 Squadron had lost two Hurricanes: Pilot Officer Sclanders was shot down and killed by Me 110s over Caterham, and Sergeant Lonsdale baled out over the same location.

At the end of this engagement, the Wing squadrons' combat claims were as follows:-

19 Squadron:	Five destroyed, two shared destroyed, three probables and one damaged.
310 Squadron:	Three destroyed, three probables and one damaged.
242 Squadron:	10 destroyed.
Wing total:	20 destroyed (& two shared), six probables and two damaged.

Two Spitfires of 19 Squadron had been damaged, two 310 Squadron Hurricanes were destroyed by collision, the pilot of one being killed, and 242 Squadron also lost two fighters with one pilot killed. After the action, which had progressed well south, the Wing's aircraft, low on fuel, were scattered and put down at various 11 Group aerodromes. In addition, for the same reasons, one Hurricane had forced-landed in a field. Until the Wing had reassembled at Duxford, and refuelled and rearmed, it could not operate as a Wing at Readiness.

In total, the *Luftwaffe* lost 27 aircraft this day. Of the above claims, only four can be cross-referenced against German aircraft known to have crashed in England, and a fifth is represented by the Me 110 with which Flying Officer Boulton collided. This time the overclaiming was therefore approximately 5:1. The combat claims of 242 Squadron are consistently and noticeably high when compared with the other Wing squadrons, and it should be remembered that 19 Squadron was by far the most combat experienced amongst them. It is also interesting that 242 Squadron did not claim any enemy aircraft as either probably destroyed or damaged: all were claimed and credited as destroyed, regardless of whether the pilot concerned had noted a crash location. Nevertheless the claims were again accepted at 12 Group HQ; the 242 Squadron ORB records that:-

Congratulations received from Air Officer Commanding and Chief of the Air Staff.

On September 9th, 616 Squadron was relieved at Coltishall by 74 'Tiger' Squadron. The reason for this was that under the Stabilising Scheme, the former squadron, having been badly beaten up at Kenley and withdrawn with only eight of its original members surviving, had become a 'C' unit. Duties from Coltishall included reinforcement of the Duxford Sector, and by this stage it was impossible for 616 Squadron to do this. At Kirton, away from the combat zone, it was able to devote its energies to recuperating and providing further training to replacement pilots. As a 'B' squadron, also receiving replacements but still with a high complement of combat experienced pilots, 74 Squadron was able to operate from Coltishall and cater for all eventualities.

74 Squadron was an experienced, regular fighter unit adequately upholding its proud Great War traditions. Reformed at Hornchurch in 1935, the squadron received its Spitfires in February 1939. On the third day of the war, the squadron had 'put up a black' when its Spitfires mistakenly intercepted Hurricanes over the Thames Estuary, shooting down two in the war's first incident of 'Friendly Fire'; there would be countless others by 1945. During the Dunkirk evacuation, 74 Squadron had operated from Hornchurch and claimed many successes. In the early part of the Battle of Britain, the 'Tigers' again operated from Hornchurch until being withdrawn to Wittering in 12 Group on August 14th, and from there, onwards to Coltishall.

The 29-year-old South African CO of 74 Squadron was amongst the most experienced Fighter Command pilots at that, or indeed any other, time: Squadron Leader AG 'Sailor' Malan DFC*. Malan was a short service commission pilot who had joined the RAF in 1936, and 74 Squadron in December of that year. In March 1939 he became a flight commander, and saw much action over Dunkirk, claiming the five victories for which his DFC was awarded. He had even destroyed an He 111 at night during the *Luftwaffe's* first major night attack on June 19th, 1940; that victory earned him a Bar to his DFC. On August 8th he was promoted and received command of the squadron. By the time this dedicated and professional fighter leader arrived at Coltishall, his 'score' stood at least nine enemy aircraft destroyed, five damaged, one probable and three further unconfirmed victories. At Coltishall, Malan was the least senior squadron commander by some six weeks. It was during this period that he wrote his famous '10 Rules of Air Fighting' which were distributed throughout Fighter Command.

Throughout the Battle of Britain, Squadron Leader Malan was a fighter leader without parallel in Fighter Command. Here was a truly exceptional fighter pilot, leader and man in every way. Flight Lieutenant Bob Poulton, when a 22-year-old Pilot Officer, was posted from 64 Squadron to join 74 Squadron at Biggin Hill in November 1940; he paid tribute to 'Sailor' Malan, saying that quite simply:-

... he was good, very, very good indeed.

The following day, September 10th, 242 Squadron remained at Coltishall, but Squadron Leader Bader flew to 12 Group HQ at Hucknall where he and Air Vice-Marshal Leigh-Mallory discussed the Wing's progress to date and considered future possibilities. It is a great pity that no record of their conversation was either recorded or preserved.

On this dull day, the enemy largely rested and there were no major raids. 611 Squadron had again flown down to Fowlmere, where they were joined by 14 Spitfires of 74 Squadron which represented Coltishall's contribution in the absence of 242 Squadron. Apart from Blue Section of 611 Squadron investigating an X Raid over 12 Group, which transpired to be a friendly aircraft, the squadrons on duty in the Duxford Sector were not called upon.

For some reason, Squadron Leader Bader did not fly at all on the following day, September 11th, when 242 Squadron again remained at Coltishall; it is noteworthy that whenever the CO was absent, the squadron did not proceed to Duxford. Again, Squadron Leader Malan led 74 Squadron to join the Spitfires of 19 and 611 Squadrons at Fowlmere. One flight of 266 Squadron (now a 'B' unit), which although officially based back at Wittering had operated from 242 Squadron's Dispersal at Coltishall since September 8th, also flew down to the Duxford Sector. A new feature of Air Vice-Marshal Leigh-Mallory's reinforcement policy was that on this day the Poles of 302 'Poznan' Squadron also joined the squadrons on Readiness at Duxford. This put the equivalent of three Spitfire and two Hurricane squadrons at the disposal of the Sector Controller, some 50 fighters in all.

302 Squadron pictured at Leconfield, September 4th, 1940. As with the Czechs, the 'Double-Banking' policy of English/Polish personnel was implemented; seated, centre, is Squadron Leader Jack Satchell, together with his British flight commanders, Flight Lieutenants Thomson (fourth left) and Farmer (fourth right).
(Author via Mr A Markiewicz)

Like the Czechs, the Poles had escaped after their homeland had been invaded, and had arrived in the UK after the fall of France. 302 Squadron had formed at Leconfield on July 13th 1940, was equipped with Hurricanes and also operated a system of 'double-banking' with English-speaking officers. For example, whilst the Polish CO was Squadron Leader Mieczyslaw Mumler, his British counterpart was Squadron Leader WAJ 'Jack' Satchell. The latter was, in fact, quite old, at 32, to be a fighter pilot; during the Battle for France, he had been a Controller at Merville. The Poles had become operational on August 19th, but had yet to see action.

The weather only slowly improved throughout the day on September 11th, so the first and only major raid did not come until 1545 hrs. Over the next hour, 250 aircraft intruded over south-east

England, although only around 30 are believed to have reached London. Over England, the *Luftwaffe* was met by Fighter Command's squadrons, now operating in pairs. At 1530 hrs, Squadron Leader Brian Lane led eight Spitfires of his own 19 Squadron, together with six of 266, off from Fowlmere as the lead unit in an all-Spitfire Wing, the other squadrons being Malan's 74 and McComb's 611. Lane's instructions were to patrol in a southerly direction towards the Thames Estuary. At about 1550 hrs, whilst flying at 20,000' over south-east London, the Spitfires sighted 100 enemy aircraft approaching them from the south. This time factor of 20 minutes is significant when considering the Wing's previous interception times involving slower Hurricane units. The approaching enemy formation was described as consisting of '15-30 Do 215s and a number of He 111s at 18,000' and a mass of Me 110s stepped up behind at 20,000', with a large number of Me 109s behind them at 24,000'. 74 and 611 Squadrons executed a left-hand turn, attacking on the beam of the enemy formation. As 611 Squadron later reported, 'from the moment of contact with the enemy it was impossible to keep formation and general melee ensued'. Squadron Leader Lane led 19 Squadron in a head-on charge against the He 111s.

Sergeant Bernard 'Jimmy' Jennings of 19 Squadron fired at an He 111 during Lane's initial charge, but later attacked the rearmost machine of 15 Me 110s. The Spitfire pilot reported that:-

..... this one fell back from the rest of the formation with smoke pouring out of his starboard engine. I did another attack from above and behind and he crashed in a wood, south of the Ashford railway line between Sittingbourne and Maidstone.

This was an aircraft of 9/ZG26 which crashed at Barnes Cote, Harvel. Both crewmen were killed.

Flight Sergeant Unwin, flying Spitfire P9546, QV-H, was shot down, however, as the pilot recalled for me 50 years later:-

I attacked a Dornier over London but was stupid enough to be shot down by the gunner they carried in a dustbin below the fuselage. I landed in a field near Brentwood in Essex and was taken to RAF North Weald by the army. With the aid of a fitter plus spares, 'QV-H' was repaired and I flew it back to Duxford two days later. One bullet had penetrated the armoured windscreen, however, so as this could not be repaired on station. P9546 was then flown away to a Maintenance Unit.

Unwin's forced-landing was much commended in the 19 Squadron ORB:-

Flight Sergeant Unwin made a wizard forced-landing with undercarriage down!!!!

Squadron Leader Malan's pilots had also made claims, but the only victory possibly substantiated was Flight Lieutenant Johnnie Freeborn's Me 110 which he reported as having crashed off Dungeness. Certainly a machine of II/ZG76 had ditched in the Channel, its crew later being rescued by the *Seenotdienst*.

In what was 611 Squadron's first engagement of a massed formation, McComb's pilots had also been in the battle's midst; Sergeant 'Sandy' Levenson attacked several enemy aircraft, including a 'Ju 88' which he actually flew alongside as the raider lost height. As he did so, his Spitfire was hit by AA fire and as black smoke poured from beneath the instrument panel he broke off to forced-land near Kenley. A nearby searchlight post then informed Levenson that the bomber concerned had crashed in flames a few miles south of Kenley. This was an He 111 of 3/KG26 which crashed at Lingfield. This raider was also featured in the combat reports of at least eight other RAF fighter pilots!

611 Squadron lost a pilot killed, Sergeant FER Shepherd, who baled out over Croydon with his parachute in flames. His Spitfire crashed into an Anderson shelter and sadly killed two civilians therein; such was the peril of living below an aerial battlefield.

The 266 Squadron pilots involved made no claims, but one of their Spitfires was lost, shot down by an He 111, although Pilot Officer Roach baled out safely over Billericay, Essex.

After the action, the Wing's total claims were around 13 enemy aircraft destroyed and five damaged. Against this, two Spitfires were lost with one pilot killed, and four more Spitfires were damaged. Three of the Wing's combat claims can now probably be confirmed, although again due to the number of claims made by pilots generally, it is impossible to be certain about these. It is noteworthy, however, that in the absence of 242 Squadron, the total number of Wing claims on this sortie was more realistic than on the previous two occasions. Of the 23 aircraft lost by the *Luftwaffe* in total on September 11th, 14 came down either on British soil or near the coast.

Squadron Leader Malan returned with his Spitfires directly to Coltishall after the action. For some reason the 'Tigers' did not operate from the Duxford Sector again, despite remaining at Coltishall until October 15th, on which date the squadron returned south for its second tour of Battle of Britain duty in 11 Group.

It is not known why neither 310 nor 302 Squadrons flew with the Wing formation on September 11th, but between 1845 and 1930 hrs the Czechs patrolled North Weald at 20,000' without meeting the enemy. It has been claimed that the discussions between Air Vice-Marshal Leigh-Mallory and Squadron Leader Bader, which took place at Hucknall on the previous day, concluded with the decision to increase the number of squadrons in the Wing. If this was indeed so, why did the five squadrons available at Duxford on September 11th not fly together? I would suggest that the arrival of 302 Squadron at Duxford on this day was merely to increase the number of squadrons available in 12 Group's southernmost Sector in view of the recent heavy fighting over the London area.

At 11 Group HQ, Air Vice-Marshal Park was having to think and respond quickly to the enemy's changing tactics. The move of most Me 109s to the Pas-de-Calais on August 28th, in preparation for the heavy assault against south-east England and London in particular, meant that Fighter Command's tactics had to be adapted accordingly. On November 7th, 1940, Park reported on enemy tactics during this phase:-

Enemy Tactics.

The normal attack was by formations of long-range bombers, escorted by strong formations of fighters as experienced in the previous phase of operations up to September 10th. Bombing attacks were mostly high level attacks with only a few at medium altitudes.

Method of Attack.

The enemy has attempted in this phase to draw our fighter patrols off from his bombers by high altitude diversions as he had attempted to do unsuccessfully prior to September 10th. Increasingly high fighter screens were sent inland to draw off and contain our fighters, whilst the bomber formations, closely escorted by further fighters, endeavoured to sweep in some 6,000'-10,000' below.

The majority of attacks approached in two or three waves at varying intervals of time, on a much wider front and at heights varying between 16,000 and 20,000 feet for bomber formations. Small formations sometimes broke off from the main raid immediately fighter opposition was encountered and, descending to lower altitude, made clever use of cloud cover to attack objectives in the London area. Owing to extreme difficulty in reporting the tracks of these split raids, they frequently reached their objectives without effective interruption, and sometimes made their escape to the coast without being engaged.

As our successes against these bombers increased, there was a noticeable increase in the ratio of enemy fighters to bombers, the ratio in the latter part of the phase being about 4 fighters to 1 bomber.

<u>Employment of Enemy Fighters.</u>

The favourite practice was to send a very high fighter screen over Kent from 15 - 45 minutes ahead of bomber attacks, presumably to draw up our fighter squadrons and exhaust their petrol before the main attack crossed the coast. At other times the high fighter screen arrived only a few minutes in advance of the bomber formations with close escort. Fighter escorts normally consisted of two parts: (a) a big formation above and to the flank or in rear of the bombers, and (b) smaller formations of fighters formating with the bombers on the same level or slightly below. The latter formations endeavoured to prevent head-on attacks by our fighters against the incoming bombers.

Regarding his own squadrons, he added:-

<u>Method of Employing our Squadrons.</u>

The general plan adopted was to engage the enemy high fighter screen with Pairs of Spitfire squadrons from Hornchurch and Biggin Hill half-way between London and the coast, and so enable Hurricane squadrons from London Sectors to attack bomber formations and their close escort before they reached the line of fighter aerodromes east and south of London. The remaining time to intercept the first wave of the attack by climbing in pairs formed a third and inner screen by patrolling along the line of aerodromes east and south of London. The fighter squadrons from Debden, Tangmere, and sometimes Northolt, were employed in Wings or three squadrons in pairs to form a screen south-east of London to intercept the third wave of the attack coming inland, also to mop up retreating formations of the earlier waves. The Spitfire squadrons were re-disposed so as to concentrate three squadrons at each of Hornchurch and Biggin Hill. The primary role of these squadrons was to engage and drive back the enemy high fighter screen, and so protect the Hurricane squadrons, whose task was to attack close escorts and then the bomber formations, all of which flew at much lower altitude.

Air Vice-Marshal Park's brilliant and rapid flexibility is amply reflected in the above paragraph, proving that the AOC 11 Group fully appreciated the benefits of attacking in strength when circumstances dictated. There was certainly no aversion, therefore, to using Wings of three squadrons from the Group's northerly Sectors of Northolt and Debden, the distance from those stations to the southerly combat area providing the squadrons involved with time to climb appropriately. It could be argued that the Air Vice-Marshal would have welcomed assistance from a *Pair* of Spitfire squadrons operating from Duxford, especially as experience indicated that such a formation could be over London in 20 minutes. Describing the use of Wing formations by 11 Group, Park went on:-

When early warning had given adequate time, and cloud conditions were suitable, squadrons were employed in Wings of three against enemy bomber formations and their close escort.

Being located outside the area normally patrolled by enemy fighter screens, the squadrons from Debden, Northolt and Tangmere were not infrequently employed in Wings of three squadrons. These Wings were successful in engaging retreating bomber formations, who normally lost their escort before reaching London, because of the vigorous action of Spitfire and Hurricane squadrons working in pairs against incoming raids.

Experience showed that even small Wings of three squadrons were not effective against high fighter patrols, and the Spitfire squadrons were therefore used in pairs.

From Debden, the Hurricane-equipped 17 and 73 Squadrons were briefed to act in concert as a two-squadron Wing. On September 11th, this formation patrolled over the Thames Estuary and intercepted Me 110s of ZG26; in total, five were claimed destroyed, but the fighting was so intense and the 110 losses acute enough to make it virtually impossible to confirm who-got-which of the enemy aircraft known to have crashed in England. Two Hurricanes were damaged, and a third destroyed. This increase in formation strength by Air Vice-Marshal Park was well thought out, as confirmed by his Instruction to Controllers No 16 (issued on September 11th):-

Engagement of Mass Attacks.

The enemy has recently dropped his plan of making two or three separate attacks by two or three hundred aircraft in one day. Recent attacks in the 11 Group area have been made by three or four hundred aircraft in two or three waves following in quick succession, the whole engagement covering between 45 to 60 minutes.

The object of the following instruction is to ensure that we meet the enemy in maximum strength, employing our fighter squadrons in pairs of the same type where possible.

READINESS SQUADRONS:

Despatch in pairs to engage first wave of enemy. Spitfires against fighter screen, and Hurricanes against bombers and close escort.

AVAILABLE 15 SQUADRONS:

a) Bring to Readiness in pairs;
b) Despatch in pairs to engage second wave.

AVAILABLE 30 SQUADRONS :

a) Bring to Readiness;
b) Despatch singly to protect aircraft factories or sector aerodromes, or to reinforce squadrons already in the air.

If there is a third wave and it is necessary to despatch these squadrons, they should be sent in pairs as follows:

DEBDEN and NORTH WEALD squadrons together.
HORNCHURCH and BIGGIN HILL squadrons together.
KENLEY and NORTHOLT squadrons together.

TANGMERE SQUADRONS:

When not required to protect the Portsmouth-Southampton area in conjunction with 10 Group squadrons, the Tangmere squadrons should be employed within the Kenley or back Tangmere Sector to engage enemy formations that approach London from the south, or endeavour to pass round the south of London to attack aircraft factories at Kingston, Brooklands and Langley.

Whenever time permits, the Readiness squadron and the Available 15 squadron should be despatched to work as a pair after having rendezvoused at base.

RENDEZVOUS OF SQUADRONS:

The Group Controller must name the base over which pairs of squadrons are to rendezvous, as they normally occupy separate aerodromes within a Sector. Sector Controllers should inform Group Controller immediately a pair of squadrons have rendezvoused over any given point. Group Controller should then detail these squadrons to a raid and leave the rest to Sector.

SELECTION OF SQUADRON TO LEAD A PAIR OF SQUADRONS:

The detailing of the directing squadron should be done by Sector Controller, who should know which squadron is best suited to lead. Sector Controllers must also repeat to the squadron being led all orders issued to the directing squadron in case these units become separated by clouds. Sector Commanders must impress on Squadron Commanders the importance of leading squadrons in a pair joining up and maintaining contact with the squadron being led.

On September 11th, 10 Group had again reinforced 11 Group. Amongst Brand's squadrons was 238, freshly returned to the fray having been at St Eval in Cornwall for two months. The squadron lost three Hurricanes on this day: two pilots were missing, the other wounded. Again, the change in the battle's tempo had been found to be traumatic. From then until October 31st 1940, the squadron lost eight pilots killed, five of them over 11 Group. At the time, Air Commodore Harry Fenton was 238's CO:-

Our routine was to rise before first light, about 0330 hrs, have a coffee and then go to dispersal. We then spent the day there, being scrambled at intervals in either squadron or section strength. We shared Middle Wallop with 609 Squadron and so took it in turns to spend every third day down at Warmwell undertaking convoy protection patrols. That was during the early days, but I was shot down and wounded on August 8th, returning to the squadron on September 12th. By that time 238 had been back at Middle Wallop for two days but we already had two pilots missing from action over 11 Group: David Hughes, an able flight commander, and a Polish pilot, Duszynski, whom I had not met. As you rightly say, the tempo of combat had totally changed.

Flight Lieutenant Gordon Batt was then amongst Fenton's NCO pilots:-

When we returned to Middle Wallop in September, the size of German formations had increased: the bomber formations were usually 50-60 strong, in an oblong block and in close formation, and above them were Me 110s, and Me 109s higher still. To counter this, we often flew together with one of Wallop's Spitfire squadrons. Our CO was the senior squadron commander and so we usually led, our Hurricanes attacking the bombers whilst the Spitfires held off the escort. It

Sergeant Gordon Batt of 10 Group's 238 Squadron; the rear-view mirror was a personal improvement - purchased from Halfords!
(Author via Flight Lieutenant LG Batt

certainly did my morale a hell of a lot of good, God and Hitler knew what it did to theirs! The only snag was that as 238 were first to attack, I never had the opportunity to look back - there must have been chaos! Towards the end of August and throughout September, we were frequently called to the west of London area. The Controller would give us a commentary regarding what was going on generally, and, whilst we held off at 20,000', could hear him directing 11 Group squadrons into action. From our position west of London, we could see the ack-ack bursting over the capital, and condensation trails of the Spitfires, Hurricanes and Me 109s; the boys of 11 Group were obviously holding their own and we were sensibly being held in reserve. When we were vectored, the Controller would say something like: '25 Bandits Angels 20, heading straight for you, they're all yours!' It really was slick control.

In his November 7th report, Air Vice-Marshal Park commented favourably upon the reinforcements received by 11 Group:-

During this phase of heavy attacks on the London area, there were occasionally heavy diversionary attacks on the Portsmouth area, when 10 Group rendered invaluable assistance by despatching squadrons singly or in pairs to reinforce the Tangmere Sector. During mass attacks on London, valuable reinforcements were provided by Nos 10 and 12 Groups. On numerous occasions two or three squadrons were provided by No 10 Group for the close protection of aircraft factories and airfields west and south-west of London. These squadrons several times intercepted bomber formations that had broken away from the main raids and endeavoured, without escort, to attack aircraft factories and aerodromes, making use of cloud cover.

The Air Vice-Marshal's further remarks concerning 12 Group will be dealt with at a more chronologically appropriate juncture. However, as regards the assistance from 10 Group, it is clear that Air Vice-Marshal Brand, by sending his squadrons either singly or in pairs, was working along the same lines as the AOC 11 Group; 10 Group's squadrons therefore fitted perfectly into Air Vice-Marshal Park's tactics.

September 12th, 1940, according to the 611 Squadron ORB, was 'a cold day, clouding over with rain in the afternoon'. The weather hampered the enemy's air operations, and the day represented a welcome respite for Fighter Command. Nonetheless 12 Group's fighters gathered in the Duxford Sector: 611 joined 19 at Fowlmere, and 242 and 302 flew south to Duxford itself where they spent an uneventful day with 310 Squadron before returning to their home bases. The 19 Squadron ORB remarks:-

Red Section of 'A' Flight on patrol but no E/A sighted. Eight new (to us) aircraft arrived for the squadron today. We need them badly. P/O Jones, Sgt Charnock and Sgt Lloyd posted to the squadron. All operational.

The Stabilising Scheme was obviously working. Charnock was an experienced pilot, having been commissioned in 1925, but had been cashiered by order of General Court Martial on December 12th, 1930, for low-flying. The outbreak of war was his salvation, but although the RAF accepted his return, it was, unlike Bader's, as an NCO pilot. Charnock subsequently joined 64 Squadron, flying Spitfires, and served throughout the squadron's busy period at Kenley between May 16th and August 19th, 1940. Thereafter the squadron was relieved by 616 Squadron and pulled out of the line to re-form, as a 'C' unit, at Leconfield. Pilot Officer Richard Jones had been posted to 64 Squadron at Kenley, directly from 5 OTU, and Sergeant Lloyd had joined the squadron at Leconfield, also straight from OTU. By the time these three pilots reached 19 Squadron, Charnock and Jones had already seen combat, and Lloyd was at least considered combat ready. Flight Lieutenant Richard Jones recalls an amusing story from his days at Kenley:-

We of 64 Squadron at Kenley in 11 Group were visited early in August 1940, by the Air Minister, Sir Archibald Sinclair. We were all lined up to meet him, standing in front of our Spitfires. He congratulated us on the work we were doing and in his opening words thanked us, *the Hurricane pilots of 12 Group*! Obviously, I thought to myself, the man doesn't know the difference between Hurricanes and Spitfires, much less Group boundaries!

It rained again on September 13th, and there was little flying. 611 Squadron was at Fowlmere and sent two sections off to investigate an X-Raid, but the Spitfires were recalled virtually immediately. 242 Squadron was at Duxford, and the ORB records uneventful patrols over 'London and North Weald'. 302 Squadron was officially detached to Duxford from this day, during which it did not fly, as did neither 19 nor 310 Squadrons.

On September 14th, the weather improved slightly, although 611 Squadron, again at Fowlmere, recorded:-

Cloudy but good visibility. Still cold. The squadron at G1 again all day, returning after dark, having done a variety of patrols without action.

At 1550 hrs, the Duxford Wing was sent off to patrol London at 23,000', but although there were five fighter squadrons at Readiness in the Duxford Sector, 611 Squadron did not join the formation. Squadron Leader Bader therefore led off a four squadron strong Wing which included the Poles for the first time. The enemy was not seen, but the Czech Sergeant Marek, on loan to 19 from 310 Squadron, crashed in Sussex and was killed as the result of oxygen system failure.

During the evening, Squadron Leader Bader led the same squadrons off on a further patrol. Although instructions remained to patrol north of the Thames Estuary, the 19 Squadron ORB provides the first hint that the Duxford Wing was starting to act as an independent entity and contrary to the System:-

Squadron again on patrol with Wing. Over Kent and almost France, still no E/A seen.

Further frustrated by the lack of action, Squadron Leader Bader was now clearly and openly disregarding orders. Flying over the sea was already an area of concern, Air Vice-Marshal Park having issued explicit instructions to his Controllers on this matter in an effort to preserve his limited resources. Whilst such a press-on and offensive spirit might have been considered commendable by some, such actions threw the System into confusion. 'Teddy' Morten recalls Squadron Leader Bader's attitude:-

On one of the many occasions on which Bader tackled me in the Mess regarding the 'Hun in the Sun' etc, he said ' "Morty", you know that yesterday you told the Wing to patrol North Weald at Angels 20?'
'Yes', I said.
'Well, d'ya know where we were upon reaching required height?'
'No', I said.
'Over *Reading*! We were looking down on the patrol area, up sun and all eyes "skinned"!'

On September 14th, Squadron Leader Bader was awarded the DSO, and Flight Lieutenant Eric Ball, the commander of 242 Squadron's 'A' Flight, received the DFC. Bader's decoration was a great morale booster; Flight Lieutenant Ron Rayner, who later flew with the Tangmere Wing during Wing Commander Bader's leadership in 1941, recalls:-

What you have to remember is that we were really up against it, on our own. We expected to be invaded and to have to fight on the ground like on the Continent. The story of a legless fighter pilot, and a squadron commander at that, was a great propaganda coup, it was tremendously inspiring to everyone.

Although the weather had improved by September 14th, and the enemy was more active, the scale of attack remained reduced by comparison with the previous week's effort; the 19 Squadron ORB perceptively recorded:-

Saving up for "der Tag" evidently.

How right that statement was.

According to the HQ Fighter Command Intelligence Officer, Sunday, 15th September 1940, dawned fair, becoming 'fair to cloudy during the morning with some showers mainly in the North and West and with cloud at 2,000 to 3,000 feet lowering to 1,000 to 2,000 feet and showers.' From first light onwards, standing patrols of RAF fighters were up over the coast between Land's End and Harwich. In addition, each Sector Station kept at least one squadron at Readiness, to scamble at a moment's notice. Between 1000 and 1100 hrs there were 'extensive enemy patrols in the Straits of Dover'. By 1050 hrs, the RDF screens were indicating a large raid moving out across the Channel, and five minutes later, all of 11 Group's squadrons were at Readiness. The size of the raid fast approaching indicated that reinforcements from neighbouring Group's would be necessary: at 1130 hrs the Duxford Wing, comprising 19, 242, 302 and 310 Squadrons, was scrambled; 611 Squadron, which was flying in from Digby, joined the Wing over Duxford a minute later. Such a rendezvous could only be described as fortuitous and is further evidence that the Big Wing was a more *ad hoc* formation than claimed by previous accounts.

At 1133 hrs, an enemy formation crossed the coast between Dover and Folkestone, being followed three minutes later by two further formations which flew in over Dover and the South Foreland. The enemy then flew a 'dog leg' course, first northwards towards the Thames Estuary, then turning south or south-west before reaching the north coast of Kent, then west to Maidstone before finally spreading out to fly over the entire London area. The raiders' selected targets were gasworks and industrial targets and docks in the London area. To meet this attack, 20 squadrons from 11 Group had been scrambled in addition to the Duxford Wing's five, and 10 Group's 609 Squadron - some 312 Spitfires and Hurricanes.

Again, however, Squadron Leader Bader was to disregard his allocated patrol line and led the Wing south in search of action, having seen AA shells exploding. The questions that should be asked are, why with attacks being made on London itself, was not 12 Group automatically vectored to the capital instead of North Weald; did this mean that perhaps the System was too inflexible? The fact remains that although we armchair strategists have the benefit of hindsight, Air Vice-Marshal Park could never discount the possibility of raids in strength north of the Thames, as has been previously stressed. Nevertheless, at 1209 hrs, 24 Do 17s of KG76 were at 16,000' over Brixton; the Duxford Wing was 3,000' above and up-sun, with an elapsed time of 38 minutes from scramble. The Dorniers were first subjected to a head-on charge by two 11 Group squadrons, 257 and 504, and so Bader had to hold off until this attack had concluded.

In the hectic combat which followed, Squadron Leader Bader attacked a Do 17 which had already been damaged by other fighters. A crew member baled out, but his parachute became entangled around the stricken bomber's tail. Bader claimed it as destroyed. Several other 242 Squadron pilots claimed Dorniers destroyed, but without exception all were hacked down jointly by many other fighters, such was the confusion of battle with so many attacking simultaneously. Although Pilot Officer Hart claimed a 109 which he saw crash into the sea, no likely candidate can be found amongst German loss records.

310 Squadron ORB:-

This was a busy day - one of the busiest and most successful that the RAF have had since the outbreak of war. The squadron, with the CO leading, took off at 1130 hrs to patrol North Weald. The squadron, with 19, 242 and 302 squadrons were flying in a Wing formation by sections in line astern, with 242 Squadron in the van. It had been arranged that the SPITFIRES (19 and 611 Squadrons) were to attack the fighter escort, the HURRICANES (242, 310 and 302 Squadrons) tackling the bombers. On approaching London from the North, the Wing sighted AA fire to the South and on investigation found a formation of Do 215 at 22,000'. The leading squadron vectored to attack from the west. Heavy AA fire compelled 'A' Flight of 310 to break away Westwards thereby losing sight of E/A. They returned to base. 'B' Flight of 310 Squadron thereupon cut in and attacked with 242 Squadron flying on their port beam. On sighting the attack, the enemy turned South and tried to evade. After the first attack, 'B' Flight broke up and did not reform, returning individually between 1230 and 1335 hours. From all accounts almost the whole of the enemy formation, amounting to 18 or 20 Do 215s, were destroyed in this engagement, which was one of the few instances in which we held the advantage in numbers, but this fact also had its disadvantage because no individual pilot could claim one bird as his own. All our pilots returned in safety. This highly satisfactory engagement took place over KINGSTON-ON-THAMES at 22,000' in fine weather.

302 Squadron:-

Five Do 17s, two Do 215s, one Do 215 (shared) destroyed (one He 111, two Do 17s, one Do 215, one Me 109 probables). Attacks commenced at 1210 hrs over SE London at 17,000'.

One of KG76's Dorniers was flown by *Feldwebel* Wilhelm Raab, a veteran of the campaigns in both Poland and France, in addition to numerous sorties over England. High above Brixton, Raab's bomber was attacked by numerous RAF fighter pilots: first Sergeant Tyrer of 46 Squadron, then Flight Lieutenant Rimmer of 229 Squadron, and Flight Lieutenant Peter Brothers and Pilot Officer Mortimer of 257 Squadron. As the Dornier dived for cloud cover, Flight Lieutenant Powell-

Sheddon and Pilot Officer Tamblyn of 242 Squadron attacked next. The CO of 19 Squadron, Squadron Leader Brian Lane, then also saw and attacked the Dornier, at first unaware of the attack in progress by the Hurricanes; realising that he had 'jumped the queue', he followed the Hurricanes and took his turn to fire. Lane was unable to tell, however, whether he or the two 242 Squadron Hurricanes were responsible for the hits he could see on Raab's aircraft. Descending at 100 feet per minute, the Dornier dropped out of the cloud and, after being attacked by more fighters, Raab ordered his crew to bale out before tumbling into space himself. At 1230 hrs, Squadron Leader Lane watched the pilotless bomber narrowly miss a house and explode on impact at Underriver, south of Sevenoaks in Kent. Raab's fate certainly confirms the 310 Squadron statement that 'no individual pilot could claim one bird as his own'.

KG76 suffered at the hands of Fighter Command, six of their number crashing on English soil. Amongst these was probably the most famous German casualty of the Battle, the Dornier which crashed on Victoria Station having been attacked by numerous fighters. The pilot, *Oberleutnant* Zehbe, landed by parachute at Kennington where he was roughly handled by a civilian mob (later dying from injuries received). Amongst the 10, 11 and 12 Group fighters which engaged this raider were at least four pilots of 310 Squadron.

Some of 19 Squadron's Spitfires managed to engage the 109s, as had been planned; at 1210 hrs, over Westerham, Kent, Flight Sergeant Unwin engaged 3/JG53's *Staffelkapitän*, *Oberleutnant* Haase, in a dogfight:-

> I was Red Three with Flight Lieutenant Lawson. We sighted the enemy aircraft which were flying in vics of three. The escorts dived singly onto us and I engaged an Me 109 with a yellow nose. I gave one burst of six seconds and it burst into flames. The pilot baled out and the enemy aircraft crashed between Redhill and Westerham.

Haase was killed as his parachute failed to open. As other Me 109s dived on 19 Squadron, Sergeant David Cox climbed and flew south. A few minutes later he found six 109s of 2/JG27 flying in the same direction. Simultaneously the Germans saw the Spitfire, and so Green 3 attacked from astern. Cox's target immediately half-rolled and dived away. Four of the fighters then broke off and continued south, no doubt low on fuel, but the sixth attacked Cox head-on. As his assailant reared up to pass over the fleeting Spitfire, Cox climbed and turned sharply, attacking from below. The 109 dived through cloud, pursued by the VR Spitfire pilot who, upon emerging below, saw his victim's wreckage burning in a field. This was at Lodge Wood, near Uckfield, and the pilot, *Unteroffizier* Walburger, was captured unhurt.

611 Squadron ORB:-

> 611 Squadron joined Wing of Hurricanes over Duxford at 15,000' at 1131 hrs then climbed to 27,000' to the left and above the Wing which was at 22,000'. When SW of London, 50 enemy bombers and 30 Me 109s escorting above were sighted coming from south. The Wing went into attack the bombers and escort turning South East. 611 Squadron kept beside the Me 109s which were to the west and above. After the Wing attack had broken up bomber formation, the Me 109s did not come down. After waiting for about seven minutes, S/Ldr McComb informed Wing Leader that he was coming down, and gave order echelon port. The Squadron proceeding at the time south east and up sun of the enemy. The Squadron in line astern, three sections of four aircraft executed a head-on attack down onto a formation of about 10 Do 215s and Do 17s. Then flying at 18,000' in a south easterly direction. S/Ldr McComb attacked Do 215 head on, hits observed, no results. Pulling up he made a beam attack on an Me 110 which turned in its

track and went down. The Squadron formation then broke up. S/Ldr McComb chased an Me 109 which was in a dogfight with a Hurricane, but could not catch up with them as he was too far behind. He then proceeded to the coast in the hope of attacking homing lame ducks before returning to base. P/O Williams after making his attack with the Squadron but without any observed results, saw a Do 215 attacked by six fighters crash into a wood near BISHOPSBOURNE, KENT. Two of the crew baling out. P/O Lund dived into initial attack but enemy aircraft passed through his sights before he could fire. P/O O'Neill attacked 6 or 7 times a Do 215 which had fallen behind the enemy formation. Four Hurricanes also attacked at same time. He chased this enemy aircraft as far as DUNGENESS where three other Spitfires carried on the attack. He then returned to base, being short of petrol and ammunition. F/Lt Leather carried out a head on attack on three Do 215s. No results observed. He then attacked a Do 215 at rear of large formation using up remainder of his ammunition. The port engine exploded and stopped. A number of other fighters also attacked this enemy aircraft and Red 2 reports seeing two crew bale out and machine crashed near BISHOPSBOURNE, KENT. Landed G1 at 1240 hours.

So far, Raab's Dornier had also appeared in the combat reports of two pilots from 611 Squadron; how many others it featured in is anyone's guess. The 611 Squadron report continues:-

P/O Pollard, after firing a short burst in the initial dive attack, chased, in company with one other Spitfire and a Hurricane, a Do 215. Between Rochester and Herne Bay, enemy aircraft lost height, smoke coming from port engine. Crew of two baled out and aircraft crashed on edge of a wood about four miles south of Herne Bay. He landed at Detling at 1305 hrs having lost his bearings, later returned to G1.

This was a 3/KG76 Do 17Z which was also engaged by Pilot Officer Meaker of 249 Squadron, and both Flight Lieutenant Ken Gillies and Pilot Officer 'Bogle' Bodie of 66 Squadron. The Dornier crashed in flames and exploded at Sturry. 611 Squadron:-

Yellow 3, P/O Brown after initial dive attack on pulling out saw no enemy aircraft. After circling for about 10 minutes he returned to home base. P/O Walker after initial dive attack on pulling out saw no enemy aircraft. He developed engine trouble and had to force land at West Malling at 1235 hrs. F/Lt Stoddart fired one quick burst in initial dive attack, and then had to take evasive action in order to avoid attack from Me 109s. He circled for some time and then returned to base. F/Sgt Sadler after initial dive saw 12 Do 215s going south east so executed two frontal attacks on leader. Enemy aircraft believed hit but no results were seen. Abandoned chase at Lympne being short of ammunition and petrol. P/O Dewey fired a short burst at a Do 215 but observed no results. After circling for some time returned base. Sgt Levenson broke formation to attack an Me 109 but enemy aircraft got away. He then flew towards large formation of Do 215s flying at 18,000'. After sighting one Do 215 by itself at 14,000' he rolled over and carried out an old astern attack diving onto the enemy. Got in a long burst and both enemy aircraft motors were smoking when he broke away. Climbing again, he carried out the same attack. He broke away when both engines and both mainplanes immediately behind them were on fire.

For the equally overworked *Luftwaffe*, the presence of so many RAF fighters, which had harried them constantly from crossing the English coast to leaving it some while later, was at the very least alarming. The crushing effect that the arrival of Bader's 50 fighters had on the Germans' morale must never be underestimated. The combined success of Fighter Command and other defences during that morning's action had resulted in few casualties and little damage being caused. Two bombs had fallen on Buckingham Palace, however, thus showing the King and Queen to be in the fight alongside humble Eastenders.

The Prime Minister, Winston Churchill, had chosen this particular morning to visit the 11 Group Operations Room at Uxbridge. As he watched squadrons being flung into battle, the Prime Minister asked Air Vice-Marshal Park what reserves he had; 'None, Sir', the AOC 11 Group replied, but to put that statement into context, he meant, of course, that all of *his* Group's squadrons were airborne. Certainly all of the Command's 'A' squadrons were committed to battle on this day, but those aircraft represented less than half of the total available, which included also 'B' and 'C' squadrons. It is likely, however, that Park had been so bold as to commit his entire force during this action owing to the protective cloud layer which covered his airfields and thus concealed them from high altitude attack whilst his fighters were being 'turned around'.

Not long after the Wing pilots had straggled back to Duxford individually, the RDF screens indicated further formations moving out from Calais. Between 1410 and 1435 hrs, eight or more formations of German bombers and their escorts crossed the English coastline between Rye and Dover, heading for London. It has been claimed previously that the Duxford Wing was scrambled too late for its next action, but in view of the fact that its last fighter had only touched down from the first engagement at around 1335 hrs, I doubt whether it would have been humanly possible for the Wing to have taken off any earlier than the 1405 scramble it was given. As it was, 611 Squadron left two of their Spitfires behind at Fowlmere as they were still refuelling.

As Squadron Leader Lane later wrote, the Wing 'ran into the whole Luftwaffe over London. Wave after wave of bombers covered by several hundred fighters'. Unfortunately, the 'whole Luftwaffe' was some 4,000' above the Wing. As the Duxford fighters climbed, the inevitable 109s plunged down and, as Bader yelled 'Break up!', the Wing scattered. Again the Wing had been unable to deliver a concentrated attack against the bombers, but as it was engaged by numerous Me 109s so other RAF fighters were able to get through to the bombers. A typically confused and extremely violent combat then took place between the opposing fighters, but few individual combats lasted more than 20 seconds - with so many fighters filling the sky, any pilot who concentrated on his target for longer ran a great risk of collision; again the 611 Squadron ORB provides a stirring account of a Spitfire squadron in action:-

611 Squadron ran into several formations of bombers before sufficient height could be reached so ignored them, attempting to get height in Westerly direction to keep Me 109s off Wing. The squadron consisted of 8 aircraft in three sections flying line astern. It was not possible to out climb the Me 109s and the Wing appeared to be both attacking and being attacked. When at 20,000' over West London, the Squadron Leader sighted a formation of 25 Do 17s proceeding South unmolested and being by then separated from the Wing, gave the order Sections Echelon Right. The Squadron dived down on the formation, coming out of the sun. At the end of the general attack, Me 110s came down. S/Ldr McComb attacked rear E/A. Rear gunner ceased firing and smoke appeared from port engine. He then pulled up into a loop and dived again in inverted position. Guns worked perfectly in this position and E/A went down in flames. Result of attack is confirmed by Yellow 2 and Yellow Leader. S/Ldr McComb then blacked out badly and came to in the clouds. After looking around and seeing nothing he returned to base.

This was a Dornier of 9/KG2 which did indeed crash in flames at Cranbrook.

P/O Williams carried out a No 3 FC attack on an He 111. A second burst at 80 yards was given but no result observed. E/A returned machine-gun fire. He was unable then to return to Squadron which had now broken up, but observing two enemy formations, he made an astern attack on No 3 of the last section of the formation of Do 215. The formation turned north but Red 2's target fell out, losing height. He then carried out another attack finishing his ammunition. E/A descended into the clouds, one engine stopped, Red 2 following. Cloud was 2,000' thick and on emerging no E/A was visible but two minutes later he saw enemy airman descending by parachute. Latter landed on edge of wood corner of Hawkhurst Golf Club about 15 miles North of Hastings.

Pilot Officer Williams had also attacked the Cranbrook Do 17Z.

F/Lt Leather followed Red Leader into attack astern and took machine next to his as his target was already aflame. He fired all ammunition and when broke away the Do 17 was in flames. He then was forced to land at Croydon at 1540 hrs and later flew to G1 rejoining the Squadron.

P/O Brown had first to evade enemy fighters and then put one short burst into the Do 215 already attacked by Red Leader which had one engine out of action. Oil or glycol from E/A covered up windscreen and so he had to break away. Then he attacked one E/A which broke away from formation using deflection. E/A went into a steep spiral dive with escape hatch over pilot's seat open. No further results seen as large formation of Me 110s appeared and Yellow 2 escaped into cloud.

P/O Lund attacked a Do 215 which was also being attacked by several other aircraft. He saw flashes of fire and smoke coming from E/A. While climbing back to main formation of bombers, one Me 110 came down on him so he fired one short burst before turning away and down. As the E/A passed his port side, black smoke was pouring from engine. No more E/A seen after this so he returned to base.

F/Sgt Sadler after attacking with Squadron, saw a Do 215 break away and begin losing height. He made two attacks on this E/A, his second attack being made at 50 yards. A Hurricane also attacked after him and the E/A apparently badly disabled disappeared below cloud.

P/O DH O'Neill lost touch with Blue Leader but after circling for about 6 minutes had to evade 8 Me 110s into cloud. Up again out of cloud saw Me 109s attacking one Hurricane and attacked one of these over Faversham without observing result although E/A took evasive action. After being attacked by another Me 109, he returned to base landing, however, by mistake first at Debden.

Sgt Levenson after attacking without visible result an Me 109 and a crippled Do 215 found himself at 10,000' over Brooklands aerodrome. He then saw about 50 Do 215s guarded by 2 Me 109s overhead. He climbed to 1,000' below formation and delivered a quarter frontal attack opening fire first at 100 yards, developing this into normal quarter attack at about 200 yards when all his ammunition was exhausted. He observed ammunition hitting leading E/A and the leading vic of 4 A/C broke away to port, smoke coming from engines of No.1 and No.2. No further result was seen but he assumed that No 1 was out of action. F/Lt Stoddart and P/O Dewey, owing to refuelling, took off 15 minutes after the squadron. The weather above cloud was perfect with visibility good.

Squadron Leader Lane reported:-

At approximately 1440 hrs AA fire was sighted to the south and at the same time a formation of about 30 Do 215s was seen. I climbed up astern of the enemy aircraft to engage the fighter escort which could be seen above the bombers at about 30,000'. Three Me 109s dived on our formation and I turned to starboard. A loose dogfight ensued with more Me 109s coming down. I could not get near to any enemy aircraft so I climbed up and engaged a formation of Me 110s without result. I then sighted 10 Me 109s just above me and attacked one of them. I got on his tail and fired several bursts of about two seconds. The enemy aircraft was taking violent evasive action and made for cloud level. I managed to get in another burst of about five seconds before it flicked over inverted and entered cloud in a shallow dive, apparently out of control. I then flew south and attacked two further formations of about 30 Do 215s from astern and head on. The enemy aircraft did not appear to like the head on attack as they jumped about a bit as I passed through. I observed no result from these attacks. Fire from the rear of the enemy aircraft was opened at 1,000 yards. Me 110s opened fire at similar range but appeared to have no idea of deflection shooting.

Squadron Leader Lane's combat represented the only protracted dogfight between the opposing fighters on this day. The melee generally dictated the maxim of Malan's 10th Rule of Air Fighting: 'Go in quickly - Punch hard - Get out', as the 109 pilots themselves knew only too well.

Flight Sergeant Unwin was Lane's Red 3; he reported sighting 'thousands of 109s'. When the Wing was attacked, at close range 'Grumpy' fired a three second burst at a 109 which half-rolled and dived steeply into the clouds. Although the Spitfire pilot pursued his prey, he lost the 109 at 6,000' when his windscreen froze up. Climbing back up to 25,000', a *Rotte* of 109s appeared above him, flying south. Unwin gave chase and caught both over Lydd. The first consequently burst into flames and went down vertically, and the second crashed into the sea. It is likely that these two 109s were from I/JG77: *Oberleutnant* Kunze, of the *Geschwaderstabschwarm*, was killed when his aircraft crashed at Lympne, as was *Unteroffizier* Meixner who crashed into the sea off Dungeness at about 1455 hrs. This brought Flight Sergeant Unwin's total of Me 109s definitely destroyed this day to three.

As the Me 109s once more rained down on 19 Squadron, Green 1, Flying Officer Alan 'Ace' Haines, attacked a 3/LG2 machine flown by *Unteroffizier* Klick. The enemy machine's radiator was badly damaged so Klick had no option but to make a forced-landing at Shellness where he was captured. Haines went on to engage an Me 110 which he also claimed as destroyed when he saw it crash on a French beach (probably one of two likely aircraft, both of LG1). Green Section's other two pilots, Flight Sergeant Harry Steere and Pilot Officer Arthur Vokes, were also successful; the latter wrote in his log book:-

'B' Flight attacked 6 Do 17s, one breaking away chased by F/Sgt Steere and self. One Jerry baled out. One Me 110 surprised me and bored a hole in starboard wing. After two or three turns I got on his tail and gave him everything. Dived vertically into cloud, starboard engine smoking. One probable Me 110. Hundreds of Jerries!

The Me 110 could also have been a machine belonging to LG1, as the 13th *Staffel's Kapitän* crashed at Hothfield, near Ashford.

Sub-Lieutenant 'Admiral' Blake noted the quantity of enemy aircraft engaged as 'innumerable', but nonetheless dived to attack six Dorniers which had become detached from the main formation. He then attacked the 109s which came down from above, firing at one particular machine twice, after which the 109 'burst into flames'. This was possibly a machine of 9/JG51 which crashed near Brenchley at 1420 hrs. The pilot, *Feldwebel* Klotz, was killed. Blake next joined a queue of fighters attacking an He 111, but was forced to land at Rochford as his Spitfire had been hit and was smoking badly. Upon landing he was told that the He 111 had crashed into the Thames Estuary. In fact, this machine of 1/KG26 forced landed below the high water mark at Asplin's Head, Foulness, at 1500 hrs. The crew were all captured.

Pilot Officer Arthur Vokes
(Author's Collection)

Pilot Officer Wallace 'Jock' Cunningham also engaged the 109s, and consequently sent a 7/JG51 machine hurtling earthwards to crash at Nelson's Park, St Margaret's-at-Cliff, near Dover, at 1450 hrs. The pilot, *Leutnant* Bildau baled out and was captured.

Sergeant Jack Potter, however, chased the enemy far out across the Channel but was shot down by *Feldwebel* Luders of 6/JG26. He forced landed on the beach near Calais and 19 Squadron were later notified of his capture.

Sergeant Jack Potter; again note the unusual battledress.
(Author's Collection)

Squadron Leader Bader's personal combat report describes the situation as the engagement commenced:-

On being attacked from behind by Me 109, I ordered 'Break Up!' and pulled up and round violently. Coming off my back partially blacked out, nearly collided with Yellow 2 (Pilot Officer Crowley-Milling). Spun in his slipstream and straightened out at 5,000' below without firing a shot. Climbed up again and saw E/A twin engined flying westwards. Just got in range and fired a short burst (3 secs) in a completely stalled position and then spun off again and lost more height.

Crowley-Milling was naturally startled at having narrowly avoided a collision with his leader, but still managed to latch on to the tail of a 109, remaining in situ despite the German's evasive tactics. Delivering a 'good burst', he ignited the cockpit area and watched the 1/JG3 fighter crash at St Michael's, Tenterden. The pilot, *Oberfeldwebel* Hessel, baled out and was captured.

Yellow 1, Pilot Officer Stansfeld, joined two other Hurricanes on an attack against a II/KG53

He 111. The enemy bomber forced-landed on West Malling airfield and featured in the combat reports of at least 10 RAF fighter pilots!

Although 310 Squadron had been briefed to attack the bombers, the 109s' intervention dictated otherwise, as the ORB records:-

The Squadron, which had been detailed to attack the bombers, were themselves attacked by the Me 109s as the Wing formation was broken up. F/Lt JEFFERIES ordered the squadron to climb to 24,000' into the sun when another large formation of E/A were seen approaching from the south. The squadron delayed the attack until they turned and when they faced West a head-on attack was launched out of the sun.

Amongst the intricate contrails, Sergeant Hubacek's Hurricane was singled out by none other than Major Adolf Galland, *Kommodore* of JG26:-

After an unsuccessful 10 minute dogfight with about eight Hurricanes, during which much altitude was lost, with the *Stabstaffel* I attacked two Hurricanes about 800m below us. Maintaining surprise, I closed on the wing man and opened fire from 120m, as he was in a gentle turn to the left. The enemy plane reeled as my rounds struck the nose from below, and pieces fell from the left wing and fuselage. The left side of the fuselage burst into flame. The enemy section leader was shot down in flames by my wing man, *Oberleutnant* Horten.

Galland's *Katchmarek* had hit the 310 Squadron CO, Squadron Leader Hess, who apparently landed by parachute at Billericay, 'little the worse except for bruises'. It is clear that neither Hess or Hubacek knew what had hit them, the former reporting that he had been the victim of an 'exploding cannon shell in mid-air', whilst the latter 'had the impression that I heard machine-gun fire behind me. I looked back several times but did not see anything. I re-trimmed the aircraft but at that moment I was hit - I do not know by what'. Sergeant Hubacek baled out, his Hurricane crashed near Chatham and he was taken to the nearby RN hospital with a slight leg injury.

Some of 310 Squadron's pilots did manage to get through to the bombers: Sergeant Prchal joined in the queue attacking the Asplin's Head Heinkel, and Sergeant Furst, together with Flying Officer BD Russel of 1 (RCAF) Squadron, destroyed a Stab/KG53 He 111 which crashed and exploded in the shell filling area of the Woolwich Arsenal. Sergeant Rechka also had a hand in the destruction of the Asplin's Head He 111, and Pilot Officer Fejfar claimed a Do 17 which forced-landed on the Isle of Grain; the latter bomber also featured in the claims of at least three Spitfire pilots from 41 and 603 Squadrons.

Squadron Leader Satchell had climbed his Poles of 302 Squadron hard after 242 and 310 Squadrons. As Satchell tried to attack a formation of bombers, he was in turn attacked by a 109 which overshot; the Hurricane pilot gave chase, fired, and the 109 rolled onto its back, diving earthwards. The Me 109 was fitted with a fuel-injected engine, and on entering a dive could leave the RAF fighters which were hampered by their gravity-affected float carburettors, such a manoeuvre being the standard *Jagdwaffe* evasive tactic. As the enemy pilot pushed forward his throttle, black smoke was momentarily thrown out of the exhausts, thus giving the impression that the 109 was diving out of control and on fire. It is likely that this was the case in respect of the machine engaged by Squadron Leader Satchell.

Some of the Poles managed to get at the bombers, Flight Lieutenant Chlopik leading Red Section into the attack against them. Chlopik attacked a Dornier which other pilots later reported as having disintegrated. Red 1 was hit by return fire in a later combat, however, and baled out. Tragically his parachute failed to open. Pilot Officer Lapka was also shot down by a Do 17's return fire, but he baled out safely, his Hurricane crashing at Pitsea. Sergeant Kowalski attacked a straggling Dornier from 30 yards, blowing its tail off. Later, a machine-gun panel came open, affecting the flying characteristics of his aircraft, so the Pole forced-landed in a field.

After the engagement, the Duxford Wing pilots returned individually, landing at various times from 1500 hrs onwards. Understandably, in view of the hectic fighting which involved many fighters from both sides, claims were much exaggerated. When the Intelligence Officers had finished their calculations at Duxford, based upon the pilot's individual combat reports in both engagements, the following claims were confirmed:-

19 Squadron:	12 destroyed, two shared, four probables, one damaged.
242 Squadron:	11 destroyed.
302 Squadron:	12 destroyed, one shared, two probables.
310 Squadron:	Four destroyed, one shared.
611 Squadron:	Six destroyed, one shared, four probables.
Total:	45 destroyed, five shared, 10 probables, one damaged.

and losses:-

19 Squadron:	Two Spitfires damaged, one lost, pilot POW.
242 Squadron:	Two Hurricanes damaged, one lost, pilot baled out injured.
302 Squadron:	One Hurricane damaged, one lost, one pilot killed.
310 Squadron:	Two Hurricanes lost, one pilot wounded.
611 Squadron:	One Spitfire damaged.
Total:	Six fighters damaged, five destroyed, two pilots wounded, one killed, one POW.

The following day, the *Times* newspaper claimed that Fighter Command had destroyed a total of 175 raiders on September 15th, for the loss of 30 RAF fighters and 10 pilots. A day later, the British victory claim had risen to 185 (178 by fighters, 7 by AA guns). In fact, the *Luftwaffe* had lost 56 aircraft in total, so the original figure represented an overclaim of 3:1, which under the circumstances was acceptable given the figures of previous engagements. The Germans had actually lost, therefore, less aircraft on this day than on August 15th (75) and 18th (69). The RAF's reported losses were virtually 100% accurate, however, as 29 aircraft and 12 pilots had really been lost. Interestingly, the Germans claimed 79, again representing an overclaiming ratio approaching 3:1.

The fighting on September 15th, 1940, now celebrated annually as 'Battle of Britain Day', was decisive as by dusk Hitler was convinced that despite Goering's assurances, the *Luftwaffe* could not gain aerial supremacy over England to facilitate an invasion that year.

At Duxford, with the overclaiming (which decreased by a factor of 3 actually gives the Duxford Wing 15 destroyed against five fighters lost), the Station was cock-a-hoop; Pilot Officer Vokes wrote proudly in his log book:-

Duxford 50 certs!

310 Squadron ORB:-

The day's 'Bag' for the station amounted to the respectable total of 44 enemy aircraft destroyed, 8 shared and 8 probables, fairly conclusive proof of the efficiency of the Wing formation.

The 12 Group AOC sent the following message:-

To OC Duxford for 19, 242, 302, 310, 611 Squadrons, from AVM T.LEIGH-MALLORY. 15.9.40. Germans have made a great effort today and you have played a notable part in frustrating it. Heartiest congratulations to you all on splendid results.

In the Big Wing, Air Vice-Marshal Leigh-Mallory and Squadron Leader Bader had clearly rejected the strict ground-to-air control system formulated by Air Chief Marshal Dowding and Air Vice-Marshal Park. This lack of team spirit, with the Big Wing acting independently of the System, was to confuse and agitate the defences. On September 15th, although requested to patrol airfields north of London, the Wing had proceeded directly across London to attack raiders already being intercepted by 11 Group squadrons.

On September 17th, Air Vice-Marshal Leigh-Mallory submitted a report concerning the actions fought by his 12 Group Wing so far (September 7th, 9th, 11th & 15th).

In this report, as a consequence of the Wing's first three engagements, Air Vice-Marshal Leigh-Mallory concluded that:-

(I)   During the first three Wing formations, the following two main difficulties were experienced:-

   (a)   The fighters who were attacking the bombers got unduly interfered with by enemy fighters. This would appear due to the fact that there were not sufficient fighters both to neutralise the enemy fighters and to attack the enemy bombers successfully.

   (b)   It was also found that after the Wing attack had been delivered, there were many enemy bombers who had become detached and were easy targets, but who could not be attacked because there were no fighters left with sufficient ammunition to carry on the engagement.

(II) As a result, the following conclusions were arrived at:-

   (a)   For an operation of this type to be really successful, three objects have got to be achieved:-

      (i)   to neutralise the enemy fighters while the attack on bombers is being made;
      (ii) to break up the bomber formation;
      (iii) to shoot down the bombers after (ii) has been achieved.

   (b)   From the size of enemy formations we have met up to the present, it was considered that at least two Spitfire squadrons are required to neutralise the enemy fighters.

   (c)   In addition to the two squadrons required to neutralise the fighters, at least three squadrons are required to break up the enemy bomber formations and carry on the main attack on them.

   (d)   It was hoped that when the bomber formations had been disintegrated, one of the two squadrons neutralising the fighters might be able to detach itself and shoot down isolated bombers.

BATTLE FOR LONDON

In his report on the afternoon action fought on September 15th, Air Vice-Marshal Leigh-Mallory stated that the Wing had been caught at a tactical disadvantage owing to not having been scrambled until 1430 hrs; this was untrue, as the Wing squadrons started going up at 1405 hrs, immediately after they had been 'turned around' from the earlier action. By now, the Wing had claimed a total of 105 enemy aircraft destroyed, 40 probables, and 18 damaged, offset by six pilots killed or missing, five pilots wounded, and 14 fighters destroyed. On paper, without claims being properly cross-referenced, the 12 Group Wing was performing brilliantly.

Air Vice-Marshal Evill was sceptical regarding the 12 Group claims, and in his covering letter to Air Chief Marshal Dowding accompanying Leigh-Mallory's report, he wrote:-

The figures of enemy losses claimed in the table attached to the report can, in my opinion, be regarded only as approximate.

It will be shown from these figures that the losses inflicted on the enemy were not increased in relation to the number of fighters engaged on the latter patrols when a larger number of squadrons took part. Nevertheless, the losses incurred by the Wing were reduced and I am, in any case, of the opinion that the AOC 12 Group is working on the right lines in organising his operations in strength.

The Commander-in-Chief responded:-

I am sure that L-Mallory is thinking on the right lines, but his figures do not support his theory.

More aircraft per squadron were brought down by the entire strength of three squadrons (though few bombers).

Little check is put on the estimate of 310 Squadron who are exuberant in their claims.

One can generally tell from reading the combat reports what degree of reliability to attach to claims - some of which are more thoughtful wishing.

Dowding concluded that Leigh-Mallory's report should be forwarded to the Air Ministry but with a note added to the effect that the claims 'must be regarded as approximate'.

It seems a little unfair that Air Chief Marshal Dowding should have singled out 310 Squadron as being 'exuberant in their claims', as research indicates that 242 Squadron were by far the worst offenders; this must have been apparent even at the time.

At the Air Ministry, Air Vice-Marshal Douglas, like Leigh-Mallory, accepted the Big Wing's claims without question. They both agreed that targets should be left to ground defences, and a concentrated attack made on the enemy - if necessary - *after* he had bombed.

Despite all, however, Fighter Command had won the Battle for London, by day at least, although there was still much fighting ahead. Whilst the pilots continued to fight bravely, behind the scenes in the corridors of Whitehall the political battle was only beginning.

CHAPTER SEVEN

Autumn Leaves

Although the enemy continued to raid London during the night of September 15th/16th 1940, Bomber Command was also active over Occupied Europe. Some 200 sorties were flown against concentrations of invasion barges at Antwerp, Ostend, Boulogne, Flushing, Calais and Dunkirk. Over Antwerp a particular 83 Squadron Hampden was hit by flak: the rear gunner baled out, but the wireless operator/air gunner, Sergeant John Hannah dealt with the resulting blaze using just two fire extinguishers and his log book; for this act of gallantry, the 18-year-old received the Victoria Cross. It was imperative to keep up the pressure on the invasion ports, but the only way was by night.

Dawn on September 16th was overcast and stormy, resulting in few sorties being flown by the *Luftwaffe*. The usual fighter squadrons gathered in the Duxford Sector that morning, but there was little activity and no requests for assistance by 11 Group. There was one Wing patrol, as the 310 Squadron ORB relates:-

The squadron, led by the CO, took off at 0740 hrs to patrol LONDON at 27,000'. This again was a Wing formation, the squadrons employed being the same as yesterday. They landed at 0845 hrs without having made contact with the enemy. The weather deteriorated about 1000 hrs and there was some rain and considerable mist. This provided a respite which did not come altogether amiss.

Squadron Leader Bader's log book indicates that he led the Wing on this patrol, in his words, of 'North Weald'. Another question now arises: as enemy air activity was absolutely minimal, and there were no requests for assistance, why was the 12 Group Wing patrolling over the 11 Group area? This is undoubtedly an indication of Air Vice-Marshal Leigh-Mallory's growing confidence.

On September 17th, the weather remained overcast with strong winds and rain. Only one major raid was launched against England, a fighter sweep of southern Kent from 1500 - 1600 hrs. Each wave consisted of two *Gruppen* of Me 109s, each the equivalent of a three-squadron Wing formation. Previous accounts have claimed that the squadrons of the Duxford Wing were amongst the Fighter Command units which engaged this *Freie Jagd*, but in fact the 12 Group 'Balbo' saw no action. Although the Duxford Wing was scrambled at 1515 hrs to patrol London, the enemy was not sighted and the Wing landed at 1645 hrs. The action was in fact much further south, and in the main the AOC 11 Group wisely kept his fighters on the ground. In view of this, and considering the established policy of forward interception followed by reinforcement, one could be justified in asking why the Duxford Wing was up at all. The 310 Squadron ORB, interestingly, describes the sortie as an 'offensive patrol again in Wing formation'. The use of the word 'offensive' is significant, as this adequately describes the spirit of Squadron Leader Bader's freelance fighter sweeps well south of his allocated patrol areas. Both Air Chief Marshal Dowding and Air Vice-Marshal Park remained acutely aware, however, that they were fighting a crucial *defensive* battle.

September 17th saw the award of two gallantry decorations to the Duxford squadrons: 310's Flight Lieutenant Jefferies received the DFC, and 19's Flight Sergeant George Unwin the DFM, his squadron's ORB commenting:-

Good show! Ten certain Huns to his credit.

The majority of George Unwin's claims can be verified today, and there can be no doubt that this award was much deserved; the first NCO pilot ever to fly a Spitfire, 'Grumpy' was amongst the most experienced Spitfire pilots in the RAF at this time.

On September 18th, the *Luftwaffe* commenced with a fighter sweep of some 60 Me 109s, which were engaged by about the same number of 11 Group fighters. Two 109s were lost against five Spitfires. At 0920 hrs the Duxford Wing was scrambled to patrol at 25,000' over the Thames Estuary: 'Quite a lot of cloud. No E/A sighted. Great amount of condensation plumes' (19 ORB). A second 'Wing Offensive Patrol' (310 ORB) took place at 12 noon, but again without contact. The next raid, at 1230 hrs, consisted of a very small formation of Ju 88s escorted by over 100 Me 109s which bombed Chatham and Rochester. It was quite clear to Air Vice-Marshal Park that the number of bombers involved represented no real threat, and that the 109s were only a menace if he scrambled fighters to engage them. Sensibly he did not therefore respond to this particular raid. It is puzzling again, therefore, why the Duxford Wing should have been on an 'Offensive patrol' over the Thames Estuary. The day's final attack came at 1630 hrs when the unescorted Ju 88s of III/KG77 - fresh to the battle - mounted an attack on Tilbury Docks. Park's reaction was swift and decisive: 14 of his squadrons intercepted.

At 1616 hrs, Squadron Leader Bader led the Hurricanes off from Duxford; 242, 302 and 310 Squadrons then headed south whilst the Fowlmere Spitfires, 19 and 611 Squadrons, slid into position above them. According to the 19 Squadron combat report the Wing's instructions were to 'patrol Hornchurch at 20,000 feet'. The 242 Squadron report confirms, however, that the Wing actually 'started to patrol centre of London to Thameshaven at 24,000 feet', above a cloud layer. Again, Squadron Leader Bader was in effect leading the Duxford Wing on a fighter sweep. Also, as on previous sorties, AA bursts above cloud to the south-west indicated the presence of enemy aircraft below. Bader immediately set off down through the cloud in pursuit, being followed by the other Hurricanes and 19 Squadron whilst Squadron Leader McComb and 611 Squadron remained on patrol above. Consequently the Duxford Wing intercepted III/KG77 south of the Thames Estuary.

242 Squadron combat report:-

12 Group Wing turned NW and sighted e/a flying in two formations close together about 20-30 e/a in each, unescorted, at 15-17,000'. They were approaching first bend of Thames West of Estuary near Gravesend and were South of Thames when attacked. Attack was launched in a dive from East to West turning North on to the enemy. Conditions were favourable to 12 Group Wing which was screened from above by cloud, whilst e/a presented excellent target against white cloud base.

Red 1, S/Ldr DRS Bader made a quarter attack turning astern at leading three Ju 88s, hitting the one on the left of this section. This Ju 88 turned in left hand dive with port engine afire and disappeared down towards north bank of Estuary West of Thameshaven.

This Ju 88 was of 8/KG77 and crashed off Sheerness. It is believed, however, that this aircraft had previously been damaged by Spitfires of 11 Group's 92 Squadron, and, in addition to Squadron Leader Bader's, it also featured in the reports of 302 Squadron's Pilot Officers Pilch and Karwowski. Two other 11 Group pilots also attacked this machine. Again it is interesting that the 12 Group pilots' combat reports do not mention the presence and involvement of other squadrons, unless, owing to the sky being filled with so many of their own Spitfires and Hurricanes, it was impossible to tell.

The 242 Squadron report continues:-

Red 1 lost about 3,000' regained control and proceeded SE and found a lone Do 17. He closed to short range and fired short burst. E/A did not return fire; instead rear gunner baled out immediately, getting his parachute entangled in tailplane. The Dornier immediately fell in succession of steep dives and two other members of crew baled out. E/A disappeared into vertical dive into cloud at 4-6,000' and Red 1 considers it crashed either in estuary or South of it, near Sheerness.

This was another 8 *Staffel* machine which also crashed into the sea, off the Nore, Sheerness. *Oberleutnant* Fuchs was the unfortunate crew member whose parachute fouled the tailplane, and he was consequently killed. Again, this bomber was also attacked by a variety of RAF fighter pilots, including Flying Officer Kowalski and Sergeant Paterek of 302, and Pilot Officer Hill of 92 Squadron.

Although Squadron Leader Bader's Hurricane was fitted with a camera-gun, he inadvertently switched on the navigation lights instead during this combat. Bader's Red 2, Pilot Officer McKnight, dived on a 'Do 17' from above and behind, set the starboard engine on fire and watched the crew bale out, this probably being the first machine also attacked by Red 1. McKnight then joined a Spitfire to attack a Ju 88, the crew of which baled out, the aircraft crashing north of the Thames. The likelihood is that this was a 9/KG77 bomber, also attacked by 19 Squadron's Sergeant Plzak, which crashed at Vange Creek, Pitsea Marshes, near Basildon. *Feldwebel* Graf baled out and was captured, the rest of the crew being killed.

Pilot Officer Campbell overshot his target during the squadron's first diving attack, but then fired at a Ju 88 which he left falling out of formation with both engines alight. He then engaged at close range another Ju 88, which had already been attacked by a Spitfire, and again saw his target burst into flames. A third bomber then received Red 3's attention, with smoke subsequently issuing from its starboard engine, but the Hurricane was then caught in cross-fire and hit in the mainplane. Campbell broke away, turning to assist a Spitfire which was attacking a Ju 88; he also engaged this enemy aircraft which he saw falling in flames. Other 242 Squadron pilots reported similarly hectic multiple combats, but Pilot Officer Hart described seeing his victim 'crash north of the Thames', this also being the Vange Creek Ju 88.

The Hurricanes of 310 Squadron followed Flight Lieutenant Jefferies into the attack, and he shared a 'Do 17' with Pilot Officer Bergman, Pilot Officer Fechtner and Sergeant Prhcal. This was possibly another 9/KG77 Ju 88 which crashed at Cooling, south of the Thames.

On this occasion, 19 Squadron was being led into action by Flight Lieutenant Wilf Clouston, commander of 'B' Flight. He attacked a Ju 88, setting its starboard engine on fire. The crew baled out, and the Spitfire pilot reported that the bomber crash 'behind some houses, either at Tilmanstone or Eastry to the west of Deal'. This was actually the aircraft of the III/KG77 *Gruppenkommandeur*, Major Klehs, who was killed when his Ju 88 crashed at Eastry Mill. Klehs had also been attacked by Flight Lieutenant Lawson, Pilot Officer Cunningham and Sergeant Lloyd.

Flight Sergeant Steere, Blue 2 in 19 Squadron, attacked an 'He 111' which had already been engaged by Green 1, Flying Officer Haines, and the former pilot watched this aircraft (actually a Ju 88) crash 'near the south coast of the Thames, probably close to the Isle of Sheppey'. This raider, of 8/KG77, did indeed crash on Sheppey, at Mocketts Farm, Harty.

Flight Sergeant Unwin claimed an Me 110, which both he and a pilot of 66 Squadron saw crash near Eastchurch. There were no Me 110 losses this day, however, and as the only enemy machine down on Sheppey was the Ju 88 also engaged by Flight Sergeant Steere, we must assume that it is this aircraft which 'Grumpy' also attacked. Pilot Officer Dolezal engaged a 'Heinkel' which

Pilot Officer Frantisek Dolezal, a Czech serving with 19 Squadron.
(Author via Flight Lieutenant RL Jones)

he saw 'spin into the sea', but this was probably one of the four KG77 Ju 88s which came down in the Thames Estuary. Sergeant Plzak also claimed a 'Heinkel', which crashed near Gillingham, but this was actually the Ju 88 down at Cooling. Flight Lieutenant Lawson, Red 1, forced landed at Eastchurch airfield, having been hit in the glycol tank, but the squadron was otherwise intact.

Above the clouds, '611 Squadron kept the 109s in play, without however firing a shot' (ORB).

Back at Duxford and Fowlmere there was jubilation. Such an interception of unescorted bombers was every fighter pilot's dream! The claims were, however, to coin Air Chief Marshal Dowding's phrase, 'exuberant':-

19 Squadron:	Five destroyed, three shared, one probable.
242 Squadron:	12 destroyed.
302 Squadron:	Seven destroyed, two probables and one damaged.
310 Squadron:	One shared.
611 Squadron:	Nil.
Total:	24 destroyed, four shared, three probables and one damaged.

In total, the enemy lost *eight* Ju 88s in this engagement, although the Wing certainly had a hand in the destruction of at least six. The overclaiming ratio was thus approximately 4:1.

Without the dreaded 109s, the Wing's losses were just two aircraft damaged (Flight Lieutenant Lawson of 19 Squadron who forced-landed at Eastchurch, and Sergeant Paterek of 302 Squadron who did likewise near Danbury). In addition, 11 Group suffered one aircraft damaged and another lost, with all pilots safe. It was a very successful engagement whichever way one looks at it, but in view of the number of 11 Group fighters acting against the unescorted bombers, it is doubtful whether the Big Wing had any significant effect on the outcome.

Back at base, 242 Squadron alone received the inevitable messages of congratulations from both the Secretary of State for Air and the CAS.

On September 19th, high winds, low cloud and heavy rain over England greatly reduced enemy air activity which was confined to isolated raids by solitary aircraft. Squadron Leader Bader took 242 Squadron down to Duxford again, but the squadron made no patrols. During the morning, Squadron Leader Blackwood led Red Section of 310 Squadron on a patrol of base below cloud, as an enemy aircraft was reported in the vicinity, but no contact was made. 'B' Flight of 302 Squadron had more success when it intercepted a 1/KG77 Ju 88 which consequently crashed and burnt out at Bury St Edmunds.

The most important feature of this day for the 12 Group Wing was that 611 Squadron's place was taken by 616. From the following day onwards, the former unit commenced sending a flight to Ringway, near Liverpool, to provide protection to both that great port and convoys. This task led to 'A' Flight being detached to Ternhill, in north Shropshire; although the squadron continued to meet very small formations, lone reconnaissance aircraft or nuisance raiders, its part in the Battle of Britain proper was over.

Several previous accounts have claimed that 616 Squadron contributed just one flight of aircraft to the Duxford Wing, but in fact this was not so: at 0653 hrs on September 19th, 14 Spitfires of 616 Squadron left Kirton for Fowlmere. After the squadron's stint in 11 Group, it was rebuilding with a new CO, Acting Squadron Leader Howard Frizzelle 'Billy' Burton, formerly a flight

Squadron Leader HF 'Billy' Burton, CO of 616 Squadron. (Author via Mrs Jean Allom)

commander with Rupert Leigh's 66 Squadron. Again there was a Cranwell connection: Burton had also won a King's Cadetship, and upon passing out in 1936, was awarded the coveted Sword-of-Honour. Burton had then flown Gauntlets with 46 Squadron, during which time his log book records the following assessment:-

As a fighter pilot: Above the average.
As a Pilot-Navigator: Above the average.
In Air Gunnery: Exceptional.

In June 1939, Burton was posted to 12 Group HQ on Operations Staff Duties, so was known personally to the AOC. Three days after war broke out, he took command of 'B' Flight in 66 Squadron. During the *Blitzkrieg* of May 1940, he destroyed an He 111 off the Hague, and another over Dunkirk on June 2nd. On June 19th he claimed a Ju 88 over the French coast. This 24-year-old was undoubtedly amongst the most promising young officers in 12 Group.

Burton's pilots included some Auxiliary survivors of the 11 Group fighting, including Pilot Officer Lionel 'Buck' Casson, 26, an experienced fighter pilot, and Pilot Officer Hugh 'Cocky' Dundas, 21. Both had participated in the Dunkirk air operations, but the latter had been shot down by Major Werner Mölders, *Kommodore* of JG51, on August 22nd; that particular sortie was one of the first made by 616 Squadron from Kenley. Dundas had baled out with difficulty, dislocating his shoulder in the process. He had not returned to the squadron until September 13th, but for him, flying with Douglas Bader was an inspiration which would restore his confidence and raise his morale enormously.

There was no action to be had for 616 Squadron on their first day of duty in the Duxford Sector, and so at 1906 hrs the 'South Yorkshire' Spitfires touched down back at Kirton.

By this time, political influence was being exerted in favour of the Big Wing by none other than the 242 Squadron adjutant, Flight Lieutenant Peter Macdonald MP. In the House of Commons he had spoken 'earnestly' with the Under-Secretary of State for Air who suggested that he should see the Prime Minister himself. Macdonald spent over an hour with Mr Churchill, who was 'gruff' at first but then 'thawed'. Allegedly, the next day the Prime Minister began 'sending for various group commanders', but it is not known who they were, except that the Commander-in-Chief and AOC 11 Group were not included. It seems likely that both Air Vice-Marshal Leigh-Mallory and the DCAS, Air Vice-Marshal Douglas, were interviewed. If so, such disloyalty to the Commander-in-Chief was inexcusable. Dowding did not learn of this behind-the-scenes political move until 1968, when he was stunned: 'It does rather take your breath away.' He went on:-

> Of course so long as a squadron adjutant pays attention to his Service responsibilities there's no harm done. Those responsibilities are clearly defined. But it is another matter when a squadron adjutant, serving under my command, starts by-passing the correct procedure and chain of command in order to get the ear of politicians. I think it was impertinent and quite extraordinary behaviour in engineering things in this way. And all done without my knowledge. No one could deny a Member of Parliament the right to attend to matters that were in his political sphere. But was it right for him to introduce this purely technical matter of the tactical use that was being made of my command into such a political atmosphere?

The answer to that question is that Macdonald's actions were wholly inappropriate, not to mention insubordinate. Air Vice-Marshal Leigh-Mallory and his supporters nevertheless now enjoyed the benefits of a political line of communication and influence. The shadowy figures were certainly gathering in the background.

With the daylight bombing offensive having failed, the *Jagdwaffe* had resorted to flying *Freie Jagd* operations over southern England on a regular basis. Whilst this was welcomed by the *Kanaljager*, who for weeks had been frustrated by their close escort role, Goering decided that one *Staffel* in each *Jagdgeschwader* would be converted into the *Jagdbomber*, or 'Jabo', role. The operational value of the fighter-bomber was undeniable, but only presupposing a surplus of aircraft. The *Jagdflieger* were furious that their new found freedom was to again be limited, especially as they had done everything possible to increase the performance of their aircraft to keep pace with a progressive enemy. The Me 109 could only carry one SC250 HE bomb, so even a complete *Staffel* could cause little damage. The strategy, however, was that whilst Fighter Command could ignore fighter sweeps, it would be unable to do so if some aircraft within the formation carried bombs. The guinea pigs for this new idea were elements of *Erprobungsgruppe* 210, and *Lehrgeschwader* 2. In mid-September these units were moved into the Pas-de-Calais, largely to be escorted by Major Galland's JG26. Within the fighter units, the leadership was bitterly criticised for this move which represented the first crisis between the *Jagdwaffe* and the *Oberkommando der Wehrmacht (OKW)*.

The first *Jabo* 'Tip n'run' raid occurred on September 20th, when 22 II/LG2 fighter-bombers, protected by numerous fighters, made a sortie to London. Not knowing of the enemy's new plan, the RAF Controllers did not react, and were therefore surprised when II/LG2 swooped down and dropped bombs on the capital. The 11 Group Spitfire squadrons from Biggin Hill and Hornchurch were scrambled late, and the enemy fighter escort pounced on them over the Maidstone area. The first British pilot to die that day was 222 Squadron's Pilot Officer Laurie Whitbread, shot down by *Hauptmann* Hans 'Assi' Hahn of II/JG2 *Richthofen*; Whitbread crashed at Higham, near Rochester, at 1115 hrs. At the same time, the Duxford Wing was scrambled.

Squadron Leader Bader was instructed to patrol Hornchurch at 25,000', but in his log book recorded that the patrol was of 'London'. Despite being airborne for one hour and 45 minutes, the enemy was not sighted. Over the Maidstone area and south-east coast, the two fighter forces had clashed briefly but bitterly: for the loss of just one Me 109 and its pilot, the *Jagdflieger* had destroyed seven RAF fighters, killing four pilots. It was a salutary reminder for Air Vice-Marshal Park of the *Jagdwaffe's* skill and experience. From now on, no enemy formations could be ignored and so Fighter Command entered another exhausting phase.

That evening, Squadron Leader Bader did not return to Coltishall with 242 Squadron, but instead diverted to 12 Group HQ at Hucknall, where he remained overnight. Presumably he again met with Air Vice-Marshal Leigh-Mallory, and again it is likely that their conversation went unrecorded; certainly no record of it has survived.

Early in the morning of September 21st, Squadron Leader Bader returned to Coltishall before leading his squadron back to Duxford at mid-day. Squadron Leader Burton led 12 Spitfires of 616 Squadron to Fowlmere at 0844 hrs, but the Wing was not scrambled until 1815 hrs. Once more instructions were to patrol Hornchurch at 20,000', but Squadron Leader Bader led his fighters over London and the Thames Estuary between 25,000 and 27,000'. The enemy was not sighted, for the day was another of reduced enemy air activity.

On September 22nd, Squadron Leader Bader led 242 back to Duxford, and Burton's 12 Spitfires of 616 Squadron returned to Fowlmere. Contemporary documents are confused regarding the day's events; the 310 Squadron ORB states that 'No patrol took place', and 302's records simply 'No flying'. The 19 Squadron ORB records four patrols over base at Section strength (three Spitfires), during the first of which a Do 215 'came out of cloud and dropped 10 28lb bombs at 'B' Flight's dispersal, destroying one aircraft. Red Section chased it into cloud, F/Lt Lawson firing one burst at it'. The 616 Squadron ORB states that 'there was one scramble with the Wing over the Thames Estuary at 25,000', but enemy not sighted'. 242 Squadron's records are generally sadly lacking in detail, and on this occasion the ORB merely notes that 'Patrols carried out with 12 Group Wing but no combat'. As three of the Wing's five squadrons fail to mention a Wing patrol, did 242 and 616 Squadrons perhaps operate on this occasion as a two-squadron Wing? That night, both 242 and 616 Squadrons remained at Duxford 'owing to unfavourable weather conditions' (616 ORB).

Although the weather remained poor, September 23rd was another day of enemy fighter sweeps, and between 0930 and 1045 hrs some 200 German fighters roamed over Kent to the outskirts of London. At 0935 hrs, the Duxford Wing, comprising 19, 242, 310 and 616, patrolled over base at 20,000'. The Wing was then vectored to the Thames Estuary at 25,000', but the enemy was not sighted. Of interest is that on this sortie, 310 Squadron was led in the air by Wing Commander Woodhall himself. Two further Wing patrols were conducted at 1150 and 1810 hrs, but again there was no contact. Upon conclusion of the last patrol, 242 and 616 returned directly to their home bases, and whilst 310 Squadron landed at Duxford, 19 Squadron patrolled overhead at 20,000'. Squadron Leader Lane's pilots later reported having seen a single aircraft which dived 'at very high speed into cloud, heading in a SE direction. Thought to be an Me 109 on reconnaissance duty'. It is unlikely, however, that an Me 109 would have been flying so far north.

Despite the lack of action, 19 Squadron received good news: Flying Officer Haines and Pilot Officer Cunningham were both awarded the DFC.

The enemy's tactics on September 24th remained much the same as for the previous day, although it must be remembered that London and other targets were being hammered by night. The usual squadrons gathered at Duxford and Fowlmere, and at 0845 hrs the Wing patrolled north of the Thames Estuary. During that sortie 19 Squadron had lost the main formation, owing to thin cloud up to 27,000'; the ORB recorded 'Ideal morning for bombing but no E/A seen'. At 1150 hrs, the Wing went up to patrol the same area, but the 19 Squadron ORB records 'No E/A seen. Ran into

No 11 Group Wing. Almost a party'.

After the war, Myles Duke-Woolley, who was given command of 11 Group's 253 Squadron in late September 1940, submitted notes to the Air Ministry on his Battle of Britain experiences. In these, he makes reference to an incident such as that mentioned by 19 Squadron:-

Very often in those days, liaison between the Groups was not water-tight and one occasionally never knew before take-off that the 12 Group 'Balbo' would be in the area. The incident I remember was in late-ish September when I was leading 253 on a standing patrol over Canterbury. Normally these patrols were at 15,000', but I seized the opportunity for practice, and was at 28,000' in our new formation. Huns were reported to be approaching the area, but no more precise information was given regarding height, direction or numbers. We accordingly increased height to 31,000', and seeing nothing to the East and South I gazed North, almost immediately seeing a black mass bearing down from the direction of London, and so handsomely below us. I recognised the a/c soon after as the 12 Group 'Balbo' but they looked so determined that I felt they must be after some specific raid: I therefore felt that they might lead us to something interesting, and turned in behind them as a sort of voluntary top cover. Feeling friendly disposed myself towards them, I never thought they would mistake me for a German formation, but I forgot to realise that our formation was still unpublished, that Hurricanes just <u>did</u> <u>not</u> operate at 30-grand, and that the '109' <u>did</u> look rather like a Hurricane. The 'Balbo', of course, did mistake us and thought they were about to be 'bounced' - so they orbited. I thought they were orbiting to intercept my raid, and so orbited too. When the 'Balbo' straightened out to climb to 'engage' me, I naturally followed suit. They, equally naturally, had no intention of climbing up on a straight course to be bounced. Thus, for some minutes, there was complete stale-mate, until the 'Balbo' started to get short of fuel and retired in good order to the south.

About a fortnight later I read a letter from 11 Group analysing in caustic terms the operation of the 'Balbo'. I remember that about eight of its trips were mentioned, the main point stressed being the comparatively short effective time on patrol. With some horror I saw one trip described under 'Remarks' in roughly these words: 'Six squadrons attempted to patrol for 15 minutes in Canterbury area, but mistook an 11 Group squadron already on patrol for German a/c and returned in disorder to their bases'. The story got around the station and was received with huge delight by ground-crew as well as aircrew. I remember feeling myself that my innocuous patrol report could link me with the 11 Group report, and that if any fur was flying I was possibly going to be in the middle somewhere: the role of 'evidence' in a head-on collision between two AOCs seemed to me about as profitable as an advertisement I recalled for Cadbury's chocolate entitled 'Talking of Sandwiches' and depicting two burly giants simultaneously barging a weedy individual from opposite directions!

On at least one occasion, Air Vice-Marshal Park had asked whether the Wing was in position as requested above the Hornchurch - North Weald line, only to be told that in fact it was over Kent. It is clear from the evidence of 10 Group pilots that their squadrons advanced to the appropriate patrol line as requested, where they held off until called into action by the 11 Group Controller. Air Vice-Marshal Park had every right to expect that 12 Group's Wing would do the same and not either go off on freelance fighter sweeps or after distant enemies already being engaged by 11 Group fighters.

September 24th also saw a development in the political battle. Air Vice-Marshal Douglas informed Air Vice-Marshal Saundby, ACAS (Tactics), that he had received a number of criticisms from several sources regarding Air Vice-Marshal Park's tactics. It is not difficult to hazard an educated guess as to the identity of at least one of those 'sources'. Saundby instructed Group

Captain HG Crowe, the Deputy Director of Air Tactics, to inquire into the allegation and report accordingly in due course. When the ACAS (Tactics) forwarded Crowe's consequent report to Air Vice-Marshal Douglas, he asked him to read not only Air Vice-Marshal Park's report on the air fighting of August and September, but also Air Vice-Marshal Leigh-Mallory's report on Wing patrols dated September 17th. The Big Wing had gained another important ally.

However, when reporting on this phase of the Battle of Britain, Air Vice-Marshal Park wrote the following concerning the use of Big Wing formations:-

..... Had No 11 Group delayed in engaging the enemy until its squadrons had been assembled in Wings of four or five squadrons, there would have been no opposition to the first wave of bomber formations, who would have had time to escape without interception. With the available force massed into a few Wings of four or five squadrons, a proportion of the second wave would have been intercepted and severely punished. The third wave of enemy bombers would, however, have had unopposed approach to the vital points of London, as the 11 Group squadrons would have been on the ground re-arming and refuelling. After six months experience of intensive fighting, I have no hesitation in saying that we would have lost the battle of London in September if No 11 Group had adopted as standard the use of Wings of four or five squadrons as has been advocated in various quarters since that critical battle was won.

On September 25th, the weather closed in over the Midlands and Squadron Leader Bader had to abandon 242 Squadron's flight to Duxford and returned to Coltishall. Squadron Leader Burton's 616 Squadron successfully completed the flight from Kirton to Fowlmere, however. Despite Bader's absence, 19, 310 and 616 Squadrons patrolled Duxford and Debden between 0900 and 0940 hrs, led by Squadron Leader Blackwood of 310. Yet again no enemy aircraft were seen, and this was to be the Wing's only patrol of the day. The Poles of 302 Squadron ceased their attachment to Duxford on this day, and returned to Leconfield, never again to operate with the Big Wing.

Bad weather continued to keep 242 Squadron at Coltishall on September 26th, but Burton's Spitfires again managed the flight from Kirton to G1. For the Fowlmere Spitfires there was to be no activity, however, and the Duxford Sector's only sortie was flown by Blue Section of 310 Squadron which patrolled base below cloud for 30 minutes without incident. The autumn cloud conditions, coupled with the height at which the enemy fighters now operated, were causing problems for the System. Air Vice-Marshal Park reported:-

The great increase in the number of enemy fighters employed and the beginning of the autumn cloud conditions, above which the enemy fighters flew at great altitudes, increased the difficulties of obtaining accurate information. The Observer Corps found it impossible to distinguish between enemy bombers and enemy fighters. In an attempt to overcome this difficulty and to improve detailed information generally, special fighter reconnaissance patrols were introduced to patrol at high altitudes and to report by R/T details of enemy formations coming in.

During this phase and particularly during the latter part of it, RDF warning deteriorated considerably. This, coupled with the increasing altitudes at which the enemy fighter patrols approached, made the problem of intercepting from the ground more and more difficult. Our fighters operating from coastal aerodromes were frequently meeting enemy fighters above them, particularly when our own fighters were on the climb preparatory to being detailed to intercept raids. For this reason squadrons were being withdrawn from the forward coastal aerodromes in Kent to bases farther back from which they were better able to climb sufficiently high before intercepting.

A series of Day Patrol Lines were introduced on September 21st between London and the

Kentish coast, behind which squadrons attained their height, and assembled in Pairs or Wings of three squadrons. Whenever inland tracks of raids became confused, our squadrons were detailed to Patrol Lines and kept informed of the approach of enemy raids as far as practicable. After assembling on back Patrol Lines the squadrons were moved on to forward patrol lines.

The Air Vice-Marshal's report on the 'Method of Employing our Squadrons' makes illuminating reading:-

The general plan adopted was to engage the high fighter screen with Pairs of Spitfire squadrons from Hornchurch and Biggin Hill half-way between London and the coast, and so enable Hurricane squadrons from London Sectors to attack bomber formations and their close escort before they reached the line of fighter aerodromes East and South of London. The remaining squadrons from London Sectors that could not be despatched in time to intercept the first wave of the attack by climbing in Pairs formed a third and inner screen by patrolling along the line of aerodromes East and South of London. The fighter squadrons from Debden, Tangmere, and sometimes Northolt, were employed in Wings of three or in Pairs to form a screen South East of London to intercept the third wave of the attack coming inland, also to mop up retreating formations of the earlier waves. The Spitfire squadrons were re-disposed so as to concentrate three squadrons at each Hornchurch and Biggin Hill. The primary role of these squadrons was to engage and drive back the enemy high fighter screen, and so protect the Hurricane squadrons, whose task was to attack close escorts and then the bomber formations, all of which flew at a much lower altitude.

It is quite clear from the foregoing that 11 Group's northerly airfields operated Wings comprising three squadrons when conditions were appropriate. This was not influenced by anything other than the changing battle and again reflects the flexibility of the AOC 11 Group. Furthermore, the use of Spitfire squadrons by Park had to be correct.

On September 26th, 24 Blenheims of Bomber Command were sent to attack German minesweepers in the Channel. Fighter cover was requested, but the rendezvous was not made. Air Vice-Marshal Douglas asked Air Chief Marshal Dowding why. Also, on the morning of September 24th, a *single Anson* had been sent to attack 'E'-Boats but had itself come under fire. The DCAS asked whether fighter escort had been provided, and if not why not?

On September 27th, the weather improved sufficiently for both 242 and 616 Squadrons to fly down to Fowlmere and Duxford respectively, where they, together with 19 and 310 Squadrons, remained on Readiness throughout the day. At 0815 hrs, a large formation of Me 110s and 109s swept over south-east England where they were engaged by 11 Group squadrons. Nevertheless the enemy aircraft remained over England, milling around without attacking any specific ground targets. Their intention, it seemed, was to exhaust the RAF fighters, thus ensuring that they would be being 'turned around' when the next, heavier, raid was sent against London.

At mid-day, some 300 enemy aircraft approached between Dover and Lympne, heading for Chatham. The bombers, Ju 88s of I and II/KG77, were late at the rendezvous and were without close escort. Some 120 Spitfires and Hurricanes fell on them: 11 Ju 88s were lost. The frantic assistance calls by the *Kampfliegern* brought many Me 109s and 110s rushing to the scene, and a huge combat developed over 'Hellfire Corner'.

At 1155 hrs, the Duxford Wing was scrambled, and 19, 242, 310 and 616 Squadrons were instructed to patrol the London area whilst the 11 Group fighters were in action over the Dover area. Squadron Leader Bader heard over the R/T that enemy formations were south of the Thames Estuary, so he 'patrolled South of the Estuary'. 'South of the Estuary' would appear to be a slight understatement as the Wing sighted enemy aircraft over 'Dover - Canterbury'. A large formation of Me 109s were 'just milling around' at 18 - 20,000'. Having been climbing for many miles, the Wing was at 23,000' and so had the height advantage. Squadron Leader Bader then led the Wing up-sun before delivering a surprise attack, ordering the Wing to 'break up and attack as they liked'. The Wing Leader later reported:-

I chose an Me 109 which was passing underneath me and turned behind and above him and gave him a short 2 seconds burst with the immediate result that he became enveloped in thick white smoke, turned over and dived vertically. I did not follow it down, but as it was the first 109 shot down it was seen by P/O Crowley-Milling, P/O Bush, and F/Lt Turner, in fact almost the whole squadron. I also had my camera gun in action which will give further confirmation.

No-one saw the Me 109 crash, however, and there would appear to be no appropriate candidates amongst those enemy fighters which crashed in England during this engagement. Squadron Leader Bader fired at several more fleeting 109s, causing 'white vapour and black smoke' to issue from one, which also covered his Hurricane windscreen with oil. This 109 was last seen over the Channel, 'gliding down quietly and apparently under full control with his engine dead'. Many *Luftwaffe* fighters were to crash-land on the French coast after this action, no doubt amongst them this anonymous enemy pilot.

After the combat, Squadron Leader Bader reported seeing the 'burning wreckage of an Me 109 on the ground just south of Canterbury.

During what was by now a typical cut-and-thrust fighter combat, Pilot Officer Bush of 242 Squadron fired a long burst at a 109 which broke up and crashed into the sea. The reported location of the combat was 'between Dover and Gravesend'. Due to the numbers of enemy fighters which met this fate, it is impossible to identify which one Bush shot down without a more specific location. Pilot Officer Latta claimed a 109 destroyed which crashed into the Channel

Pilot Officer JB Latta of 242 Squadron.
(Author via Douglas Bader Foundation)

5-10 miles off Dover, and a second which crashed 5-10 miles inland of Dover; strangely, no candidate can be found for either of these claims. Unfortunately the squadron lost Pilot Officer Homer who, in fighter pilots' parlance, became a 'flamer' over Sittingbourne.

When the Wing's initial attack commenced, Squadron Leader Blackwood of 310 Squadron experienced engine vibration so sensibly broke away. Later the trouble was found to be caused by the 'gravity petrol feed', but it was too late for Blue 1 to rejoin the Squadron. Instead he joined up with another Hurricane and patrolled the mouth of the Thames, but without result. Blue 2, Sergeant Kaucky, attacked an Me 109, but a 'Spitfire dived on the same E/A and shot it down!' Sergeant Kominek claimed an Me 109 which 'dived vertically into the sea some five miles SW of Dover', and a 'Do 17' probable, although the latter was more likely an Me 110. The 109 concerned is believed to have been of 9/JG3, and the pilot remains missing. Flight Lieutenant Sinclair, Red 1, had to bale out for the second time during the Battle of Britain (ORB):-

.... was attacked by a 109 before he broke formation and the first burst destroyed his ailerons and the second set him on fire. As he was unable to invert his aircraft he had some difficulty in extricating himself as the machine was in a steep dive. He did, however, succeed in doing so and landed, unhurt, in the branches of a fir tree near CALLAM from which some farm hands helped him to mother earth. The aircraft was practically burnt out before it crashed.

For 310 Squadron, this was not a very successful action owing to the pilots suffering gun stoppages. Kominek's 109 was in fact the squadron's only claim.
616 Squadron ORB:-

It was in the second scramble (of the day) that the Squadron had their only engagement with the enemy when flying in the Wing. The squadron took off at 1142 hrs and positioned themselves at 25,000' above and behind 19 Squadron who were in turn above two squadrons of Hurricanes. They were flying East when a raid of 50 plus of Me 109s were sighted and engaged. Our squadron was unfortunately in a very bad position as 12 or more Me 109s dived down and attacked them out of the sun. P/O DS Smith who was weaving behind the Squadron was caught unawares and shot down. He made a forced landing but was seriously wounded. He was taken to FAVERSHAM Cottage Hospital, but unfortunately died the next day. P/O Holden claimed an Me 109 destroyed and Sgt Copeland an Me 109 probable.

Flight Lieutenant Ken Holden of 616 Squadron.
(Author via Air Vice-Marshal JE Johnson)

The 19 Squadron ORB reported that over Canterbury the Wing had intercepted 'approx. 20 bombers and innumerable fighters'. The 'bombers' are now believed to have been Me 110s. Nevertheless, 19 Squadron was attacked by the 109s from above. During the ensuing combat, Sergeant Jennings attacked the leader of five 109s:-

I saw him turn to starboard with white smoke coming from his engine. I followed him down and saw thick black smoke coming from the engine in place of the previous white smoke. As I followed him down I saw tracers pouring past me and found the other four 109s coming down after me. I turned to starboard and dived away. I pulled up and saw a Spitfire or Hurricane in flames, spinning down. The pilot jumped out and I followed him down to the ground. He landed OK in a clearing near a big wood.

Jennings had probably seen the descent of either Flight Lieutenant Sinclair of 310 Squadron, or Sergeant David Cox, a fellow 19 Squadron pilot, who baled out and landed at Wye:-

Upon scramble, I had jumped into the nearest Spitfire, 'QV-L', as mine would not start. This aircraft was nearly always flown by Sergeant Plzak, our 6'6" Czech who had dubbed me 'Little Boy'. To save time I buckled on his parachute, which was already in the cockpit - more of that later!

We were top cover of the Duxford Wing but were attacked by a large number of Me 109s in the Dover area. After some hectic moments avoiding being shot down, I found myself more or less on my own between Ashford and Folkestone. I then saw towards Folkestone a Hurricane being attacked by four Me 109s. Before I could give any assistance, which was my intention having got within a few hundred yards of the scrap, the Hurricane went down in a vertical dive inland.

(The Hurricane was probably Flight Lieutenant Sinclair's, which crashed at Godmersham, a few miles north of Wye).

The four Me 109s then turned their attentions to me. They knew their stuff as two got above me and two below. Naturally I had some hectic moments of turning this way and that as they came at me in attacks from all directions. I remember doing quite a lot of firing of my guns, but I think it was more in the hope of frightening them or raising my morale than in any real hope of shooting anything down!

All of a sudden there was a loud bang in the cockpit and for a second or two I was dazed. When I became normal again there was a lot of smoke about and my Spitfire was in a steep climb. As I lost flying speed I opened the hood, turned the aircraft over, undid my straps, and fell out, quickly pulling the ripcord of my parachute. When the canopy opened it gave me a severe jolt and several days later a lot of bruises showed on my chest and shoulders. Remember that the parachute harness was fitted for a man of 6'6" - I was lucky not to fall out of it!

As I floated down a 109 came and had a look at me and then flew off. It was then that I felt a lot of pain in my right leg and saw lots of holes in my flying boots out of which blood was oozing. Ground observers said that I took about 15 minutes to come down as I was so high up - I know that it was jolly cold up there when I came out of the aeroplane. I landed in the corner of a ploughed field near a farm. By this time I was feeling rather rough and must have looked it as the farmer handed me a bottle of whisky, from which I took a large swig. I was later taken to hospital at Walsford where a surgeon from Folkestone Hospital extracted several large pieces of cannon shell from just below my knee cap down into my ankle. I was in hospital about six weeks and off flying until December 1940.

Pilot Officer Eric Burgoyne's 19 Squadron Spitfire was also hit by the 109s, but sadly this pilot crashed and was killed at Coldred, just inland of Dover. Squadron Leader Lane himself had a lucky escape, but not at the hands of the enemy. Two days previously the squadron had begun re-equipping with Mk II Spitfires, one of which the CO was flying in this combat. After firing two short bursts, Lane's Spitfire became uncontrollable and skidded away, the pilot using all his strength to recover. This was only achieved at 3,000', by which time Lane was considering baling out. Back at Fowlmere the aircraft was found to have a misshapen rudder and a wrongly adjusted trim tab which prevented one elevator functioning correctly.

Flight Sergeant Unwin, also of 19 Squadron, engaged an Me 109 in a protracted dogfight lasting some 10 minutes and which took the Spitfire pilot dangerously near the French coast. Eventually Unwin fired a 30 degree deflection shot: the 109 stalled and spun into the sea.

September 27th was the heaviest day of fighting for some time. The Wing's claims were as follows:-

19 Squadron:	Seven destroyed, one 'possible'.
242 Squadron:	Four destroyed, two probables and one damaged.
310 Squadron:	One destroyed.
616 Squadron:	One destroyed, one probable.
Total:	13 destroyed, three probables, one 'possible' and one damaged.

Due to the confusion of the combat it is again difficult to verify individual claims, but four Me 109s did crash on English soil; although times are vague, it is possible that up to eight 109s crashed into the sea, and that a further seven arrived back at their bases in a damaged state. However, not all of those in the latter two categories might have been as a result of this particular engagement, and again we must remember that 11 Group squadrons were also engaged. The overclaiming ratio was thus probably about 3:1.

The Wing's losses were two pilots killed and one wounded, with four aircraft lost and two damaged. Squadron Leader Bader reported that:-

12 Group Wing as a whole did well.

The evidence from both the 310 and 616 Squadron ORBs is that those units would not have agreed with him.

On this day, Flight Lieutenant Stan Turner, and Pilot Officers Noel Stansfeld and Willie McKnight of 242 Squadron were awarded DFCs.

On September 28th, both 242 and 616 Squadron returned to the Duxford Sector, but despite two Wing patrols over the Thames Estuary, the ORBs report that the enemy was not engaged. According to the 616 Squadron ORB, there was 'very little flying owing to bad visibility'. Nevertheless, contemporary official records can be confusing and incomplete for obvious reasons; the log book of Richard Jones, at the time a Pilot Officer in 19 Squadron, indicates that on this day he was shot down in Spitfire P7432: 'Shot down and crash landed at Hawkhurst, Kent. Killed three sheep. What a bloody mess!!!' Over half a century later, he remembered the incident:-

When patrolling the Tenterden area at 29,000', the Controller informed us that as there were apparently no enemy aircraft in the vicinity we could return to 'Pancake'. I was 'Arse-End Charlie' and relaxed slightly as we dived to 20,000'. Suddenly about four feet of my starboard wing just peeled off - my initial thought was that it was a poor show on a new aircraft. Then a loud bang and a hole appeared above the undercarriage. I was obviously the target of an enemy fighter up-sun. Immediately I took evasive action, simultaneously my engine cut for good and I was suddenly in a high speed stall and spin. My radio was u/s so I was unable to inform the squadron who returned to base blissfully unaware that I had been shot down.

I recovered from the spin at about 10,000' - the aircraft was not responding to the controls - I realised too that the hood was completely jammed. I subsequently crash-landed with a dead engine in one of only two suitable fields in a heavily wooded area just outside Hawkhurst. Unfortunately I did so amongst a flock of sheep and I regret that several were killed. I was rescued by the Army and first taken to the Hawkhurst doctor who treated a flesh wound to my leg, then to the Mess prior to returning safely to Fowlmere.

My Spitfire had a broken propeller and radiator, a few holes and some missing parts, but was otherwise relatively undamaged.

The weather was so bad the following day that 242 Squadron remained at Coltishall. Neither 19 nor 310 Squadrons flew at all. At Kirton, 616 Squadron were notified that their presence was no longer required at Fowlmere. Squadron Leader Burton's pilots had flown a total of eight Wing sorties but had met the enemy only once when one pilot was lost against one Me 109 claimed destroyed and a probable. The Wing now consisted of the original three squadrons, 19, 242 and 310, so it is fair to say that on this day, with the autumn leaves, the Big Wing proper passed into history.

Big Wing Spitfire pilots at Readiness, Fowlmere, September 1940. Those identified are, from left, feet on table: Squadron Leader 'Billy' Burton (616), Flight Lieutenant Colin Macfie (616), Squadron Leader Brian Lane (19), Pilot Officer Hugh Dundas (616).
(Imperial War Museum)

Although September 29th remained quiet from a flying perspective, there was to be another development in the political battle. Following the failure of Fighter Command's SASO, Air Vice-Marshal Evill, to resolve matters between the AOCs of 11 and 12 Groups in August 1940, Air Vice-Marshal Park recognised that matters were getting worse and wrote again to HQ Fighter Command. This time his letter was addressed not to Evill, the Old Cranwellian Assistant Commandant, but to Air Chief Marshal Dowding himself.

Park explained that when the scale of attack dictated, he had worked out a system with Air Vice-Marshal Brand for 10 Group to supply a maximum of four squadrons for reinforcement. Due to Brand's own defensive commitments, these were only requested when targets south-west of London were threatened. For two months this arrangement had worked admirably, not least because these two commanders agreed that it was:-

..... essential to get a small number of squadrons quickly to the point requested than to delay whilst his squadrons are forming up in Wings, which would mean their arriving at the scene of battle after vital objectives have been bombed and the enemy was retreating. The latter action undoubtedly secures a better 'bag' of enemy aircraft but does not achieve our main aim, which is to protect aircraft factories and other vital points from being bombed by day.

Arrangements with the AOC 12 Group, Park continued, were unsatisfactory. The old coals of the late August airfield bombing were raked over once more, although as we have seen it was the technical limitations of the System rather than either of the Groups concerned which were to blame. Park quite rightly complained about the Wing's freelance fighter sweeps over southern England which had proceeded despite his specific request for 12 Group to protect his airfields north of the Thames. This action by the 12 Group Wing, he pointed out, had confused the Observer Corps, 11 Group Controllers and fighter squadrons.

Air Vice-Marshal Evill added comment to this letter before it was given to the Commander-in-Chief. The SASO confirmed that although Air Vice-Marshal Leigh-Mallory did send individual squadrons to reinforce 11 Group, it was true that he generally sent the Big Wing. Evill agreed that it was 'entirely wrong' for the 12 Group formation to 'rove without control over 11 Group's sectors' and he 'presumed' that Dowding would 'wish this stopped'. Evill did, however, give support to the Big Wing concept by claiming that Park tended 'to ignore the value of utilising the large formation when time permits'. As 11 Group was nearly always outnumbered, Evill considered that by using the Big Wing approach, there were occasions when that situation could be reversed. Park should, in the SASO's opinion, have organised things so that he could have used Leigh-Mallory's strength.

Air Vice-Marshal Leigh-Mallory received a copy of Air Vice-Marshal Park's letter on October 8th. Research indicates that his response concerning late calls were inaccurate. He emphasised that if warning was given when the enemy built up over the Pas-de-Calais, the Wing would have ample time to get to Hornchurch and at an appropriate height to intercept. Lord Dowding himself later commented:-

It was contrary to the whole structure of the Command and it takes into consideration only what was in the interests of the Duxford Wing.

Air Vice-Marshal Leigh-Mallory's report finally claimed that although the Wing had been in action over east Kent, this was only when either drawn south by combat or when so vectored by the 11 Group Controller. When this response was received at Bentley Priory, Air Vice-Marshal Evill and Air Commodore Lawson checked but found Leigh-Mallory's final claim to be untrue. Clearly the typewriter combat was increasing in intensity.

On September 30th, the Duxford Wing made one patrol over Hornchurch at 20,000' but landed without incident. This was also a significant date in the Battle of Britain, however, as the raid by KG55's He 111s against the Westland Aircraft Factory at Yeovil (although nearby Sherborne town was hit by mistake) represented the last daylight massed bomber raid. To deal with this attack, 10 Group had called for assistance from 11 Group, and the Tangmere squadrons sallied forth over the West Country. Four Heinkels were lost during this raid, after which the *OKW* at last accepted the folly of sending poorly-equipped, massed formations over England in daylight. Consequently the He 111 was withdrawn from the arena to operate thereafter only at night. The emphasis of the aerial assault on Great Britain had already shifted to *Nachtangriff*, which suited the *Kampfliegern* far better as the night defences remained in their infancy. The night sky presented the raiders with difficulties in navigation and target location, but these were soon solved via the use of radio guidance beams. Likewise, Air Chief Marshal Dowding, ever the technocrat, knew that the answer to the night bombing problem lay with the new Beaufighter and its Airborne Interception (AI) radar; neither were yet ready, although AI equipped Blenheims were valiantly holding the fort.

Although the danger of invasion had passed, Dowding and Park were about to face the enemy within.

CHAPTER EIGHT

Meeting of Infamy

By October 1st 1940, the question of Wing tactics was increasingly on the minds of many officers of Air rank. On this day, Air Vice-Marshal Park sent a memorandum to all his Sector Station Commanders; it was comprehensive and set out clearly the conditions under which it was practical for 11 Group to operate *three-squadron* Wings, and when it was not:-

Wing Formations.

There is a feeling among pilots in some squadrons that the only way to defeat the enemy raiders against this country is to employ our fighter squadrons in Wings of three squadrons. The object of this Note is to explain why such formations have been used off and on during the past five months, yet have not been made the standard method of grouping our fighter squadrons in home defence fighting.

2.　During the operations by 11 Group over France and Belgium, squadrons were originally employed singly. When the enemy opposition strengthened, squadrons were employed in pairs. Moreover, when squadrons could only raise three sections each, they were employed in Wings of three squadrons. The conditions were that our squadrons were being operated on a pre-arranged programme and could be allotted to their tasks some hours in advance and were normally collected and despatched from forward aerodromes on the coast. This gave ample time for squadrons to be arranged into pairs of Wings, under conditions which do not obtain in the defence of this country, when the enemy can and has made four heavy attacks in one day, giving only the minimum warning on each occasion.

3.　In spite of the favourable conditions during the operations over France, for the employment of Wings of three squadrons, the best results during the whole of this operation were obtained by squadrons working in pairs. Whenever possible, two pairs of squadrons patrolled the same restricted area; two at high altitude to engage enemy fighter patrols, and two about 5,000 to 8,000' lower to engage the enemy bombers, which, in those days, did not normally employ close escorts as they were operating over their own territory.

4.　Experience in home defence during the last two months' intensive operations has shown that there are many occasions in which the use of Wings of three squadrons is quite unsuitable, because of cloud conditions and lack of time, due to short warning of the approaching attack.

5.　Experience over many weeks has shown that when there are two or more layers of clouds, the squadrons of a Wing have great difficulty in assembling above the clouds at a rendezvous, also in maintaining touch after passing through clouds when on patrol. Instead of devoting their time to searching for the enemy, squadrons have frequently had to devote much of their attention to maintaining contact with other squadrons of a Wing of three. Unless the sky is relatively clear of clouds, pairs of squadrons have been more effective in intercepting the enemy.

6.　Quite apart from cloud interference, the lack of time due to short warning of the approach of raids frequently renders it inadvisable to detail Wings of three squadrons. Experience has shown that it takes much longer to despatch, assemble and climb to operating height, a Wing of three squadrons than one of even two pairs of squadrons. Frequently Wings of three squadrons have been attacked by enemy fighters whilst still climbing or forming up over their Sector aerodromes. It has been found better to have even one strong squadron of our fighters over the enemy than a Wing of three climbing up below them, in which attitude they are peculiarly vulnerable to attacks from above.

7.   In clear weather when the enemy attack develops in two or three waves, there is often time for the squadrons or Sectors on the flank of the attack, e.g. Debden, Northolt, Tangmere, to be despatched as Wings of three squadrons to meet the third incoming wave or to sweep across and mop up the retreating enemy bombers and close escort. There is rarely time for London Sectors to get Wing formations up to the desired height before the enemy reaches important bombing targets, e.g. factories, docks, Sector aerodromes.

8.   Until we have VHF in all squadrons, it is not practicable for three squadrons in a Wing to work on a common R/T frequency; at least, that is the considered opinion of the majority of squadron and sector commanders. Pairs of squadrons can and do work successfully on a common frequency whenever the State of Preparedness in a Sector permits. Here again some squadron commanders prefer to be on a separate R/T frequency in order to have better intercommunication within their squadrons.

CONCLUSION:

9.   As a result of five months' intensive fighting in No 11 Group, it is clear that Wings of three squadrons are not the most suitable formations under many conditions of TIME and WEATHER. On the whole, squadrons working in pairs have obtained better results in home defence, especially as our practice since July has been to detail two or more pairs of squadrons to intercept raids in massed formation. However, when conditions are favourable, squadrons will continue to be despatched in Wings of three, but the only person to decide whether Wings or Pairs of squadrons should be the Group Controller. He has the complete picture of the enemy's movements on a wide front from Lowestoft to Bournemouth, and must quickly decide whether the time and cloud conditions are suitable for pairs of Wing formations. Squadrons must, therefore, continue to study and develop fighting tactics in Wings of three squadrons, which will probably become more common in the spring of 1941.

10.   Two copies of this note are to be distributed to each fighter squadron, and one copy is to be read by each Sector Controller.

Three copies of the foregoing were also sent to Bentley Priory.

Many previous accounts have claimed that the Big Wing controversy arose because Air Vice-Marshal Park had a total aversion to using such a formation. His report of October 1st disproves this. It is quite clear that he enjoyed an enviable understanding of fighter tactics, and was quite prepared to use Wing formations in the *right* circumstances; likewise, he knew when *not* to use them. On the other hand, Air Vice-Marshal Leigh-Mallory and Air Vice-Marshal Douglas were advocating Wing use as *standard* practice, something which was quite impractical. Air Vice-Marshal Park had clearly identified that the Wing formation was best suited to *offensive* tactics, when the attacker could choose to operate under appropriate conditions of time and weather. His remarks concerning the future use of Wings are remarkably perceptive.

On October 1st, the Duxford Wing patrolled North Weald but without result. Such uneventful patrols were to be the norm for Bader's pilots as the autumn waned, with both the weather and the enemy's tactics becoming unsuitable for Wing operations.

On October 3rd, Air Vice-Marshal Leigh-Mallory visited 19 Squadron at Fowlmere, as the ORB reported:-

Visit from AOC discussing new tactics, principally against fighter formations and night interception. Many solutions discussed and information of the new devices and ideas being put forward and being developed for night interception.

Flight Lieutenant 'Teddy' Morten, of Ops 'B' at Duxford, recalls the AOC's visits:-

The AOC of 12 Group and the Station Commander, Wing Commander Woodhall, were very close, and on the former's many short visits to Duxford the pair of them would walk the station hangars talking 'shop'. The same loyal and close relationship existed between 'LM', 'Woody' (the 'Boss Controller') and Douglas Bader. I know. I was there.

On October 5th, 19 Squadron's Pilot Officer Vokes collected a cannon-armed Spitfire from the Air Fighting Development Unit, 'which has to be tested thoroughly'. A new booster coil helped push the cartridge in as the spring in the magazine ran down, while the feed chute had a wider sweep and went through one of the wing struts. The development of the cannon-armed Spitfire to a standard of operational acceptability was becoming increasingly urgent. On the same day, Wing patrols were carried out over Debden and North Weald by 19, 242 and 310 Squadrons with the addition of 266 Squadron's Wittering-based Spitfires which had flown down to operate from Fowlmere.

The operation of Wing formations near or over the sea was another concern of Air Vice-Marshal Park, as indicated by a further memorandum issued from Uxbridge to all 11 Group Sectors on October 5th:-

The opinion has recently been expressed that a Wing formation should not be led out of parachute dropping distance from the land. It would appear that this attitude of mind, which is quite new, regarding flying by aircraft of Fighter Command over the sea may have been induced by the fact that during recent months we have been forced to fight a defensive battle over our own territory.
2.   This is, however, quite a passing phase, during which the enemy has attempted to obtain air superiority over this country and to carry out mass bombing attacks by day, in the course of which he has been severely handled and has suffered very heavy losses. We must now look forward, perhaps quite soon, to such improvement in the air situation that we shall once more take the offensive in the air and put strong formations over the Channel and later over the enemy's coastal aerodromes to shoot him down as he assembles and climbs up, in the same way as he has recently done over SE England.
3.   It is, therefore, most important that all squadrons and pilots should realise that their duties will occasionally take them over the sea even though at present we do not normally pursue the enemy more than 15 miles to sea. Moreover, the improved arrangements for the rescue of pilots who have fallen into the water should enable a much higher percentage of rescues to be made than was the case during the Dunkirk and subsequent operations - such as those over Cherbourg.
4.   Finally, it is pointed out that were the practice to be followed of only flying so as to be out of parachute dropping distance of the sea, a north-westerly wind of 30 mph would prevent our aircraft at 21,000' from flying much further south-east than Ashford, for example; for a parachutist from that height takes about 17 minutes to descend to earth.
5.   Two copies of this letter are to be passed to each fighter squadron and spare copies retained for fresh units arriving to reinforce in exchange for some of our present squadrons.

A commendable feature of Air Vice-Marshal Park's leadership of 11 Group was the way in which he sought to fully brief his personnel on various operational matters, such as in these reports of

MEETING OF INFAMY

October 1st and 5th. The same cannot be said of Air Vice-Marshal Leigh-Mallory's running of 12 Group; Wing Commander Frank Brinsden:-

I do not believe that any of us in 12 Group at squadron pilot level realised that we were engaged in a full scale battle, nor how important the outcome would be if lost. Intelligence and general briefing was sadly lacking.

By October 5th, the Battle of Britain had entered its final phase, during which the enemy largely undertook high altitude fighter sweeps punctuated by fighter-bomber attacks on London. As a result of the increased speed of the enemy formations, and the shorter warning therefore given by RDF, from early October onwards 11 Group had found it necessary to introduce Standing Patrols by either one or two Pairs of squadrons above the Maidstone line. Immediately an attack's approach was detected, these patrolling squadrons were ordered up to 30,000' to contain the enemy's highest fighters and provide cover to additional squadrons scrambled to meet the threat. The new enemy tactics demanded a much higher state of Preparedness throughout 11 Group, and the Standing Patrols greatly increased the volume of operational flying by Park's pilots (which now ranged from 45-60 hours per squadron, per day).

On October 6th, Air Vice-Marshal Park issued the following instructions regarding the use of Wing Formations in 11 Group:-

When the sky is mainly clear of clouds and the Group Controller receives ample warning by RDF of the forming up and approach of mass attacks over the French coast or from the south, some squadrons will be despatched in Wings of three units. Moreover, this type of formation will continue to be used to bring Sectors in the North and South of London in to meet the third wave of a prolonged attack or to 'mop' up raids that are retreating after having been engaged by other squadrons around London.

2.   As a result of practical experience during the last five months by Squadrons, Sectors and Group Headquarters, the following brief instructions are issued. As further experience is gained by Squadrons working in Wing formations, fresh and more detailed instructions will be issued for the benefit of all concerned. Much of that which follows applies to squadrons working in pairs; the normal formation for reasons already stated in my letter 11G/486, dated October 1st.

Leadership:

3.   The squadron and leader of the Wing must be decided by the Sector Commander before the beginning of daylight operations each day. After a heavy engagement it may be necessary to change the leadership, when the strongest squadron should be appointed to lead the Wing.

Take-Off:

4.   Squadrons should take off separately and not form up in Wing on the ground.

Assembly:

5.   The Group Controller will order the place and height of rendezvous, according to the cloud conditions and the proximity of enemy raids. The rendezvous will, whenever possible, be well inland in order to enable squadrons to join up at the height ordered before engaging the enemy. The Wing Leader must report immediately the Wing assembles, and Sector Controller

is to report to Group Controller, who will then detail Wing to a raid or a patrol line above the enemy raids.

Failure to Assemble:

6. If slow take-off or unexpected cloud conditions unduly delay the assembly of the Wing when enemy raids are approaching important targets, the Group Controller may be compelled to detail one or more squadrons of the intended Wing to intercept approaching raids to break up or harass bombers before they reach the target. In this event, it will be necessary for squadrons having VHF to revert from common frequency to their own R/T channel.

Rendezvous:

7. Group Controller will normally select an aerodrome or other good landmark well back from the approaching enemy raids.

R/T Frequencies.

8. Until all squadrons have VHF it is not considered practicable for all units in the Wing to work on a common R/T frequency. This ruling is based on the experience of many squadrons in several Sectors over a long period. On the introduction of VHF, squadrons will work on a common R/T frequency as soon as they assemble as a Wing. If the Wing becomes broken, squadrons should revert to their own R/T frequency to facilitate communication with the Sector Controller.

Formation:

9. The leading squadron will normally be lower than the two following squadrons. Sectors, however, are to try out stepping down one or more of the following squadrons.

Tactics:

10. Before leaving the ground it is essential that the three squadrons shall know which unit is to take on the bombers, which to attack the escort, and lastly which squadron is to act as above-guard or screen to hold off enemy high fighter screen. As the enemy close escort may be above the bombers, in rear, or on a flank or even ahead, and on other occasions may fly weaving between the bomber sub-formations, it is not always possible to lay down rigidly beforehand which Squadrons in the Wing will attack bombers or their escort. This makes it all the more necessary for the general tactics of the Wing to be discussed and decided on the ground before a patrol.

Look-out Guards:

11. Each squadron should provide its own look-out guards, especially for the period prior to assembly, and after the Wing has become split up by an engagement with the enemy. The Wing should normally have one squadron slightly in the rear and above to act as cover to the whole Wing against very high enemy fighters.

Pip-Squeak:

12. Each squadron is to provide one aircraft with pip-squeak to enable fixing at Sector Operations Room.

The Sun:

13. The Wing formation should whenever possible patrol across the direction of the sun. Enemy fighters attacking out of the sun will then be offered only deflection shots at our fighters.

Section Formation:

14. When in Wing formations, Sections should normally be composed of four aircraft, consisting of two pairs of fighters. Each squadron should, therefore, have three sections of four aircraft.

Assembly After Combat:

15. It is not considered necessary or advisable for squadrons to try to re-form Wing after a general engagement takes place over enemy territory or over the sea, then it may be advisable to lay down beforehand the Wing rendezvous.

Breaking Off from Wing:

16. If squadrons are detailed to be detached from the Wing formation, Sector Controller should give the order 'X Squadron break away, Vector ....', and then inform the Wing Leader that X Squadron has been ordered to break away.

From these instructions, it is again clear that Air Vice-Marshal Park had every intention of utilising three-squadron Wings when circumstances were applicable. Also, great thought had been given to this use of Wings, and it is commendable that again a full briefing was distributed to all Sectors. This is in direct contrast to Air Vice-Marshal Leigh-Mallory's arrangements which were apparently made behind closed doors at Hucknall and for the ears of but a select few; Air Vice-Marshal Park's actions, however, were not contrary to the wishes of his Commander-in-Chief.

Regarding the use of Wing's in 11 Group, Air Vice-Marshal Park was later to report that he had 'learned the following lessons' regarding Wing fighting:-

a) There are relatively few days in Autumn when cloud conditions are suitable for formations of Wings;
b) A much longer time is required to despatch, assemble and climb Wing formations.
c) The employment of Wing formations considerably reduced the duration of fighter patrols.
d) Mass formations of even three squadrons are slow and cumbersome, and likely to be out-flanked so fail to intercept the faster German fighter formations;
e) Better results can be obtained by two Pairs of squadrons than by four squadrons operating in a Wing;
f) The delay caused by the use of Wing formations would on many occasions allow enemy fighter-bomber raids to attack vital objectives and escape without interception;
g) All squadrons must be trained to fight and fend for themselves as squadrons before

attempting to work in mass formations or Wings.

Wing Commander Douglas Blackwood, CO of the Duxford Wing's 310 Squadron:-

There was never really time to get 3 or 4 squadrons off the ground and into some shape and form to attack the usual mass of enemy aircraft effectively. On one or two occasions I, as deputy senior Squadron Commander, was detailed by Bader and the AOC to lead the formation, so I know a little about this difficulty. Of course Douglas Bader was at the front and so he never saw the 'Tail End Charlies' - it was chaos at the back with chaps being left behind and all sorts. Remember, of course, that the Hurricane had not the power of the Spitfire.

On October 10th, Air Vice-Marshal Park wrote to the Commander-in-Chief requesting that 12 Group take a larger share of the fighting. He nevertheless pointed out that some 12 Group squadrons would have to exchange with some currently war-weary 11 Group squadrons. The only alternative, he suggested, was for the 12 Group Wing to operate under the control of the Biggin Hill or Kenley Sector for a short period each day. Here Keith Park raised a noteworthy point. Despite the policy of rotating squadrons through the line, the AOC 12 Group had never sent 19, 242, 302, 310 or 611 Squadrons to serve in 11 Group. Had he done so, it would have been interesting to see how certain of them fared; even at this late stage in the Battle, the change from 12 to 11 Group operations remained traumatic.

On October 13th, Air Vice-Marshal Evill sent Air Chief Marshal Dowding a set of minutes regarding various aspects of the battle to date. Amongst his concerns the SASO mentioned that beyond daily Group and Squadron combat reports, Bentley Priory had:-

... no regular source of information as to how Groups are operating. We do not know whether their squadrons are sent up singly or in twos or threes, or to what heights they are sent. We have no indication as to how squadrons in the air are disposed or whether factory areas are specifically covered. There is, in fact, no general statement of the action taken. For instance, though No 12 Group's Wing was called in on the afternoon of 11th October, as is indicated in their Form "Y", there is no mention in 11 Group's report that they called for this reinforcement or what they did with it.

We have, I know, received - after calling for it - a report from 11 Group on their method of operation in the first six weeks of this battle, which contains very valuable information as to methods adopted by 11 Group in that period. We have also received from Leigh-Mallory reports as to why and how he employs his Wing, and reports from Park as to why he does not. Apart from these communications we do not know a great deal about the way in which they conduct operations and there is certainly no recognised routine for reports from Groups as to what they are doing.

I fully understand that you delegate the tactical conduct of operations to the Groups, and that we must neither bother them with demands for a lot of written information nor show a lack of confidence in their conduct of operations, which would, indeed, be entirely unjustified in view of the results which they have achieved.

Air Vice-Marshal Park's reports are, in fact, comprehensively detailed, and do not state 'why he does not' employ a Wing. Extracts from these reports have already been quoted, and 11 Group's tactics would appear to have been clearly defined yet flexible according to the situation faced at any given time. Could it have been that Air Vice-Marshal Evill sensed the political danger which lay ahead, to which he had, perhaps unwittingly, contributed?

Whilst Air Vice-Marshal Park attempted to achieve a rapport with 12 Group, the Air Ministry was preparing a critique of his tactics. On October 14th, Air Vice-Marshal Stevenson produced an 'Air Staff Note on the Operation of Fighter Wings' for the DCAS, Air Vice-Marshal Douglas; it was based on Air Vice-Marshal Leigh-Mallory's report of September 17th. Where appropriate Air Vice-Marshal Park's hand-written notes have been added in italics:-

It has become apparent that on some occasions our fighters have been meeting the enemy on unequal terms both as regards numbers and height. In order to overcome or reduce this disadvantage, fighters must be operated in tactical units large enough to deal effectively with enemy formations and these units must be so controlled that they encounter the enemy without tactical disadvantage.

2.   It is the purpose of this note to examine the circumstances in which fighter units of more than single squadrons should be operated and to evolve general principles for their employment.

3.   It would be well first to summarise the disadvantages under which our own fighters have in some instances operated. These are briefly as follows:-

(i)   Numerical Inferiority: Squadrons have been sent up singly or in pairs to meet large formations of bombers escorted by still larger formations of enemy fighters. The operations of three squadrons have not been effectively co- ordinated with the operations of other squadrons in the same group, and adjacent groups, with the result that fighters have operated independently and ineffectively.

Pairs of Spitfire squadrons engage high fighter screen. Pairs of Hurricane squadrons to each raid and escort. Wing formations from Tangmere, Northolt, Debden, North Weald. Not 'adjacent Groups', only 12 Group.

(ii)   There have been few opportunities for fighter formation leaders to discuss or concert operations with the leaders of other fighter formations.

Group and Sector Conferences are frequent.

(iii)   Fighters are frequently told to patrol at a height which puts them at the mercy of high flying enemy fighters.

See Instruction to Controllers No 25.

(iv)   Fighters are vectored towards enemy formations in such a way that by the time they reach the plan position of the enemy, they are below him.

For many units assemble at height over base or on their patrol line.

(v)   The limitations of HF RT preclude the possibility of operating a number of squadrons on the same frequency.

4.   Examination of these disadvantages leads us to recommend the adoption of the following

principles for operating fighter squadrons larger than squadrons.

Is an aim to engage bombers before they reach target?

FIGHTER WING.

5.   The minimum fighter unit to meet large enemy formations should be a Wing of three squadrons.

Depends on time available and clouds. Impossible for London Sectors!

"BALBO"

6.   When necessary, to secure superiority in numbers or to reduce inferiority as far as possible, a force of two fighter Wings should be operated as a tactical unit. This tactical unit of two Wings will be referred to in this paper as a "balbo".

Too clumsy and rigid for Home Defence fighting.

COMPOSITION OF A WING.

7.   A Wing should be of three squadrons of the same type and if possible Mark of aircraft.

Yes.

8.   All squadrons of a Wing should operate from the same aerodrome, or failing this, from aerodromes within 2 or 3 miles of each other.

No. Dispersment reduces vulnerability.

COMPOSITION OF A BALBO.

9.   A balbo should be of two Wings. One wing may be of one type of aircraft and the other wing may be of another. Wings composing a balbo should be so disposed that the Wing having the aircraft of higher performance is further back from the zone of operations.

CONTROL OF A WING.

10. In order to ensure sympathetic and effective control of the Wing, one of the squadron commanders from the squadrons composing the Wing should supervise the controlling of the Wing from the Sector Operations Room.

Continuous Watch in daylight?

CONTROL OF A BALBO.

11. The Wings composing a balbo will come from different sectors. The control of each Wing will be supervised by a squadron commander from the Wing, but the Group Headquarters

should detail one of the Sectors to co-ordinate the operations of the 2 Wings of the balbo. The D/F positions of both Wings should be shown in the Operations Room of the Controlling Sector.

VARIATIONS IN CONTROL NECESSITATED BY VHF OR HF R/T.

12.   VHF facilitates the control of balbos, but if squadrons are fitted with HF it is considered that difficulties in inter-communication are outweighed by the advantages in meeting large enemy formations with large fighter formations.

CONTROL OF BALBOS WITH VHF R/T.

13.   All the squadrons in each Wing should operate on sector frequency (Button "B") and would have to be controlled on this frequency. Inter-communication between Wings in a balbo would be by means of the Command frequency through aircraft on watch on this frequency.

Yes.

CONTROL OF BALBOS WITH HF R/T.

14.   Squadrons should operate on their squadron frequency; inter-communication between squadrons by R/T is impracticable except through ground stations. It will frequently happen when using HF that balbos will pass out of R/T range of their Sectors. When this happens it may be confidently expected that weather will be such that large enemy formations will be clearly visible from a distance, and vectoring, therefore, will be unnecessary.

Yes.

15.   The control of balbos operating at a distance from their controlling sectors even with VHF is complicated by the sectors not having operations tables big enough to show the whole area over which balbos may have to fight. It is recommended that smaller scale "balbo tables" should be provided to show the tracks of enemy formations of more than say 50 aircraft. These tables should be small-scale replicas of the Fighter Command table, (say 10 miles to 1"). Consideration would have to be given to the method by which this information might be passed to Sectors.

One Group must control all squadrons in its Sector.

UNITY OF WINGS.

16.   "Esprit de wing" and consequent operational efficiency would be fostered by regarding Wings as units and moving them complete from one station to another when rest or reinforcement is necessary, but this is obviously impracticable at present. It would be difficult to engender in a balbo the same spirit of unity which should inform a Wing, but much could be done to promote good co-operation by encouraging personal contact between the pilots and particularly the leaders of the squadrons concerned.

LOCATION OF WINGS.

17. Wings should be located at stations from which they can gain advantage in height over the enemy before they meet him, without having to turn. This may be impracticable except in special cases.

GROUP COMBINED TACTICAL PLAN.

18. The tactical plan on which the primary Group should work ought to be based on the principle that although the aim is to destroy enemy bombers, the enemy fighters must be contained to enable the bombers to be destroyed.

Need to protect vitals of area?

ROLE OF WINGS

19. The Wing with higher performance aircraft should take on enemy fighters. The Wing with the lower performance aircraft should take on bombers, if any.

Yes.

20. If the strength of enemy formations is low enough to warrant the use of only one Wing, the Wing Leader should use his judgement in deciding what proportion of his force to devote to enemy fighters.

Yes.

Air Vice-Marshal Park had all the answers to the areas of importance contained within the Air Staff Note. I think it abundantly clear by now that tactically his thinking was absolutely sound, which leads me to conclude that his critics were motivated by *personal* and *political* ambition.

The Air Staff Note was circulated with a covering letter from Air Vice-Marshal Stevenson notifying the AOCs of 10, 11 and 12 Groups that the CAS intended to hold a conference at the Air Ministry on October 17th to both discuss fighter formation tactics and hear a report from Air Chief Marshal Dowding regarding the progress of night interceptions. The Air Staff Note, however, was to 'form the basis for discussion'.

On October 14th, the Agenda for the forthcoming conference was also published; again, Air Vice-Marshal Park's personal notes appear in italics:-

Is it agreed that the maximum fighter unit to meet large enemy formations should be a Wing of three squadrons?

To meet enemy bomber formations only.

Is it agreed that a larger fighter formation than a Wing should operate as a tactical unit? If so, is it agreed that this unit should consist of two Wings?

Not over UK but on offensive sweeps.

By what name should such a unit (referred to in this Agenda as a "BALBO") be known?

Are any insurmountable obstacles foreseen in operating all the squadrons of a Wing from the same aerodrome?

No, but congestion, take-off delay and all being bombed on the ground together should be considered.

Is it agreed that the Wing and "Balbo" should be controlled by a Squadron Commander from one of the squadrons composing the formation?

No, by Ground Sector Controller.

Are there likely to be any difficulties in co-ordinating the operations of the two Wings or "BALBO"?

Yes, limitation of R/T, and clouds.

In weather conditions which enable the enemy to operate in mass formation, it is likely that the fighter leader may be able to dispense with Sector Control. Is it agreed that in these conditions he should inform the Sector Controller and take over control of the Wing or "BALBO", being informed by the Controller of the location, size, speed, course and height of the enemy mass?

These conditions are best suited for Sector Control as he gets good information from Observer Corps, Recce aircraft, AA units and Group HQ.

Has the conference any comments on the method of R/T control of "BALBOS" described in paras 12 to 15 of the attached Air Staff Note.

VHF as common frequency.

Can Wings be regarded as permanent units and moved complete when necessary, from one station to another?

No, unless squadrons are added.

Is it agreed that Wings should be deployed at stations from which they can gain advantage in height over the enemy without having to turn?

No, depends on length of warning.

Short report by C-in-C Fighter Commander on present position regarding night interception.

On October 15th, Air Vice-Marshal Park sent a memorandum to his Sector Commanders, the following being an extract therefrom:-

USE OF WING FORMATIONS AGAINST PRESENT ENEMY TACTICS.

The use of Wings of two or three squadrons is effective against enemy <u>bombers</u> with close fighter escorts for the following reasons:

(a)   Much more warning from RDF plots is received whilst the enemy bomber and fighter formations are assembling over the French coast; this gives the Group Controller plenty of time to order squadrons up to operational height, in some cases well before the enemy raids commenced to approach our coast;

(b)   The bomber formations fly mostly between heights of 15,000 to 20,000';

(c)   Formations of enemy bombers and escorting fighters can be sent over to this country only in good weather conditions which are suitable for interception by Wings.

2.   Against the present enemy tactics, very high fighter patrols or raids, the use of Wing formations has been found to have serious disadvantages for the following reasons:

(a)   The warning received from RDF plots is insufficient to place squadrons at the required height in time to intercept the <u>first</u> wave of enemy fighters;

(b)   The heights of enemy aircraft are much greater, thus requiring more time to intercept from above;

(c)   The present enemy tactics are generally confined to days when considerable and cloud are present.

3.   Results have shown that Wings or Pairs of squadrons have only been successful in intercepting when there is a second or third wave of enemy fighters, and this can only be done if the squadrons take off and climb independently to their operational height and then effect a rendezvous. When two or three squadrons take off and climb together, the rate of ascent is found to be slower, thereby wasting valuable minutes during which time one or two squadrons, operating singly, could attain position above the enemy fighter formations.

4.   The first wave of enemy fighter aircraft has usually been intercepted only by the Spitfire squadron carrying out Standing Readiness Patrol, and sometimes by one or two Spitfire squadrons from 'Stand-by'.

5.   <u>Rigid</u> squadron formations and Wing formations have been found to be ineffective against very high fighter raids for the following reasons:

(a)   They can be broken up easily by attacks from above by small formations of enemy aircraft. Instances have occurred of even one or two enemy fighters having broken up a pair of our squadrons.

(b)   If enemy fighter aircraft happen to be below they can usually see a large formation of our fighters, and on account of their superior speed at high altitude they are able to withdraw before we can engage.

The Air Vice-Marshal went on to discuss enemy fighters tactics at great length, but added that:-

This instruction has been prepared as a result of very careful scrutiny by the Group Commander of dozens of recent patrol reports and combat reports from our twenty day fighter squadrons. Observations of our squadrons on patrol over Kent (by Park himself whilst flying in 'OK1'), and various discussions with Sector and Squadron Commanders have also been taken into account before putting this brief instruction in writing.

MEETING OF INFAMY

The first paragraph 'a' in Air Vice-Marshal Park's report requires discussion. Air Vice-Marshal Leigh-Mallory, Wing Commander Woodhall and Squadron Leader Bader all believed that the Duxford squadrons should be scrambled immediately RDF indicated the build-up of a raid over Calais; they argued that by being called off at that early juncture, the Duxford Wing could be at height and meet the raiders as they were inbound over the Canterbury area. It has already been said that this was impossible because the technical limitations of RDF meant that the System was unable to differentiate between a raid assembling and the general constant air traffic over the Pas-de-Calais. The earliest warning of a raid, therefore, was when it commenced moving out across the Channel, just seven minutes from the English coast. The content of Park's leading paragraph is open to misinterpretation: he states that warning was, in fact, received via RDF whilst the enemy formation *was* assembling over the French coast; on some occasions this gave the Group Controller '*plenty of time* to order squadrons up to operational height, in some cases *well before* the enemy raids commenced to approach our coast'. Certainly in 1939, it was reported that RDF was capable of reaching 60-70 miles inland of Calais, and could detect a single aircraft at a height of 10,000' and 100 miles away. The accuracy of the equipment was excellent: 1,000' in height, and one mile in distance at 50 miles range. Given such information about RDF, the paragraph in question may lead one to ask why, if Park accepted the Wing's worth against bomber formations, was the Duxford Wing was not fully used by 11 Group during the Battle for London? The following, however, should be borne in mind:-

1. From the time a plot was first observed on the RDF screen, it took around five minutes before the first scrambles.

2. The distance between Duxford and Canterbury is roughly 70 miles.

3. Pilot's Notes indicate that the Spitfire's average climbing speed was 180 mph. Thus it would take approximately 23 minutes to reach Canterbury, assuming a continuous climb in order enable a superior height to be achieved for the intercept. Clearly, for a number of aircraft in formation this time would be increased and when considering also the delay inherent in '1' above, the time between the first RDF plots appearing and the Duxford Wing's arrival over Canterbury could be approaching 30 minutes. It is also noted that Bader's Wing included three, slower Hurricane squadrons, which would increase this time.

4. For a German bomber formation progressing at 3 miles a minute, it would take roughly 14 minutes to fly from Calais to Canterbury.

5. Put simply, given these figures, the *enemy would be incoming over Canterbury in half the time it would take for the Duxford Wing to reach this position.*

From the foregoing mathematics, it is apparent that although Air Vice-Marshal Park used such phrases as 'plenty of time', this was only in the context of the reaction times of 11 Group itself. Such remarks in no way alter the fact that the suggested use of the Duxford Wing was both impractical and unrealistic. Ultimately there is but one conclusion: Squadron Leader Bader would never find the action he craved for in 12 Group.

On the same day that the AOC 11 Group wrote his report on the use of Wing formations, he replied to Air Vice-Marshal Stevenson regarding the Air Staff Note. He enclosed copies of his instructions to 11 Group Sectors of October 1st and 5th, and suggested that these be circulated before the conference 'in order to save a great deal of valuable time'. Remarking on his five months experience in the employment of Wing formations, the Air Vice-Marshal continued:-

Your Air Staff Note is, apparently, based on the experience of 12 Group on the five occasions in which they have reinforced my Group. We in 11 Group used Wings of three squadrons in May, June, July, August, September, and are still using them when conditions of time, space and weather make them effective.

During the last big attack by the German long range bomber force, the squadrons in 11 Group operating mostly in pairs of two squadrons destroyed 115, plus 28 probably destroyed, plus 41 shot down damaged, for a cost of 15 pilots. 12 Group employed their large Wing formation on that date .... they destroyed 13 enemy aircraft, plus 6 probably destroyed, plus 3 damaged, for a cost of 2 pilots. As you have included in the papers for the Conference detailed results by 12 Group Wings, I think you should include the attached statement .... showing the results by 10 and 11 Groups on the last big battle with bombers over England. We were both using mainly pairs of fighter squadrons as our geographical situation does not afford the time to despatch, assemble and engage with Wing formations BEFORE THE BOMBER RAIDS HAVE REACHED VITAL OBJECTIVES. I may be wrong in imagining that our primary task is to protect London, aircraft factories, Sector aerodromes, against enemy bombers, and not merely to secure a maximum bag of enemy aircraft after they have done their fiendish damage.

You must appreciate of course that *conditions of time and space do not permit of squadrons in 12 Group engaging incoming raids*, but mainly the outgoing raids after they have been attacked by pairs of Spitfire and also Hurricane squadrons located around London and have had their close escort and themselves pretty badly shaken by AA fire.

Air Vice-Marshal Park also wrote out his own 'Points for Air Ministry Conference' in which he reiterated the content of his previous reports concerning the use of Wing formations; several interesting points made were:-

Our AIM has been to engage bombers BEFORE they reach vital objectives, using maximum force in time given - Wings or pairs, or single squadron, or even Station Commanders.

FLANK SECTORS, North and South, been used in Wings of three frequently, but can only engage out-going bomb raids with good results because:-

i)   raids coming in been engaged by pairs of Spitfire and/or Hurricanes and so lost their escorts;
ii)   have been subjected to heavy AA fire.
iii) have expended much of their ammunition;

DUXFORD WINGS, 4/5 squadrons, like the Debden and Tangmere Wings have arrived in time to intercept the <u>out-going</u> bomb raids.

DANGER to MORALE of Squadrons being taught by Northern Groups that it is not safe to enter the South-East area except in Wings of 4/5 squadrons. 616, 266, 66 Squadrons from 12 Group possibly imbued with Big Wing idea not fought so well as 13 Group Squadrons trained to fight singly.

However, on the matter of training, Air Vice-Marshal Park was wrong, for as we have seen there was, despite previous claims, precious little in the use of Wing formations in 12 Group. The Points continued:-

DEBDEN squadrons found to be TOO FAR NORTH, so moved one squadron to North Weald.

DUXFORD ROVING WINGS caused considerable confusion to London defences and prolonged Air Raid Warnings through wandering uninvited and unannounced over East Kent after retreat of enemy.

REINFORCEMENTS from 10 Group; arrangement entirely satisfactory because:-
(a) they proceed to the place and height requested.
(b) they do not delay to form up Wings of 4/5, so arrive after Brooklands, Kingston, Kenley, etc have been bombed.
(c) They remain under the direction of 11 Group, so avoid confusing Observer Corps, 11 Group squadrons and ARW system.

Logically, how could *anyone* argue with Air Vice-Marshal Park?

On October 15th, for reasons which will become apparent, the 242 Squadron ORB recorded that 'Squadron Leader Bader proceeded on four days leave'.
On October 17th, the following gathered in the Air Council Room:-

Air Vice-Marshal WS Douglas:	DCAS
Air Chief Marshal Sir Hugh CT Dowding:	AOC-in-C
Air Marshal Sir Charles Portal:	AM (P)
Air Marshal Sir Phillip PB Joubert de la Ferte:	ACAS (R)
Air Vice-Marshal KR Park:	AOC 11 Group
Air Vice-Marshal Sir CJ Quintin Brand:	AOC 10 Group
Air Vice-Marshal TL Leigh-Mallory:	AOC 12 Group
Air Commodore JC Slessor:	D of Planning
Air Commodore DF Stevenson:	DHO
Air Commodore OGWC Lywood:	PDD of Signals
Group Captain HG Crowe:	ADAT
Squadron Leader DRS Bader:	OC 242 Squadron
Wing Commander TN McEvoy:	
Mr JS Orme:	Secretaries

The presence of a junior Squadron Leader at this meeting is incredible. Dowding, Park and Brand were not told that Douglas Bader would be attending, nor did they think to take pilots with them. It has previously been claimed that Air Vice-Marshal Leigh-Mallory had told Bader to attend the Air Ministry in the hope that he (Leigh-Mallory) could 'get him in'. I would suggest that in view of the circumstances of Squadron Leader Bader's leave, his friendship with
Air Vice-Marshal Leigh-Mallory, the political involvement of his adjutant, Flight Lieutenant Peter Macdonald MP, and given that the meeting was Chaired by Air Vice-Marshal Douglas, his attendance was, in fact, premeditated in every way. The minutes of the meeting would have made even more interesting reading had Air Vice-Marshal Park perhaps taken along Squadron Leader 'Sailor' Malan, who had not only fought extensively under 11 Group conditions, but also with the Duxford Wing. In addition, Air Vice-Marshal Brand could have taken Squadron Leader Harry Fenton, the CO of 238 Squadron, or George Darley who had commanded 609 Squadron until October 4th, both squadrons having frequently reinforced 11 Group.
According to Brickhill, 'Dowding looked at him (Bader) severely'; that he might, as the

Commander-in-Chief was *astonished* that *Acting Squadron Leader* Bader should be present without his permission. The situation was a clear indication of the Big Wing's support at the Air Ministry, although Air Vice-Marshal Park later summed up Bader's involvement: 'he was used to make room for Leigh-Mallory'. Dowding agreed, but added that 'Leigh-Mallory had quite enough incentive of his own, without bringing Douglas Bader in'. The Commander-in-Chief was not to learn of Leigh-Mallory's statement to Park that he would 'move heaven and earth' to get Dowding 'sacked' until 1968; afterwards things must have become much clearer:-

I do not think Bader would ever have allowed himself consciously to become embroiled in such a move. It would probably have come as a shock to him to hear that Leigh-Mallory ever entertained such an idea. It was one thing to disagree with my views, and to express criticisms forcibly, but it was another altogether to intrigue against his own Commander-in-Chief, which is why I think the latter was out of the question.

It became rapidly obvious to Dowding and Park that the intention of the meeting was to push through the use of Wing formations as future standard operating procedure regardless of the arguments in favour of flexibility based upon 11 Group experiences. The dice were loaded from the outset. For the record, the minutes of this 'Meeting of Infamy' were as follows:-

DCAS explained that he was presiding at the meeting as CAS was unable to be present owing to indisposition.

2.   There were three propositions that he would like the meeting to consider:-

(i)   We wish to outnumber the enemy formations when we meet them

(ii)   We want our superior numbers to go into the attack with a co-ordinated plan of action so that the protecting fighters are engaged by one part of our force, leaving the bombers to be engaged by the remainder.

(iii) If possible we want the top layer of our fighter formation to have the advantage of height over the top layer of the enemy formation.

3.   This was the ideal, but it was obviously not always possible of attainment. For instance, the   time factor might not allow us to do what we wanted. It might be necessary to engage before he reached some vital objective, and in such cases there might not be time either to collect a superior force or to obtain superior height. DCAS then invited comments on the propositions he had outlined.

4.   AOC No 11 Group said that with the factors of time, distance and cloud that were often involved in the operations of No 11 Group it should not be laid down as a general principle that the "Wing" of fighters was the right formation with which to oppose attacks even those made in mass. He felt that the satisfactory use of the Wing by No 12 Group related to ideal conditions when the enemy bombers were in retreat, separated from their escort. No 11 Group, using formations of one or two squadrons had, on the other hand, quite recently obtained results against bombers on their way in which compared not unfavourably with those of the Wing sorties from No 12 Group.

5.   The AOC outlined to the meeting the principle that applied in No 11 Group for operations against enemy bombers with a fighter screen; this involved the use of squadrons in pairs at

different heights to engage separately the top fighter screen, the close escort and the bombers.

6.   AOC-In-C Fighter Command said that the great problem was to obtain early knowledge as to which of perhaps many raids was the major one. The Observer Corps did good work but were often baffled by the extreme height of enemy formations. He therefore attached the great importance to the development of the GL and LC organisation; Kent and Sussex would be covered by the end of November. This beam control had, of course, the disadvantage that the plot of only one formation at a time could be brought through into a Sector Operations Room, but it would be a big help when a big raid was known to be coming in.

7.   AOC No 11 Group referred to experiments he had been making with reconnaissance Spitfires which, in favourable conditions, were useful for obtaining early reports of big formations. The general installation of VHF would give better results from this reconnaissance work.

8.   Incidentally there had been two recent occurrences of extreme experienced pilots on reconnaissance being shot down over 25,000' by raids of which the RDF had given no indication.

9.   Experience showed that this reconnaissance work was not suitable for young pilots whose commendable keenness lead them to engage, rather than shadow, the enemy.

10. Reverting to the general question of fighter tactics the AOC said that to meet the present 'Tip-and-run' raids he felt that the only safe system was that now employed in No 11 Group. The reconnaissance Spitfire section was always backed by a strong Spitfire squadron patrolling on the Maidstone patrol line at 15,000', as soon as the first RDF warning was received this squadron went up to 30,000' and then to 35,000', so as to cover the ascent of other squadrons; One of these was always at instant readiness and, generally, the present situation demanded an exceptionally high degree of readiness throughout the Group.

11. AOC No 12 Group said that he would welcome more opportunities of using the Wing formation, operating, say, from Duxford and coming down to help No 11 Group. We could get a Wing of five squadrons into the air in six minutes and it could be over Hornchurch at 20,000' in 25 minutes. If this type of counter-attack intercepted a big formation only once in ten times the effort would none the less be worth it. On two recent occasions good results had again been obtained, once against fighters alone.

12. ACAS(R) drew attention to the shortness of some of the warnings that Groups had recently received.

13. AOC-In-C Fighter Command said that he had recently given written orders than an "Arrow" should go down on the operations table on receipt of the first "Counter"; It must be realised that the enemy's approach at great height presented a difficult problem.

14. AOC No 11 Group said that he could face the problem when it was a large bomber raid that was coming in. Could it not be accepted that if his Group had, say, 20 squadrons at readiness, that was generally sufficient to meet any enemy formation?

15. Discussions followed on this question and it was generally agreed that additional fighter

support would often be advantageous, since the more we could outnumber the enemy the more we should shoot down. The AOC-in-C said that he could, with his Group Commander, resolve any difficulties of control involved in sending such support. The other main difficulties to be met, it was agreed were those involving the time factor, though in this connection it was mentioned that the Me 109s carrying bombs had not, so far, been found over 22,000'.

16. Squadron Leader Bader said that from his practical experience time was the essence of the problem; If enough warning could be given to bring a large number of fighters into position there was no doubt they could get most effective results.

17. Air Marshal Portal enquired how such a local concentration might affect the responsibility of a Group Commander for the defence of all the area of his Group. AOC No 12 Group said that satisfactory plans were prepared to meet the possibility of other attacks coming in: He was satisfied that the concentration of a Wing was not incompatible with his general responsibilities as Group Commander.

18. This raised the question of whether some of No 12 Group's squadrons might be moved to No 10 Group which was, the C-in-C agreed, at present somewhat weak should any concentrated attack develop in the West. On the other hand, the protection of the Midlands and of the East Coast convoys was a big commitment for No 12 Group. Though it was a serious limitation he had, as C-in-C, to keep in mind the necessity of meeting every threat with some force.

19. Further discussion followed in which the importance of a long warning from the RDF was stressed. ACAS(R) said that was everything was being done to get the South-East coast RDF stations back to full efficiency following the damage suffered from enemy attacks. He mentioned the recent example when a 25 minutes steady RDF warning had not been received without delay in No 11 Group. It was decided that No 11 Group should have the services of a certain member of the Stanmore Research Station who had previously been of assistance to them.

20. DCAS said that he thought the views of the meeting could be summarised as followed:

    The employment of a large mass of fighters had great advantages, though it was not necessarily the complete solution to the problem of interception. In No 11 Group where the enemy was very close at hand both the methods described by AOC No 11 Group and those of AOC No 12 Group could, on occasion, be used with forces from the two Groups co-operating.

21. The AOC-in-C said that it would be arranged for No 12 Group "Wings" to participate freely in suitable operations over the 11 Group area. He would be able to resolve any complications of control. In reply to DHO the C-in-C said that co-operation of this kind could, in the present circumstances, hardly be employed generally throughout the Command as similar conditions seldom arose elsewhere.

22. With reference to the formal Agenda prepared for the meeting, the following observations were made:-

Items 1 and 2

Items 1 and 2 formed the subject of general discussion as shown above.

It was agreed that where conditions were suitable, wings of three squadrons should be employed against large enemy formations and that where further forces could be made available without detriment to other commitments larger fighter formations than wings should operate as tactical units.

It was agreed that it would , on occasion, be convenient to operate two wings together as a unit and that, for want of a better name, such a unit should provisionally be known as a 'Balbo'

Item 3

It was agreed that it would not always be practicable to operate the combined squadrons of a Wing from the same aerodrome, particularly in winter when aircraft might be confined to the runways. It was, however, agreed that all the squadrons of a Wing should operate from the same Sector.

Item 4

It was agreed that, as was now the practice, the Wing or 'Balbo' should be controlled by the Sector Commander. It was considered undesirable for a Squadron Commander from one of the squadrons to control such a formation.

Item 5

No major difficulty was foreseen in co-ordinating the operations of the two Wings of a 'Balbo'; it was agreed that one Sector Commander should control the two Wings, and that when possible the two Wings of a 'Balbo' could work on a common frequency.

Item 6

It was agreed that, in the conditions which enable the enemy to operate in mass formation, the fighter leader could dispense with sector control and that if he was given information about enemy movements he should be responsible for leading his formation to the battle.

Item 7

It was agreed that all squadrons of a 'Balbo' could operate effectively on the same frequency with HF R/T and that by using VHF a theoretical maximum of seven 'Balbos' could be operated.

Item 8

It was not thought that Wings could be regarded as permanent units to be moved complete, but that whenever possible the same squadrons should operate together as a Wing.

Item 9

It was agreed that where practicable, Wings should be deployed at stations from which they could gain advantage in height over the enemy without having to turn.

Item 10

23. AOC-in-C, Fighter Command, in amplification of his earlier Reports, gave the meeting an interim account of the development of the AI Beaufighter. As yet, troubles with the Mark IV AI Beaufighter, and its engines, were causing much unserviceability, but he was satisfied that the system was sound in principle.

24. The method of using searchlights in clumps promised good results and was about to be developed in the South.

25. DCAS and DHO referred to the grave problem of maintaining civil morale in London, in the face of continued attack, over the two or three months that might be expected to pass before the system outlined by the C-in-C was practically efficient. To bridge the gap during the intervening period it was suggested that a temporary Wing of two Defiant and two Hurricane squadrons should be formed to specialise in night fighting on a 1914-1918 basis. C-in-C Fighter Command said that continual experiments had been made on these lines, many of them by the AOC No 10 Group who had, since the last war, been a specialist in night interception, but with the height and speed of modern night raids the old methods had not so far proved effective. He felt certain that now the only sound method would be a combination of AI and GL (or LC); his Defiant squadrons were, however, now being normally employed on night interception. While it was his considered opinion that the diversion of Hurricanes to night interception was a dangerous and unsound policy, with our present strength of fighter Squadrons, he had nevertheless agreed with reluctance to implement the Air Staff decision to do so. These aircraft he felt, might show reasonable results in clear weather when the controlled clumps of searchlights began to work round London towards the end of November, but a real solution to the problem would only be found through the logical development of a system based on the two new radio aids to interception.

26. AOC-in-C said that he would be prepared to experiment with a "Fighter Night" over London, but this was not a course he could recommend. As people heard the fighters over London they would imagine that the noise represented so many more enemy aircraft, and the experiment would be justified only if it were successful.

27. A preliminary draft of the scheme which DCAS and DHO had explained to the meeting was handed to the C-in-C Fighter Command who undertook to examine it.

Copies of the minutes were sent to the Commander-in-Chief and the three Group AOCs present, and Squadron Leader Bader.

Air Chief Marshal Dowding had actually placed little importance on the meeting prior to attending. He felt that the Germans' tactics had changed so much that any thought of using massed fighter formations was from a defensive viewpoint 'out of the question'. To Dowding, the Air Staff were not looking ahead, as the meeting claimed, but to the past. It must have rapidly dawned upon him in the Air Council Room that this was a post-mortem of Fighter Command tactics, and that both he and Park were being called to account. The Commander-in-Chief thought then that he had 'possibly made a mistake in allowing my Group Commanders so much liberty in running their Groups in their own way'. Of the two Group commanders concerned, he said:-

I was entirely on Park's side without, up to that time, having had to say much. There was no need for me to say it. He was carrying out his assigned task, and there was no need for any comment from me. But I had come by then to realise that Leigh-Mallory was not conducting the affairs of his Group in the way I expected of him. I did not want to say you mustn't do this and you mustn't do that. I expected more of my Group Commanders. And that was why, by mid-October, I had come to realise I would have to do something about what was going on and get rid of Leigh-Mallory.

Many previous accounts have blamed the Commander-in-Chief for not acting sooner, but, being involved with matters on a higher level and following his policy of delegation, Dowding was largely unaware of 'what was going on'. He could not deny, however, that Air Vice-Marshal Park had written to him in precise terms on September 29th regarding his problems with Leigh-Mallory. The Commander-in-Chief took no action, but the crux of the matter can be traced back to Park's letter to Air Vice-Marshal Evill, the SASO, who failed to resolve matters at that early juncture. For this Evill had to accept responsibility, and one could question why he chose to take no action.

In his autobiography, 'Years of Command' (see Bibliography), Marshal of the Royal Air Force Lord Douglas of Kirtleside, as the DCAS later became, referred to the 'clash of personalities' between Air Vice-Marshal Park and Leigh-Mallory culminating in 'an unnecessarily heated argument' between them 'one afternoon at the Air Ministry'. Douglas claimed that from 'that time on, I became drawn into the argument, and just as Dowding's name has since become linked with Park's, so mine has become associated with Leigh-Mallory's'. As we have seen, however, the Commander-in-Chief was perfectly happy to be 'linked' with the loyal and able Air Vice-Marshal Park. Lord Douglas also stated that 'It has since become clear that Dowding, also, was not as deeply involved in what has come to be called the "Wings Controversy" as many writers and historians would have us believe'. Nevertheless, Dowding himself later said, 'I don't see how it would have been possible for me to have become more deeply involved'.

When later reporting on the meeting, Air Vice-Marshal Douglas wrote:-

At this meeting it was confirmed that Wings of three or more squadrons were the proper weapon to oppose large enemy formations when conditions are suitable......It was my view that the best way of defending an objective was not so much as to interpose a screen of fighters squadrons between that objective and the enemy, as to shoot down a high proportion of the enemy force sent to attack it, irrespective of whether the objective was bombed on a particular occasion or not.

The correspondence he was soon to receive would indicate that Dowding, Park and Brand objected. Reflecting on this 'Meeting of Infamy' I find it incredible that such experienced fighter leaders as Dowding and Park, who had just won the greatest defensive battle in the history of aerial warfare, should have been brought to task by men of far less experience and knowledge of fighter tactics.

On October 20th, Air Vice-Marshal Park wrote to Air Vice-Marshal Leigh-Mallory saying that he would be 'delighted' to have the Duxford Wing's assistance *provided* that it patrolled where requested until engaged (as did 10 Group's squadrons when called to reinforce). The Wing's position would also have to be communicated to 11 Group Control to avoid throwing the Observer Corps and AA units into confusion as had happened on Bader's previous unauthorised fighter sweeps over Kent. The AOC 12 Group refused, however, as he believed that he could maintain R/T control from Duxford and 'fix' the Wing's position south of the Thames by Direction Finding (DF).

On October 21st, Air Vice-Marshal Park sent a statement regarding the minutes of the October 17th meeting to the Air Ministry:-

The AOC 11 Group pointed out that the Air Staff Note and proposals attached to the Agenda were based on the experience of No 12 Group using Wing formations only on five occasions, whereas No 11 Group had accumulated five and a half months' experience in using Wings of three squadrons when the conditions were suitable. The first essential is adequate time to despatch, assemble, climb and move across country the Wing formation. The short warning given to squadrons stationed around London seldom gave sufficient time for the employment of Wing formations. To be effective, Wing formations required a sky mainly clear of cloud layers. Lastly, the possibility of employing squadrons in Wing formations was dependent on the State of Preparedness of squadrons at each Sector, and this was dictated by the intensity of enemy activity.

2. The primary aim of No 11 Group has been to engage the enemy bomber formations BEFORE they reached vital objectives, such as Aircraft Factories, Ammunition Factories, London, and Sector aerodromes. When conditions were suitable, squadrons were employed in Wings, otherwise in pairs, and in emergency in single squadrons if necessary to save an important factory from being bombed. On several occasions, single aircraft flown by Station Commanders had saved Sector aerodromes by means of head-on attacks which broke up the enemy bomber formation when about to attack. The AOC No 11 Group emphasised that if he had delayed engaging enemy bomb raids until after his squadrons had been put to operating height in Wing formations, they would seldom have intercepted before vital objectives had been effectively bombed, and that to have adopted this policy would probably have led to the German Long Range Bomber force achieving decisive results in their heavy scale attacks on the South-East of England during August and September. The DCAS, C-in-C, Fighter Command, and Air Marshal Portal agreed that the AOC No 11 Group had followed the correct policy, and must continue this against future mass attacks by bombers.

3. The AOC No 11 Group described how the Sectors on the North and South flanks of London had frequently despatched their squadrons in Wings of three into Kent in order to intercept bomb raids, but owing to inevitable delay in forming up and manoeuvring in Wing formation, these squadrons arrived in time to intercept the outgoing bomb raids. These outgoing raids had been fairly easy to deal with, because during their inward journey they had already been attacked by pairs of Spitfire Squadrons and Hurricane Squadrons who had effectively dealt with the high fighter screen and close escorting fighters, and frequently broken up the bomber formations which were retreating, having expended much of their ammunition. The AOC No 11 Group pointed out that the Duxford Wing operated under these favourable conditions, and therefore it was not sound to compare their results in air combat with squadrons stationed around London, who were forced to engage the incoming bomb raids, fighter screen and close escorts. In spite of the difficult conditions under which No 11 Group squadrons fought, mainly using pairs of squadrons, the results obtained on the last two occasions when the enemy employed his Long Range Bomber force compared very favourably with the results obtain by the Duxford Wings. For example, on September 27th, No 11 Group squadrons destroyed 102, plus 28 probably destroyed for a loss of 15 pilots, and on September 30th, destroyed 31 plus 20 probably destroyed, for a loss of only 2 pilots.

4. The AOC No 11 Group mentioned the danger to the high morale of squadrons in being

taught by No 12 Group that it is not safe to enter the South-Eastern area except in Wings of four or five squadrons, and that he had had to issue special instructions to squadrons recently trained in No 12 Group and now in No 11 Group emphasising the entirely different conditions under which squadrons located around London must operate, because of the close proximity of the German Air Force.

5.   The AOC No 11 Group stated that the arrangements in the last two months for obtaining quick reinforcement from No 10 Group had been entirely satisfactory, and had on a number of occasions resulted in saving from heavy bombing the aircraft factories at Brooklands, Kingston and Langley, as well as Sector aerodromes to the West and South-West of London. The reasons for this were that No 10 Group squadrons had always proceeded immediately to the place and height requested by No 11 Group, and had placed themselves under No 11 Group's direction, so avoiding confusion to the Observer Corps, Air Raids Warning system, and No 11 Group squadrons. Moreover, No 10 Group squadrons did not delay in forming up in Wings which would have prevented their arriving in time to engage the enemy before he had bombed the vital factories.

6.   The AOC No 11 Group then proceeded to describe the confusion that had been caused to the fighter defences, the ground defences and the ARW system in the South-East through his Group not being informed when Duxford Wings had been unable to patrol the area requested, but had proceeded unknown to No 11 Group to the Kentish coast between 20,000 and 25,000', thus causing new raids to be originated by the Observer Corps and the AA units. This had not only prolonged the air raid warnings, but had necessitated the despatch of No 11 Group squadrons to intercept friendly formations which had been reported as fresh raids, indicating a third or fourth wave of attack.

7.   The AOC No 11 Group explained that he had not made a practice of calling for reinforcements from No 10 and No 12 Groups if he had adequate squadrons to meet enemy bomber attacks, because he understood that the other Groups had only sufficient squadrons to meet daylight attacks in their area. As No 12 Group stated they could always spare four or five squadrons from their area, he agreed, however, to call on them for a Wing whenever it was reported to be available in time to make effective interception, provided it would go where requested and No 11 Group could be constantly informed of the position of the reinforcing Wing.

Air Vice-Marshal Douglas refused to allow Park's comments to be added, nor did he consider the AOC 11 Group's remarks concerning the Duxford Wing's failure to do what was asked of it to be 'appropriate' to the minutes.

Air Chief Marshal Dowding objected to a statement in which it was said that he agreed with a particular point when he did not: 'Please do not say that I agree, reluctantly or otherwise. I am carrying out orders which I believe to be dangerous and unsound with our present strength of fighter squadrons.' This was also ignored.

Air Vice-Marshal Brand also suggested amendments to the minutes. These too were ignored. He also wrote to Air Vice-Marshal Park, thanking him for his 'paper on the recent results of the employment of the Duxford Wing':-

They do not surprise me, and I am fully in agreement with your conclusion regarding the operations of No 11 Group.

The only conclusion possible therefore is that the minutes were a cover-up. Air Vice-Marshals Douglas and Leigh-Mallory had orchestrated the session to promote their inflexible and impractical Big Wing tactics as Fighter Command's standard defensive method; they did so safe in the knowledge of their gathering political support.

Despite the pressures imposed by both the Germans and the 'enemy within', on October 21st Air Vice-Marshal Park made time to issue the following memorandum to his Sectors regarding '11 Group Offensive Sweeps':-

When weather conditions are suitable and enemy activities justify their use, the Group may order offensive sweeps to be made.

2.   At present during daylight there is almost continuous enemy air activity about the French coast and within the area Calais-Cap Griz Nez - Dungeness - Dover. This activity may at any time develop into a mass attack by enemy bombers under cover of fighters. The enemy cannot, however, assemble and launch mass raids from North West France later than about one-and-a-half hours before sunset and land back in daylight. It is proposed, therefore, to make use of this period whenever possible to surprise the enemy by making a sweep in strength through the Dover Straits.

3.   For this purpose a Wing of three squadrons, from North Weald or Northolt, may be ordered to provide sweeps. The executive order for the despatch of these sweeps will be issued by the Group Controller on the authority of the AOC.

4.   Wings are to assemble, squadrons in company, in the vicinity of their bases and proceed to the area of sweep at a height of 25,000'.

5.   Dispositions within the Wing, the direction and method of approach to the sweep are to be decided by the Wing Leader in the light of the weather conditions prevailing.

6.   Units comprising a sweep are not to remain in the vicinity of hostile territory, but are to make their sweep from SW to NE, engage any hostile aircraft encountered, and are to return immediately to their bases unless otherwise ordered by Group Commander.

7.   Fighter cover for the withdrawal of a sweep will be arranged on each occasion by the Group Controller as follows:-

   (i)   Two Spitfire squadrons, on common R/T frequency, patrolling one squadron at 30,000', one at 25,000', on the Canterbury patrol line during the sweep. The Group Controller is to withdraw these squadrons to the Maidstone Patrol Line as soon as the sweep has withdrawn inland over Kent.

   (ii)   Two Hurricane or Spitfire squadrons on Readiness Patrol at 15,000' on the Maidstone Patrol Line to counter any late raids by the enemy.

8.   In case of additional cover for London area being required during the course of, or withdrawal of a sweep, squadrons at the disengaged sectors will be brought to a specially high state of Preparedness.

The foregoing emphasises yet again that Air Vice-Marshal Park was more than capable of employing his fighters in strength and in an offensive capacity *when* the circumstances dictated.

On October 25th, Air Vice-Marshal Leigh-Mallory requested permission to send the Wing into Kent. Air Vice-Marshal Park agreed, and asked the Wing to patrol the Sheerness - Maidstone line at 25,000' unless the enemy was sighted. Once the Wing had passed south of the Thames, however, Uxbridge received no reports on its position. 19 Squadron ORB:-

No E/A seen, although some thought they saw a dogfight. Believed to be 11 Group.

Afterwards, Air Vice-Marshal Leigh-Mallory agreed to the operating procedures made by Air Vice-Marshal Park five days previously.

On October 26th, Sir Archibald Sinclair, Secretary of State for Air, visited both Duxford and Fowlmere to discuss the Wing situation with the 12 Group pilots. This visit was to have far-reaching effects. On this day, 242 Squadron moved permanently from Coltishall to Duxford.

Air Vice-Marshal Leigh-Mallory visited 242 Squadron on October 28th, and 'Congratulated pilots on efficiency of squadron which he said was equal if not superior to any squadron in the RAF'.

The following day the Duxford Wing patrolled the Sheerness - Maidstone line twice without event. On the day's third scramble, at 1615, 'Squadron Leader Bader's radio u/s so the Wing was unable to set favourably' (19 ORB). The 11 Group report on the day's fighting, compiled from data available immediately after the attack, provides essential information concerning both RDF warning and the Duxford Wing's involvement:-

<u>Area of Attack.</u>

1.   About 200 E/A were engaged in the attack which was made in three waves.

In the first wave about 30 E/A crossed the North Foreland at 1624 hrs, followed by a second formation of 20 which flew across the Estuary to the River Crouch. Some of these reached North Weald which was dive-bombed at about 1700 hrs.

The second wave followed almost immediately in two formations of 30 and 20 E/A, but did not penetrate further than the Dover-Deal area.

At 1646 hrs, the third wave of three formations crossed the coast and headed towards Biggin Hill. In this attack, several Italian aircraft were reported. This is the first occasion on which the Axis Partner's Air Force has been recorded as taking part in daylight raids on this country.

<u>RDF Information.</u>

2.   The first plot of Raid 50, 15 plus at 6,000', appeared over Cap Gris Nez at 1601 hrs. The raid reached North Weald about 1700 hrs.

The first plot of Raid 4, 12 plus (no height) appeared over Dunkerque at 1606 hrs. At 1617 hrs the strength was increased to 50 plus. This raid was lost in the Chelmsford area at 1648 hrs.

The first plot of Raid 3 appeared 10 miles NE of Dunkerque as 12 plus, no height, at 1607 hrs. This raid was lost over Margate at 1628 hrs.

The first plot of Raid 9 (Bombers), 20 plus, no height appeared near Arras at 1625 hrs and reached the Dover area at 1633 hrs.

The first plot of Raid 12 appeared as 4 plus, no height, at Cap Gris Nez. No RDF warning was received of Raids 60, 61 and 62, which were picked up by the Observer Corps and plotted in the Tonbridge - Dungeness area.

Observer Corps Information.

3.   Observer Corps picked up the enemy formations and plotted them accurately. The tracks of Raids 4 and 50 were lost in the North Weald area.

They reported two enemy formations which crossed the coast near Dungeness, and a third, No 60, which appeared inland in the same area. Those three raids totalled approximately 60 aircraft. Raid 61 appeared at 1646 hrs and Raid 62 at 1647 hrs.

Weather.

4.   Clouds 3/10ths at 3/4,000', thin layer at 27,000'. Visibility good below low cloud.

Action by Group Controller.

5.   At 1607 hrs, Nos 17 and 46 Squadrons were ordered to patrol North Weald at 15,000', and at 1619 hrs to proceed to Maidstone Patrol Line at 25,000'.
      At 1615 hrs, Nos 501 and 253 Squadrons were ordered to patrol Brooklands at 15,000' and at 1630 hrs to patrol Biggin Hill Patrol Line on Readiness Patrol.
      At 1621 hrs, Nos 222 and 92 Squadrons from Hornchurch and Biggin Hill respectively were ordered to patrol Hornchurch at 15,000'. At 1626 hrs, No 74 Squadron was ordered to patrol Hornchurch at 15,000'. At 1626 hrs No 74 Squadron was ordered to patrol Biggin Hill for aerodrome protection. At 1631 hrs, No 229 Squadron was ordered to patrol Northolt.
      1636 hrs Nos 249 and 257 Squadrons were ordered to patrol North Weald at 15,000' for aerodrome protection. At 1711 hrs Nos 41 and 603 Squadrons were ordered to patrol Rochford at 20,000'.
      In addition the No 12 Group Wing took off from Duxford at 1608 hrs. They originally were asked for by No 11 Group to patrol Maidstone - Sheerness, then to intercept two raids that were crossing the Thames Estuary heading for Essex before attacking North Weald. Later No 12 Group was asked to make a sweep through North Kent.

Action by Fighter Squadrons.

6.   At 1630 hrs No 12 Group Wing was reported to be over Hornchurch at 25,000', proceeding towards Sheerness. Immediately two raids that had been approaching Sheerness turned Northwards across the Thames Estuary; No 12 Group was requested to intercept these raids between North Weald and the coast, as it was feared that the enemy was about to attack fighter aerodromes in Essex. As the Duxford Wing continued, however, to proceed towards Sheerness, Hornchurch was requested to try and inform it by R/T of the new patrol line, but was unable to communicate with the Wing because of continuous R/T traffic between the Wing and Duxford. Immediately it was evident that the Duxford Wing might fail to intercept the raids, a pair of No 11 Group squadrons were ordered from East Kent to try and overtake, but unfortunately the enemy reached North Weald first and bombed the aerodrome causing some casualties and damage. The enemy, however, was intercepted by No 11 Group squadrons immediately after completing his bombing and heavy casualties were inflicted.

Clearly, the significant point in the foregoing paragraph is 11 Group's inability to control the Wing because of the 'continuous R/T traffic between the Wing and Duxford'. Air Marshal Sir Denis Crowley-Milling once enthused to me regarding 'DB's constant chatter on the R/T', which he, and other young pilots, 'found totally inspiring'. This is emphasised in the film 'Reach for the Sky', but it has not previously been indicated that this jamming of the airwaves actually prevented the Wing from being vectored against an incoming raid: loss of life was the result. Furthermore, had 12 Group been patrolling the north bank of the Thames, as the System had originally perceived, the Duxford Wing would have been well situated to intercept the raid against North Weald. The 11 Group report continues:-

Immediately it was seen that the Duxford Wing was not going to intercept the raids, 12 Group was requested to make a sweep through North Kent to intercept two more raids heading towards Biggin Hill aerodrome, but the AOC No 12 Group recalled the Duxford Wing because of a report that the weather was no longer fine at Duxford and he was afraid of difficulty in landing so many squadrons at one aerodrome. The Duxford Wing, therefore, missed an interception with these two raids which fortunately did not proceed far inland, probably because they saw additional No 11 Group squadrons climbing in the Biggin Hill area.

After describing the various 11 Group interceptions, claims were reported as:-

Enemy casualties were 16 destroyed, 6 probably destroyed and 5 damaged, for the loss of 1 RAF pilot who was killed.

In fact, eight Me 109s were lost over England, so overclaiming, in relation to aircraft destroyed, was an acceptable 2:1. The 11 Group pilot killed was Sergeant Girdwood of 257 Squadron whose Hurricane had been hit by bombs whilst scrambling from North Weald during II/LG2's fighter-bomber attack which 12 Group failed to intercept. Despite having not engaged, however, the Duxford Wing had not fared well. Shortly after take-off and just one mile from Duxford, Pilot Officer Emil Fechtner DFC collided with Flight Lieutenant Maly; the former, who had only received his DFC the previous day, was killed, and the latter was slightly injured in a forced-landing. Over Essex, some members of 19 Squadron reported seeing seven Me 109s above; back at Fowlmere, Lane's pilots waited in vain for the return of Sub-Lieutenant 'Admiral' Blake, who was acting as a weaver behind the squadron, and it was assumed that he had been picked off by the enemy fighters. The ORB recorded 'He was found near Chelmsford. It is a great loss to the Squadron as he was very well liked by us all as well as a pilot of exceptional ability'. In all probability, Blake had been shot down by *Leutnant* Hubert Huppertz of III/JG51. Ivor Linsdell had watched the action from the ground:-

I lived two miles west of Chelmsford and was in the garden when I heard AA fire and saw a smoke cloud low in the West and guessed that North Weald, about 14 miles away, was being hit. I watched the grey overcast and hoped that some action would materialise - I was aged 14 and an enthusiastic aircraft spotter! Soon an Me 109 appeared going very fast and passed over at just 200' - I could see a plume of smoke or oil streaming from underneath it. I could see the pilot clearly but he was gone in a flash, before I could wave to him, something we kids always did to any low flying aircraft. Once, to our immense joy, a Hurricane pilot slid back his canopy and raised his hand in reply to our frantic waving. We were convinced that he was telling us that he had shot a German down, he was certainly going back to North Weald after action. Within a few minutes of the 109 passing, I heard the noise of an aero-engine under stress above the clouds and to the south. Then came the hammer of cannon fire. I was looking towards Chelmsford and I saw a Spitfire emerge from the cloud blanket, diving vertically. I knew that it was not going to pull out. The engine screamed and continued for a second or two after the smoke arose, then I heard the thud of the impact. It took me less than 10 minutes of furious pedalling to reach the crash site. The Spitfire had crashed into 'Oakhurst' at London Road, Chelmsford, and the house, garage and Spitfire were all mangled together. I arrived just as two bodies were being loaded into an ambulance. A piece of wing in the garden next door was the only piece recognisable as part of a Spitfire. Some people looked around the ruins of the house whilst I scrabbled around looking for a souvenir - bullets were always highly prized. I lifted up a large garage door and there lay a forearm clad in a dark blue sleeve that had a thin gold band around the cuff. From the sleeve projected an amazingly clean white shirt cuff with a gold link; the fingers were heavily nicotine stained and on one finger was a gold ring. The sight upset me - it wasn't the first piece of human remains I had seen that summer, but I suppose it was the surprise of the discovery and knowing that it was a Spitfire pilot which so disturbed me. I put the garage door back down over the arm, crept out through the back fence and went home. At the time I knew that it was not an RAF uniform, so decided that it must have been a Czech or a Pole. The memory of that day has remained with me all my life.

The 'Admiral' was to be the last pilot lost by the Duxford Wing during the Battle of Britain.

Not surprisingly, Air Vice-Marshal Leigh-Mallory was criticised by Bentley Priory for his handling of October 29th. In addition to the Wing's failure to intercept the raid against North Weald, whilst the Wing had been over the 11 Group area, airfields in East Anglia were bombed. It led to a rebuke: 'Leigh-Mallory must not neglect his own responsibilities in future'.

In Air Vice-Marshal Park's report regarding this final phase of battle, he wrote:-

Use of Mass Formations - Big Wings and "Balbos":

The Air Ministry held a conference ... to examine a proposal that Wings should be adopted as standard formation for air fighting, and that wherever possible, Balbos - mass formations of six squadrons - should be employed against enemy raids on this country. These proposals arose as a result of the remarkable results claimed in air combat by No 12 Group, employing its squadrons in Wings of four and five squadrons on five occasions in September, operating from Duxford. Good results were reported against fighters as well as bombers.

As a result of the Air Ministry conference, the Duxford Wing was invited to operate in No 11 Group area on every possible occasion during the last half of October. In view of the results obtained in No 11 Group when employing mass formations, the operations of the Duxford Wing have been watched with close interest. The attached table of patrols by the Duxford Wing shows that in ten sorties, it effected one interception and destroyed one enemy aircraft. On only few days was the weather considered fit for the Duxford Wing to operate. On several days that were unfit for these large formations, the squadrons in No 11 Group were operating at high pressure, in pairs.

The intensity of the air fighting over No 11 Group territory during the second half of October can be gauged by the fact that its squadrons accounted for 83 enemy aircraft destroyed, plus 62 probably destroyed, plus 66 damaged; a total of 211 aircraft accounted for in the period covered by the attached table, Appendix 'B'. Moreover, during this short period, the squadrons in No 11 Group by successful interception, prevented scores of enemy raids from proceeding inland and

Appendix B.

14th October to 2nd November, 1940.

Operations in 11 Group area of Duxford BALBOS - October 1940.

	Time of Request.	Patrol Requested.	Time Plotted as Reached Patrol.	Time Withdrawn by No.12 Group.	Time on Patrol.	Interceptions Reported by 12 Group.	Remarks.
1.	11.30	Maidstone	12.15	12.20	5 mins.	n i l	Broke up and returned to base on sighting Pair of 11 Group Sqdns. above to the East.
2.	offered at 11.00	Maidstone Sheerness	12.00	12.35	35 mins.	n i l	
3.	Requested 11.21.	Patrol Maidstone Sheerness for 1 hour	12.15	12.40.	25 mins.	n i l	Withdrawn due to lack of oxygen. Later patrol requested, but not carried out owing to Duxford weather.
4.	16.30	Patrol in Kent	(assembled over Duxford only.)	-	-	n i l	Did not leave Duxford area owing to R/T trouble.
5.	Offered at 16.30	Maidstone Line	17.20	17.25	5 mins.	n i l	
6.	Requested 10.30	Maidstone then Canterbury.	11.34	11.48	14 mins.	n i l	
7.	Requested at 1315 for 1400.	Gravesend Maidstone	14.17	14.55	35 mins.	n i l	
8.	At 15.45 requested patrol from 16.30.	Maidstone Line	16.35	17.05	30 mins.	1 Me.109 destroyed at 17.00 nr. Lympne.	Requested when 25,000' over Hornchurch to intercept 2 raids crossing Thames near Sheppey which later bombed N. Weald. 2 11 Gp. Sqdns. intercepted.
9.	Requested at 1115 for 1200.	Sheerness - Maidstone.	12.09	12.35	26 mins.	n i l	Left Patrol line owing to shortage of oxygen.
10.	Requested at 1345 for 1430-1530.	Sheerness - Maidstone later Canterbury - Hawkinge.	14.46	15.30	44 mins.	n i l	Offered Manston and Hawkinge to refuel as 2 raids approaching from French Coast as Wing withdrawing.

Average Time to reach Sheerness: 56 mins.   Average Patrol: 24 mins.

Air Vice-Marshal Park's analysis of 12 Group Wing operations following the 'Meeting of Infamy'.

bombing vital objectives. On numerous occasions the enemy turned about and retreated at speed before our fighters could come within effective range.

From watching the operations of the Duxford Wings of four squadrons during the second half of October, confirmation was obtained of the lessons previously learned in No 11 Group in the employment of smaller Wing formations. Other lessons appear to have been brought out as under:-

1)   Mass formations require the assistance of good Sector Controllers if they are to effect interceptions of enemy fighter formations;

2)   Large Wings of four of five squadrons suffer serious difficulties in R/T communications;

3)   Increasing the number of squadrons in a Wing does not appear to increase the chances of interceptions or the area of search effectively covered;

4)   It is inadvisable to concentrate four or five squadrons on an aerodrome in the autumn, because all are likely to be weather-bound together;

5)   The maximum size of a Wing should be three squadrons, not four or five as previously practised in the North.

In conclusion, Air Vice-Marshal Park wrote:-

I wish to pay high tribute to the fine offensive spirit of pilots in all squadrons during the past two months of difficult fighting. During the second phase of operations, the morale of our pilots has been severely tested, because the enemy has had a great advantage in superior performance at high altitude in the Fighter versus Fighter battle. When well led, however, our pilots have out-fought the enemy at all heights. With few exceptions, Squadron Commanders and Flight Commanders have quickly adapted themselves to the changing tactics of the enemy.

The enemy's superior numbers enabled him to throw our fighter forces on the defensive, resulting in the majority of the fighting in the past three months taking place either over British territory or close to our shores. Our constant aim, however, has been to intercept the enemy as far forward as possible and make him shed his bombs harmlessly in open country or in the sea. The aim of all squadrons in the Group now is to inflict such heavy punishment that the enemy will find it too hot to send his fighter patrols or daylight raids inland over home territory, and our pilots will not be satisfied until the air over the Homeland is again free of the German Air Force.

On October 31st 1940, the Battle of Britain was officially deemed to have come to an end. Air Chief Marshal Dowding considered that the Battle had been won when Hitler's plans for invasion were abandoned, but German historians argue that the Battle was not over until May 1941 when the *Führer* turned his territorial ambitions eastward. Whichever viewpoint is accepted, the fact remains that Fighter Command had denied the numerically superior *Luftwaffe* aerial supremacy over England. Despite latter day attempts to put the Battle of Britain into 'perspective', let us be clear on two things: firstly, Fighter Command won the Battle of Britain, and secondly, without that victory there would have been no other battles. Shortly before the Battle, the Prime Minister made the prediction that 'if we fail, then the whole world, including the United States, including all that we have known and cared for, will sink into the abyss of a new Dark Age made more sinister, and perhaps more protracted, by the lights of perverted science'. Let us understand that, for that is why the world owes so much to the Few.

Unfortunately for Dowding and Park, the true architects of this great victory, the political battle was already lost.

CHAPTER NINE

A Political Disgrace

Although the Battle of Britain was officially over, there was no sudden cessation of the German fighter sweeps which had been the main feature of the enemy's tactics throughout October. In fact, the two fighter forces continued to clash over the south-east of England and the Channel until early 1941. The Duxford Wing continued its patrols, but these were to be largely uneventful.

On November 3rd, Air Vice-Marshal Douglas wrote to Air Chief Marshal Dowding enclosing a copy of notes made by the Parliamentary Under-Secretary of State for Air, Harold Balfour, following recent visits to Duxford by both Balfour and the Secretary of State for Air, Sir Archibald Sinclair. Balfour wrote that his visit confirmed what Sinclair himself had gathered a week previously, namely that the Wing was being requested too late and that it was being under-used. He accused Park of being jealous that the Wing would shoot down 'his' Germans. Wing Commander Woodhall and Squadron Leader Bader had enthused about the Big Wing to the politicians. The latter insisted that given time to gain height, he was 'absolutely certain' of 'taking enormous tolls'. In his letter, Air Vice-Marshal Douglas stated that the differences between the two Group Commanders had still not been resolved, and he was not only 'inclined to support' Leigh-Mallory but also believed that Park showed an aversion to 'poachers'. The DCAS had also communicated Mr Balfour's concern that Squadron Leader Bader might be disciplined 'for having been so outspoken'.

The Commander-in-Chief tasked his SASO to investigate the matters raised by the DCAS, and Air Vice-Marshal Evill consequently raised four points:-

(i)   12 Group was not given all available RDF information.
(ii)   12 Group was not given all available Observer Corps information.
(iii)   12 Group was not being called until it was too late.
(iv)   Consequently its opportunities were lost.

In responding, Air Chief Marshal Dowding was forced to make yet another protest. Central to that protest were two men who had reflected great courage as combat pilots: The Under-Secretary of State for Air, Harold Balfour (who had flown in the Great War), and Squadron Leader Douglas Bader. Previously, Dowding had always dealt with facts, but he now considered that the personal element had intruded too far. Just how far is reflected at the outset of Dowding's response, dated November 6th:-

I agree that this operation is causing so much friction and ill-feeling that I must withdraw the control of combined operations between Nos 11 and 12 Groups from the Group Commanders themselves and issue the orders through my own Operations Room.

Regarding Balfour:-

.... the story which Balfour has collected by his direct methods is wrong in its conclusions and in the facts on which these conclusions are based.

Dowding also pointed out that 12 Group had always received, direct from Bentley Priory, all available RDF information covering both southern Kent and Cap Gris-Nez. The claim that 12 Group was not supplied with all Observer Corps information was equally untrue; 12 Group had been using an 'unauthorised system' which had been stopped by the Southern Area Observer Corps Commandant. On the question of 12 Group being called upon late, he wrote:-

My criticism is that the recent conference and all the fuss that has been made has resulted in 11 Group calling for assistance from 12 Group not only too early, but without the slightest excuse.

As the Air Staff had apparently overlooked 12 Group's primary function and geographical responsibilities, the C-in-C pointed out that the continual use of certain squadrons with the 12 Group Wing:-

... diverts them from the normal tasks of No 12 Group which are the defence of its own area, including some highly important industrial districts..... I am inclined to the conclusion that for the moment in this present phase, the use of the Duxford Wing is a misemployment of a valuable element of our very limited strength.

Dowding had at last realised that Air Vice-Marshal Leigh-Mallory was seeking to further his own interests by exploiting every opportunity to denigrate 11 Group:-

Leigh-Mallory has many commitments of his own.....and should 'keep his eye on the boat'.

Air Vice-Marshal Leigh-Mallory at a party in 1941 with Spitfire pilots of 609 Squadron.
(Author's Collection)

Linked to the AOC 12 Group's personal behaviour was, of course, his having allowed his subordinates free expression to politicians and officials from outside Fighter Command. That political leaders were provided with such criticism, and were allowed to accept and disseminate it without consulting the Commander-in-Chief, Dowding felt most 'improper':-

There remains the question of the Under-Secretary of State listening to the accusations of a junior officer against the Air Officer Commanding Group, and putting them on paper with the pious hope that that officer will not get into trouble..... Balfour has been in the service and ought to know better.

Dowding blamed Bader for initiating a great deal of the controversy:-

.... a good deal of the ill-feeling which has been engendered in this controversy has been directly due to young Bader, who, whatever his other merits, suffers from overdevelopment of the critical faculty.

Dowding added that he had enormous regard for Bader's courage, but the matters in question had *nothing* to do with gallantry in the air. He added:-

This might give an opportunity of moving young Bader to another station where he would be kept in better control. His amazing gallantry will protect him from disciplinary action if it can possibly be avoided.

There can be no question that for Air Chief Marshal Dowding, the sooner the triangle linking Leigh-Mallory, Woodhall and Bader was broken the better.

There can be no doubt that Mr Balfour should have listened more critically to Woodhall and Bader, especially as neither had ever served in 11 Group. Nor did Balfour or Sinclair visit 11 Group to ascertain the accuracy of the allegations of poor morale in Park's squadrons. Group Captain Gerry Edge served in 11 Group throughout virtually the whole of the Battle of Britain:-

There was never anything wrong with our morale in 11 Group. Certainly we were hard pressed, but such was the nature of the Battle of Britain.

Unfortunately, Dowding's acute displeasure and *totally* justified comments were the final nail: his signature on this forthright response to the DCAS provoked the wrath of the Air Staff and politicians alike. Having sent the letter, Dowding got on with his job: the night blitz was in full fury.

As Air Chief Marshal Dowding responded to the DCAS during the morning of November 6th, the Duxford Wing was patrolling between Dover and Deal when Me 109s of II and III/JG26 swept in on a *Freie Jagd*. Although claims were made, no 109s crashed in England during this engagement. Between 1427 and 1620 hrs, 42 more JG26 Me 109s intruded over Kent. Over Canterbury, 310 Squadron was 'bounced': five Hurricanes were hit, two pilots baling out whilst the others crash-landed. Such was the ferocity of the attack that only Flight Lieutenant McKnight of 242 Squadron brought his guns to bear. He shot down *Feldwebel* Scheidt of 1/JG26, the 109 crashing at Birchington. It is believed, however, that this enemy fighter was also that claimed by 19 Squadron's Flying Officer Haines. 242 Squadron's Sub-Lieutenant Gardner crash-landed with a damaged Hurricane, and Pilot Officer Hart was killed by *Oberleutnant* Johannes Seifert, *Staffelkapitän* of 3/JG26. 19 Squadron's Flight Lieutenant Lawson was flying the new cannon-armed Spitfire, and claimed a 109 which 'literally fell to pieces', although no candidate can be found amongst actual losses. *Hauptmann* Rolf Pingel, *Gruppenkommandeur* of I/JG26 shot down and killed 19 Squadron's Pilot Officer Hradil, who crashed in flames off Southend pier. Flight Sergeant Unwin was to claim an 'He 113', but his own Spitfire was severely damaged, quite possibly being the Spitfire claimed by *Hauptmann* Gerhard Schöpfel, *Gruppenkommandeur* of III/JG26. The Wing had not fared well in this engagement against enemy fighters: two pilots had been killed, while a further five aircraft had been shot down together with one more damaged. German records indicate that the 109 shared by McKnight and Haines is the only German loss which can be attributed to the Wing.

Pilot Officer Frantisek Hradil, another Czech serving with 19 Squadron, killed in action on November, 5th, 1940. (Author via Flight Lieutenant RL Jones)

On November 8th, the Duxford Wing was patrolling over Canterbury when Squadron Leader Lane became the victim of 'Friendly Fire'; he wrote in his log book:-

Sighted Me 109s over Canterbury and turned to give chase. Hurricane squadron chased <u>us</u> and their leader put a burst into my engine!! Apparently CO of one of the North Weald squadrons. Blacked out, then minus oxygen forced-landed at Eastchurch OK. Jennings escorted me down and refused to leave me. Damn good of him.

The offending Hurricane pilot was Squadron Leader Lionel Gaunce DFC, CO of 46 Squadron. At the time, Squadron Leader Pat Wells was a Flying Officer serving with 249 Squadron, a Hurricane unit which shared North Weald with 46:-

After this incident, Squadron Leader Bader arrived from Duxford. He first approached the 249 Squadron dispersal but we told him that we knew nothing about it, so he then taxied over to 46 Squadron. Whilst he did so, we telephoned their dispersal to let them know that Bader was coming. I dread to think what happened when he get over there as he was fuming!

On November 16th, Air Chief Marshal Dowding received a telephone call from the Air Minister, Sir Archibald Sinclair, of whom he had been critical in his letter to the DCAS of November 6th:-

He told me that I was to relinquish my Command immediately. I asked what was meant by 'immediately', and was told that it would take effect within the next day or so. Since that was tantamount to being given 24 hours notice, and verbally at that, I pointed out that it was perfectly absurd that I should be relieved of my Command in this way unless it was thought that I had committed some major crime or whatever. But all I could get in reply was that the decision had been reached, and that was that, with no explanation for such a precipitate step being taken.

Sinclair also told Dowding that he was not to take any disciplinary action against Squadron Leader Bader. The Air Minister also advised that Dowding's replacement was to be none other than Sholto Douglas. The facts prove beyond question that Dowding's sacking - for that is what it was - *was* due to the Big Wing Controversy, despite what others would have us believe.

Many previous authors, particularly those sympathetic to Air Vice-Marshal Leigh-Mallory and Squadron Leader Bader, and who have allowed their judgement to be emotionally affected, have claimed that Dowding's dismissal was more a matter of his natural retirement. In August 1940, the Air Staff had extended Dowding's appointment without imposing any time limit; so far as he was concerned, having defeated the Germans during the day fighting over England, he was now in a position to develop the means of winning the nocturnal air battle. Others have argued that it was the night-bombing question which caused Dowding's downfall, as over this issue Viscount Trenchard was calling for his dismissal. Once again, however, 'Stuffy' had already researched the way forward and was awaiting the arrival of new weapons to enable victory to be achieved.

Incredibly, the Air Ministry never even sent Dowding a letter informing him that he was to give up his Command, and no mention was made of what he had achieved during his appointment and of his victory in the Battle of Britain. Dowding appreciated that if the Air Staff and politicians had convinced themselves that he was wrong about the Big Wing then he *had* to go, but 'it was the way in which it was done that hurt, as if I had been some kind of indifferent Commander.' Even the Prime Minister had no knowledge of the situation; as Churchill later told Dowding, the first he knew of it was when he read of Dowding's replacement in the papers (although coming from a man so directly involved with the aspects of high command, that has to be considered surprising). As Dowding himself said, 'They just got rid of me.'

Lord Dowding, but never a Marshal of the RAF.
(Author via Lady Odette Dowding)

On November 17th, Air Chief Marshal Dowding received a letter from the CAS:-

> With reference to your recent correspondence with Douglas about a report made by Balfour after conversation with Woodhall and Bader, the Secretary of State has directed that no reproof should be offered to either of the two officers on account of the conversations referred to.

Dowding was stunned. The DCAS had requested that he take steps to rectify the differences between the 11 and 12 Group AOCs, and he had responded in a perfectly correct manner. Clearly the Air Staff had considered the views of the Commander-in-Chief against 'those of one of my young squadron commanders. Those of the young squadron commander prevailed.'

On November 17th, Air Vice-Marshal Leigh-Mallory reported to Bentley Priory regarding the operation of the 12 Group Wing. Therein he refuted allegations made by 11 Group that the Wing largely arrived 'only in time to intercept bomber formations retreating from objectives in the London area after they had already been attacked and lost their close escort'. Although the 12 Group AOC was to claim that the Wing had engaged the enemy before 11 Group units on every occasion except the action fought on September 27th, our intensive analysis of the relevant combats indicates otherwise. Air Vice-Marshal Leigh-Mallory emphasised the problems inherent in obtaining accurate and early intelligence, the accuracy of claims having been previously confirmed by Evill some extent. The report continued:-

.... therefore whilst the enemy is employing large formations the largest formation which it is possible to control should be employed to oppose them. Up to date insufficient experience has been had with large formations, but it would seem possible to operate a formation made up of up to six squadrons operating in two Wings. Communications within and without a very large formation must of necessity be more difficult than with a small formation, but careful organisation, strict R/T discipline and the use of VHF can produce satisfactory communications.

In accepting that three squadrons, and not five or even six, were the most practical for a Wing formation, Air Vice-Marshal Leigh-Mallory had at last grasped a fundamental principle which Air Vice-Marshal Park had been reporting on for some time. In conclusion, the 12 Group AOC claimed that the operations of the Duxford Wing 'proved beyond any doubt that':-

(a)   a formation of fighters up to 60 can be controlled satisfactorily.
(b)   when such a formation does make contact with large mixed enemy formations, very
        heavy casualties can be inflicted on the enemy with very small loss to ourselves.

The subsequent operations of the Wing prove most conclusively that timely and adequate information is just as essential to the successful operation of a Wing of fighters as to any other fighting force.

The evidence presented in previous chapters concerning the Big Wing's operation and performance provides the reader with the opportunity to decide just how accurate Air Vice-Marshal Leigh-Mallory's conclusions were.

On November 25th, Air Chief Marshal Dowding was replaced as Commander-in-Chief by Sholto Douglas, who was promoted to Air Marshal. Dowding's only failing was that he should have realised how serious the 11 and 12 Group disagreement was, and *enforced* co-operation. As he himself later wrote, 'it is the Commander's job to know'; had Air Vice-Marshal Evill brought Park's letter of August 27th to the AOC-in-C's attention, he would have done.

Before leaving Bentley Priory, the outgoing AOC-in-C sent one last signal to his squadrons:-

In sending you this, my last message, I wish I could say all that is in my heart.
I cannot hope to surpass the simple eloquence of the Prime Minister's words 'Never before has so much been owed by so many to so few'. That debt remains and will increase.
In saying goodbye to you I want you to know how continually you have been in my thoughts, and that, though our direct connection may be severed, I may yet be able to help you in your gallant fight.
Goodbye to you and God bless you all.

Against his wishes, Dowding was temporarily exiled, sent to America on a mission for which he was totally unsuited. When the church bells in England rang on Christmas Day 1940 to celebrate victory in the Battle of Britain, the principal architect was many thousands of miles away and therefore well out of earshot.

Shortly before Dowding's replacement, Air Vice-Marshal Park learned that he too was to be relieved after just six months in command of 11 Group. He felt that the Group should go to Air Vice-Marshal Richard Saul, AOC 13 Group, but was 'shocked' when the coveted 11 Group went to Leigh-Mallory whilst Saul received 12 Group. In the event, Air Vice-Marshal Leigh-Mallory failed to extend the courtesy of observing the usual handover procedure, so Air Vice-Marshal Park handed over 11 Group to his SASO. On December 27th, 1940, Park became head of 23 Group, Flying *Training* Command, at South Cerney, near Cirencester, Gloucestershire.

It could not have been mere coincidence that Douglas and Leigh-Mallory succeeded Dowding and Park respectively. In view of all the foregoing evidence, I doubt whether anyone would be surprised to learn that the official account of the epic Battle of Britain, published in March 1941, failed to mention the name of Air Chief Marshal Dowding.

On January 29th, 1941, Air Vice-Marshal Leigh-Mallory conducted a paper exercise using the circumstances of an actual attack on the Sector Stations of both Kenley and Biggin Hill which had occurred on September 6th, 1940. The new AOC 11 Group totally mismanaged this exercise which had been orchestrated to prove the supposed great worth of large fighter formations. The enemy 'raid' was not intercepted whilst inbound and bombed both target airfields whilst Leigh-Mallory's fighters were still on the ground.

CHAPTER TEN

The Great Experience

Throughout the last 10 years, I have obtained the views of various former Big Wing pilots on both their leader and the 12 Group formation.

The Big Wing's pilots remember Douglas Bader:-

Flight Lieutenant Wallace Cunningham:-

Douglas Bader was a competent pilot and a good leader. Brian Lane, our CO, was calm and reassuring, in addition to being an excellent fighter pilot. There was little to choose between them, although they were very different; Douglas had great charisma, and being short of a couple of legs was very newsworthy.

Wing Commander Bernard Jennings:-

Bader's great advantage in combat was that, having no legs, he could pull far greater 'g' than able-bodied pilots before blacking out. He could therefore execute a tighter turn than anybody else and so get on his opponent's tail and hold his position. Other pilots, upon feeling the onset of a blackout had to lower the 'g' force and therefore increase their turning circle, possibly leaving themselves open to attack if their opponent could stand higher 'g'.

Wing Commander George Unwin:-

My own opinion of Bader can only be based on his performance as a pilot and leader. As a pilot he proved his ability by winning the respect of all who flew with him. As a leader I can only say that he inspired confidence and that I would happily have followed him anywhere. He

Wing Commander George Unwin DSO DFM pictured with the author at the launch of the latter's third book, 'Through Peril to the Stars', at Great Malvern, September 1993. In the author's considered opinion, George Unwin was amongst Fighter Command's greatest pilots in 1940.

was a born leader, always humorous but <u>very</u> aggressive. He didn't hesitate to put across his point of view, no matter how high ranking the person was on the receiving end. At Duxford he was tremendously popular with aircrew and groundcrew alike.

Flight Lieutenant Vic Bergman (Czech):-

We all admired Bader, his tremendous iron will, resolution and ability.

Wing Commander James Thomson:-

It was sometimes said that the publicity he was given by the media was a little 'over the top'. However, he was obviously an effective instrument in the propaganda war as well as the military one.

Warrant Officer Antoni Markiewicz (Polish):-

One thing I do remember, if we missed the Germans Bader was very displeased, and let us know in very simple language!

Antoni Markiewicz, who flew with 302 Squadron in 1940. (Author via Mr A Markiewicz)

Of the Big Wing:-

Wing Commander Douglas Blackwood:-

I suppose I would not be speaking unreasonably by saying that the Wing was eventually a failure in so much as there was never really time to get three or four squadrons off the ground and into some shape and form to attack the usual mass of enemy aircraft effectively. On one or two occasions I was detailed by Bader and the AOC to lead the formation, so I know something of the difficulty. But when we did attack a formation of enemy bombers, the Wing was extremely successful. I would say that the main reason for any loss of effectiveness was primarily due to a sort of jealousy between the AOCs of both 11 and 12 Groups. 11 Group felt that it was their responsibility to protect London without 12 Group interfering.

Warrant Officer Antoni Markiewicz:-

Whilst flying with the Big Wing in 1940 I was in favour of it. Destroying German aircraft before they reached the target, or forcing them to drop their bombs just anywhere would be a great achievement. But to use a large force to do that, left the industrial Midlands without adequate protection. It was rather risky. No doubt Fighter Command knew that, and did not want to take any chances.

The matter of leaving the Midlands unprotected is crucial. In Chapter One we have seen that before the Battle of Britain, Air Vice-Marshal Leigh-Mallory was so concerned about his meagre strength that he wrote to Air Chief Marshal Dowding to have his concerns placed on record. During the summer of 1940 the AOC 12 Group must have forgotten such concerns, as by that time he was clearly prepared to send up to five of his squadrons sallying forth over the 11 Group area.

Wing Commander Sir Kenneth Stoddart:-

Although I am now one of the very few survivors of 611 Squadron from 1940, at the time I was a junior Flight Lieutenant. We were stationed at Digby and for a period of time flew down to Fowlmere on a daily basis, returning home at dusk. The only views I may have had about 'Big Wings' or anything else in those days would have been made in ignorance; apart from Dunkirk, they were the first days that the squadron was truly involved in a big action.

Air Marshal Sir Denis Crowley-Milling:-

The 'Big Wing' interest is in the tactical argument under the circumstances that developed at one stage in the Battle of Britain, i.e. end of August and early September 1940. It was tried out on but few occasions. If the timing and positioning were right, and the enemy did what you expected, it could result in hitting the German formations earlier and with more fighters. The very first Duxford Wing of three squadrons was not used until September 7th, 1940. The vital point in the Battle of Britain was, of course, Goering's change in tactics, making the whole weight of attack against London, thus allowing our radar and front-line airfields to recover.

Denis Crowley-Milling pictured when a Wing Commander flying Typhoon fighter-bombers in 1942. (Author via Douglas Bader Foundation)

Wing Commander James Thomson:-

The Big Wing was a wonderful operation to take part in as we felt that we were answering numbers with numbers. However, subsequent study suggested that Sir Keith Park's strategy may have been the sounder. He used smaller numbers to break up the attacking formations, so disrupting their concentration of force over the target area and the effectiveness of their attack. It also enabled him to retain some aircraft for the defence of their bases during that most vulnerable operation: refuelling and re-arming.

Furthermore, the Big Wing took some time to form up and reach the area under attack; occasionally it 'missed the boat'.

The relative merits of the two methods were argued openly by the circulation of correspondence on the subject between the two Groups. Many of us felt that this was a diversion of mental effort from the main aim of defeating the Luftwaffe and was not entirely becoming of the authorities concerned.

Flight Lieutenant Ken Wilkinson:-

Fighter Command's strategy of aerodrome locations was successful in that there were very few attempts in daylight of mass bombing raids over the East Coast of England and Scotland, but the possibility always remained. The squadrons resting at Wittering, Kirton, Newcastle, Drem, Montrose, etc maintained the defence of the East Coast. Most critics seem to forget that we had a lot to defend - this aspect may have had some bearing on the infrequent calls upon the Duxford Wing. If one can be satisfied that there was little or no likelihood of a major bomber offensive from the east, then the Duxford Wing was right.

Ken Wilkinson, an NCO VR pilot with 19 Squadron in 1940.
(Author via Flight Lieutenant K Wilkinson)

Seeing these large numbers of bombers and fighter escorts, and realising that 11 Group was continually taking a pasting, there had to be some help we could give; if 60 additional RAF fighters arrived from the north in time, chances were that the *Luftwaffe* could have been deterred earlier. Being the lowest of the low (i.e. a brand new RAFVR Sergeant Pilot), I had no idea about the arguments that we are now told were taking place regarding tactics, but my personal experience tells me that Fighter Command was dedicated to protecting our country and so I am loathe to believe that <u>one</u> Group AOC was pursuing selfish interests contrary to the common objective of defeating (or negating) the *Luftwaffe*.

THE GREAT EXPERIENCE

Flight Lieutenant Vic Bergman:-

In those heady days I was a mere Pilot Officer who loved flying, loved the Hurricane, and was able to point my guns at a German target. But my English was limited. I have always had the impression that the initial interception of the enemy was left to No 11 Group. We were then to follow the raiders and damage or destroy as many as possible on their return journey.

More than once, the Wing was released for lunch when Douglas Bader 'pegged' into the dining room and called 'Come on boys, we are wanted!' That was followed by the clutter of cutlery on the unfinished plates - rush for the door, transport to dispersals, and in 15-20 minutes all 12 Hurricanes of 242 Squadron took off in formation on the grass airfield, immediately followed by ours of 310. No 19 Squadron's Spitfires from Fowlmere soon appeared overhead, their job being to protect us from the enemy fighters whilst we Hurricanes went for the bombers. It did not always work out like that, though. In mid-September our squadron was meeting a formation of Do 17s when we were jumped by a swarm of Me 109s: I was shot down.

Wing Commander George Unwin:-

It didn't take Douglas Bader long to realise that sending a squadron of fighters to take on huge bomber raids was not the answer, especially as these raids were usually escorted by fighters. As he put it - if only we had three times the number of fighters as a unit we could shoot down three times the number of enemy aircraft. In my opinion there was a further factor that was behind his argument for the Big Wing; for the first five months of his return to the RAF he had been flying Spitfires: with 242 Squadron he was on Hurricanes, and no matter what the loyal Hurricane pilots may say, it was no match for the 109. Agreed, it could out-turn the Hun but obviously this is far outweighed if the target is leaving you by 30 mph. On the other hand, the Hurricane had it over the Spitfire as a gun platform, both from the steadiness of that platform and concentration of fire. In my opinion the Hurricane was capable of shooting down bombers more effectively provided it was not interfered with by the 109s. The Hurricane casualties at this time support this argument. Once we had the Big Wing operating it was very obviously the answer in that the Hurricane casualties dropped appreciably and the number of German aircraft destroyed increased. The Wing started operating in the first week of September 1940, and was in action until November. In my opinion it was an unqualified success.

As for the argument as to the value of flying 60 fighters together, there really was no basis for this disagreement between the two AOCs, for the simple reason that it would not have been feasible to assemble such a large number of fighters from the aerodromes in 11 Group in time to intercept an incoming raid. We at Duxford and Fowlmere had a full 15 minutes of flying to arrive at the battle area (north of the Thames) and with our two aerodromes only a couple of miles apart we could easily assemble the Wing en route to London. I am convinced that the real trouble was caused by Keith Park steadfastly refusing to use the strength of Duxford to anywhere near its capabilities. Day after day we would sit at Readiness without being called on to help out. When we were called out, quite often it was merely to patrol the 11 Group aerodromes whilst their squadrons were rearming and refuelling. On other days we were too late on the scene. The most glaring example of this was when we were scrambled as a Wing and vectored to London area. After about seven minutes our Controller, using plain language, said 'They are bombing North Weald, go there quickly!' This was the day that North Weald was very heavily damaged. When we arrived it was all over, we were too late. I suggest that 60 fighters could have considerably lessened that damage. The total flying time from Duxford to North Weald is six - seven minutes.

One other very important factor was the effect the Big Wing had on the German aircrews. They had been told that the RAF was just about finished and that all would soon be over. This was to boost their morale which by this time was pretty low. Imagine their feelings when instead of being met by a depleted squadron, no less than 60 descended on them!

A further point is that throughout 1940, all squadrons at Duxford and Fowlmere were always at full strength.

Flight Lieutenant Richard Jones:-

Early in September 1940 I was transferred from 64 Squadron at Kenley in 11 Group to 19 Squadron at Fowlmere, a part of 12 Group. By then, the latter was a part of Douglas Bader's Big Wing.

Then & Now: Richard Jones
(Author)

My immediate impression was the experience of flying with a Wing comprising five squadrons of both Spitfires and Hurricanes, instead of anything between 5-10 aircraft taking off from Kenley to intercept large numbers of enemy aircraft.

To me this experience gave enormous confidence,: looking around and seeing anything from 50 upwards of fighters keeping me company! Also, I presumed that there was perhaps time being wasted in forming up etc after take-off, using valuable fuel required for the flight south. At the same time, the Big Wing must have had a great effect on the lowering of enemy morale, who, for the first time, encountered such a formidable opponent.

Flight Lieutenant Wallace Cunningham:-

Bader took over 242 (Canadian) Squadron - good pilots flying Hurricanes with a good concentration of firepower. They were a good unit to lead the attack into the large enemy formations, our Spitfires were better for attacking the escorts. Together with 310 Squadron, we had the makings of a good attacking Wing. 12 Group's forays were of value, good combats and victories, losses sustainable and gaining experience. We were in good shape to play a major part in the coming struggle. That Hitler and the OKW postponed the invasion was their error and our salvation.

THE GREAT EXPERIENCE

Wing Commander David Cox:-

When the Wing went into action the Spitfire squadron or squadrons were left to their own devices to combat the 109 escorts.

I think that five squadrons - three of Hurricanes, two of Spitfires, was too many. I remember going round and round for some 15-20 minutes waiting for the Wing to form up and get going. This resulted in the Wing often arriving late at the Patrol Line given by the 11 Group Controllers.

Wing Commander David Cox at home, 1995.

There is no doubt that some of the 11 Group squadrons blamed the Big Wing's late arrival for their airfields being bombed. This caused some bad feeling between the pilots. Even as late as the 1960s an ex-pilot of 41 Squadron nearly gave me a punch on the nose in a pub at Grimsby when he found out that I had flown with the 12 Group Wing!

I think that a Wing of three squadrons would have made better time. Why not another two Spitfire squadrons operating with us as a further Wing? They would have made the Patrol Line quicker and with the advantage of more height. However, I do think that 11 Group could have called for the Wing earlier on certain occasions.

Was the Big Wing a success? I doubt it. Its best effort was on the afternoon of September 15th when I remember the words of Bobby Oxspring, a flight commander in 66 Squadron, saying what a wonderful sight it was to see 60 fighters suddenly appear. No doubt it was a bit of a shock to the Luftwaffe!

Wing Commander Bernard Jennings:-

As I recall, the pilots had two views on the Big Wing. Firstly that it was rather cumbersome, even when led by Brian Lane, a wonderful pilot.

Secondly, if you were in one of the rear squadrons, those in front would get the first attack and we would have to go down and help them out at our best advantage. Or if we were the front squadron, then we had plenty of cover and help available.

Wing Commander Frank Brinsden:-

The constraints of Bader's ponderous mass formation were a disaster in my opinion, a retrograde step. Nothing was achieved by arriving en masse because the Wing disintegrated almost immediately battle was joined. In fact time, and therefore advantage, was lost during assembly and this compounded the effect of late scramble orders. These observations on tactics are, of course, in retrospect, but I do recall at the time feeling some unease or dissatisfaction at 19 Squadron's inability to do better.

Air Commodore Peter Brothers was a flight commander in 257 Squadron during the latter part of the Battle of Britain, and participated in 11 Group's Wing operations:-

Peter Brothers whilst a Flight Lieutenant with 32 Squadron during 1940.
(Author via Air Commodore PM Brothers)

I was surprised by Peter Townsend's suggestion in 'Duel of Eagles' that Air Vice-Marshal Park formed an 11 Group Wing to avoid criticism. He was far too strong a character to do that, and in fact exercised flexible tactics, alternating to whichever was appropriate at the time. My log book shows that most operational sorties I flew in 257 Squadron between September 28th and October 8th 1940, were in a Wing with 73 and 17 Squadrons from Castle Camps, we being based at Martlesham Heath, all in the Debden Sector and so nearly as far north of the Thames as Duxford. We then moved to North Weald and between October 9th and 27th, operated together with 46 and 249 Squadrons. All sorties are recorded as 'Defensive Wing Patrols', a total of 16.

Apart from one occasion which I have not recorded but vividly remember, our Wings saw little action. We were just below cloud when two Me 109s swept past to the left and below us, shot down two Hurricanes of 17 Squadron, which was leading, then pulled up and vanished into cloud. All far too quick for our great lumbering concentrated formation to react.

By October the period of intensive activity was drawing to a close and so we could afford wasteful standing patrols - the 'Maidstone Line at 20,000" being the usual one - and we were far enough inland to form up into a Wing when enemy activity was brewing. All this was so different from my days at Biggin Hill, Manston or Hawkinge when we were scrambled late to ensure that the raid was the real thing and not a 'spoof' to get us airborne then catch us on the ground refuelling.

Douglas Bader, a close and dear friend, based further north at Duxford, allowed his fretful anxiety to be in the forefront of the activity to cloud his judgement. Dowding's SASO, Air Vice-Marshal Sir Douglas Evill, was right when he said 'It is quite useless to argue whether Wing formations are or are not desirable, both statements are equally true under different conditions'. Those conditions were to come later to us in 11 Group.

The tactical evidence generally is overwhelmingly against the Big Wing. As we have seen, MRAF

Lord Douglas of Kirtleside attempted to largely disassociate himself from the controversy in his autobiography (see Bibliography). Air Chief Marshal Sir Trafford Leigh-Mallory was killed as the result of a flying accident in 1944 whilst en route to command the Allied Air Forces in South East Asia. It would be illuminating to see how he would have answered his critics with regard to the political and tactical issues of the Big Wing. Group Captain Sir Douglas Bader died in 1982, but reproduced below is the only known interview he ever gave to an historian on this subject; the tape was recorded by Dr Alfred Price during the course of his research for 'Battle of Britain Day' (see Bibliography):-

AP: I am very interested in the Big Wing and how one got it to work.

DB: You are the first author who has ever come to see me about it. Despite everything published about my Wing, you are the only one who has ever bothered to come and talk to me about it, and after all I am the only chap left alive who can tell you. All have, however, played on this so-called controversy between Leigh-Mallory and Park, and of course Dowding being sacked.

AP: You say "so called controversy"?

DB: Yes. I was only an Acting Squadron Leader at the time, but I got fairly close to Leigh-Mallory. He was one of these warm people, he was a tremendously good commander and everybody who served with him was very fond of him. He would come over and say, "Well done" and all that sort of thing. What happened was that on August 30th, 1940, I think it was, we got off a squadron, just 12 of us, and we had everything in our favour, the height, I knew where they were and we had the sun. We shot down a few without any problems whatsoever. When we were writing out our combat reports afterwards, Leigh-Mallory rang me up and said "Congratulations, Bader, on the squadron's performance today", and so I said "Thank you very much, Sir, but if we'd had more aeroplanes then we would have shot down a whole lot more". He asked what I meant and I explained that with more fighters our results would have been even better. He said, "Look, I'd like to talk to you about this", and so I flew over to Hucknall and I told him what I thought. He agreed and created the Duxford Wing, under my leadership and comprising 242, 310 (Czech) and 19 Squadrons. Leigh-Mallory said to try the idea and see what we could do with three squadrons. There was actually no problem at all. We usually got off the ground in four minutes, at worst five.

AP: And this five minutes is from scramble to last aircraft wheels off?

DB: Yes. Now other people, who were ignorant and didn't bother to come and see me, assumed, and therefore stated in print, that the Wing took a long time to get off the ground. Not so. As the two Hurricane squadrons got off from Duxford, the Spitfires from Fowlmere, there was no forming up as such. I just set course and kept going and everyone else just formated on my lead.

AP: Would the second squadron have taken off behind you, or in any direction regardless of wind?'

DB: 'You would have three lots of three, then they'd go off together.

AP: So it was always in threes and in line abreast.

DB: Oh yes, and as soon as the first three were getting towards the far hedge then the next three would be taxiing into position and so on.

AP: On September 15th, 1940, you did it with five squadrons?

DB: That's right, 242, 310, 302, 611 and 19, the latter two being at Fowlmere.

AP: So once off the ground, would you go into an orbit?

DB: No, I used to get off the ground and get absolutely right on course. The chaps then joined me, and the Spitfire squadrons stayed above us.

AP: As I understand it the Hurricane climbed more steeply than the Spitfire?

DB: Yes, but not as fast, you see. I usually set the pace to climb at about 140 mph. We reckoned to be at the Estuary at about 20,000 feet, and I think that it was 48 miles away.

AP: So would the Spitfires throttle back to stay with you?

DB: Yes, but they would be 5,000 feet above us. The Germans always came in at 17,000 feet, every bloody time. Our Controller, 'Woody', would ring me up and say that they were building up over the Pas-de-Calais, and I remember saying "Well why the hell don't we go off now and get the buggers whilst they're forming up?" You see the bombers would come from their bases in France and orbit the Pas-de-Calais, that area around Calais and Boulogne, and the fighters would then take off from their airfields within that area, such as Wissant and St Omer, of course the fighters had a very short range, not much more than 45 minutes. They would climb up and join the bombers and then the whole armada would set course over the Channel. If our Duxford Wing had got off when they were building up, we'd have got about 70 miles south of base, probably down to Canterbury area, and we'd have got 'em there, on the way in. We would have been at the right height and would have therefore controlled the battle. Our 60, or 36, fighters would have got 'em, absolutely bang on. The problem was, of course, that those controllers down south only had a map showing the 11 Group Sector and the north of France. You couldn't blame the controllers as none of them had been doing it for long, but you couldn't expect him to call on 12 Group, he'd say "Where the hell is 12 Group!" There was an order from Park saying that they were not to engage over the sea, so what happened was that 'Sailor' Malan, Al Deere, and all these chaps who had been at Dunkirk and were therefore a little more knowledgeable, after having been clobbered a few times due to being too low, they would climb north, away from the Germans, get height and then come back.'

AP: This idea to meet the incoming raids near Canterbury was never accepted, then?

DB: The thing was, you see, was that Leigh-Mallory was totally loyal. I used to go on at him about why we couldn't go off early and be down there, but he said, "Look, we just can't go until Air Vice-Marshal Park requests us. Do please remember, Bader, that they've got plenty of problems down there without us adding to them." You see, he was very, very loyal. He never once said anything disparaging to me about either Park or Dowding.

AP: So it would have been totally unethical for Leigh-Mallory to put his fighters into Park's area without the latter's authorisation?

DB: Quite right The thing was that the Battle should have been controlled from Fighter Co mand HQ, where they had a map of the whole country and knew the state of each squadron, instead of just the 11 Group control centre which, as I have said, focused entirely on their area. The other point is that we never suggested that 11 Group should use Wings, they couldn't, they were far too near the Germans, it was right for Park to use his squadrons as he did, and if the Battle had been controlled from Fighter Command HQ then I would not say they should have been used any differently.

AP: But Park tended not to call you in until his squadrons were committed?

DB: Yes. But what a sight the Wing must have been to those hard pressed 11 Group boys?

AP: Yes, I was recently talking to Group Captain Bobbie Oxspring and he said that on September 15th, 1940, he and another 66 Squadron pilot were weaving above their squadron, feeling very lonely, when suddenly the Wing came into view with 60 fighters!

DB: Absolutely. My point now is that all of these books have been written about the so called controversy, but history has to be put right before it is too late. The point is that we should have been called for in good time, when the enemy was building up.

AP: So you are saying that time was lost not because of the Wing taking off and forming up, but because you were not requested early enough by 11 Group?

DB: Yes, there was no time lost through us getting off. Once we were off we were off, there was no milling about, all this was done on the climb and en route. No time lost.'

AP: Could a Wing climb as fast as a squadron?

DB: No. The leader is the fellow who sets the pace, to give the blokes at the back time to settle down and so on, and obviously a squadron in a hurry was faster than a Wing because the leader had less blokes to worry about.

AP: So with your Wing off the ground, with the Spitfires as top cover you did not therefore need weavers?

DB: No, we never had weavers.

AP: So what sort of a formation would you be in?

DB: Each squadron in threes, we always climbed in line astern.

AP: So four lots in threes in line astern?

DB: Yes.

AP: And the Spitfires 5,000 feet above also in threes?

DB: Yes, always in threes, the "Finger Four" came later.

AP: And were you all on the same radio frequency?

DB: No, only the squadron commanders were on the same frequency. We had four buttons on the VHF in those days, which we had just received before the Battle of Britain. It was ridiculous anyway, trying to tune this thing with someone shooting up your backside! Anyway, the other pilots each had their own squadron frequency. The controller would talk to me on my frequency. To talk to the chaps I would have to keep changing frequency from squadron to squadron. Later of course we got it so that we were all on the same frequency. When we were above the enemy I would say "Diving, diving now, attacking now", and my section of three would go down, followed by everyone else. As soon as we had made one pass, the formation was broken up.

AP: So would you personally attempt to control the Wing once you had attacked the enemy?

DB: No. My objective was to get the Wing into the right position, and then say "Attacking now", after which it was entirely up to them.

AP: Did they await your order?

DB: Oh yes.

AP: But once you engaged, each man knew what he had to do?

DB: Yes.

AP: When 611 Squadron joined the Wing, they were actually stationed at Digby. Presumably they flew down to Fowlmere and joined you there, or did they meet you in the air.

DB: Oh no, not in the air, not possible really. We were actually based at Coltishall, so we would fly to Duxford in the morning, joining 310 who were based there, 19 Squadron of course being at Fowlmere, and 611 likewise would arrive at Fowlmere from Digby. We would then wait there and operate from there in the event of a scramble.

AP: And would it have been impossible to operate all squadrons from the same airfield?

DB: Yes, it would have taken much longer. Duxford and Fowlmere were perfect as they were only three miles apart.

AP: After an engagement, what happened?

DB: We landed back separately, you see, you might collect an odd bloke with you, but essentially you landed separately. It was actually very difficult, as all of these pilots would be calling up on the R/T for a Homing bearing, it wouldn't be dark, although sometimes hazy, and you had to find a field amongst many fields. It could be very difficult. You must also remember that a lot of these chaps were very young and actually had little experience. The Battle of Britain was won not by Malan, Stanford-Tuck and myself, who got all the accolades, it was won by kids of 19 or 20, who maybe shot down either nothing or just one before being killed themselves. They were the blokes who won the Battle of Britain. Make no mistake there.

AP: If they shot down nothing, how did they contribute?

DB: Well, by being determined, by going off to fight and being prepared to die if necessary, that's the point. The Battle of Britain was not won by one pilot, it was won by the whole nation. The Navy also had colossal losses bringing convoys in to this beleaguered island, the people on the ground who took the bombing, those are the people who won. It was a united national effort, no doubt about it. Churchill of course called us the "Few", and we loved him for it, but if we hadn't got planes and ammunition and gasoline, which was all brought in, we could never have fought in the first place. And let's not forget the nurses, the doctors, and the emergency services, they were even building Spitfires under bridges in Southampton! So don't think that it was Bader and Tuck who won the Battle of Britain, don't make any mistake on that point, it has to be said, don't just dismiss it, remember that if nothing else.

AP: On 'Battle of Britain Day', did it occur to you that it was a special day, a turning point?

DB: Nothing like that ever occurred to us, we were only thinking in terms of our own engagement, not the overall scenario. Of course we saw 11 Group fighters in the air, and we thought "Bloody good show, there they are", but my only vision was confined to my Wing getting at the enemy, not what the rest of Fighter Command was doing. Certain individual things stick in your mind, like a Spitfire diving vertically and colliding with a Dornier, Gordon Sinclair and Jefferies colliding, and so on - I couldn't warn them because I was on a different frequency, Gordon baled out but Boulton went down like a falling leaf and was killed.

AP: When you had landed, having taken losses, when the reports were made of these great combat claims, would there be a huge party at Duxford?

DB: No because in fact we didn't drink too much, after being stood down we may well have gathered around the bar or played snooker, but that was about it, no party. It never occurred to us that we would lose, although of course we didn't know what Churchill and Dowding knew.

AP: To conclude, earlier you referred to the "alleged controversy". Are you saying that you never detected any controversy between the two commanders supposedly concerned?

DB: No. Leigh-Mallory was absolutely, rigidly loyal, and I got to know him pretty well, it got beyond the stage of "Bader", it was "Douglas" and so on.

AP: Surely though an Air Vice-Marshal would feel that whatever he did at a higher level was not for discussion with a Squadron Leader?

DB: Agreed, but why didn't we all know if it was happening? There have been some appalling books written on the subject which malign me tremendously, saying that I had done my best to torpedo Park and Dowding. It is absurd to suggest that a mere Acting Squadron Leader would have such power. Some of the authors concerned should have known better. No-one but you has ever come to see me about it, as I have said.

AP: But I have heard from a former controller that Leigh-Mallory was reluctant to provide squadrons to cover 11 Group airfields.

DB: No, and let's get this absolutely right. There were actually two Wings, I had the first at Duxford and Harry Broadhurst the other at Wittering, and they also went down south into action. Leigh-Mallory would not release our squadrons to 11 Group but said that we would stay in 12 Group as the Duxford and Wittering Wings.

AP: A case of either you have a Wing or nothing?

DB: Yes. In other words he said I am not sending these squadrons down to relieve 11 Group squadrons and therefore lose them completely to 12 Group. It was simply because he wanted to keep our Wings together, which was good sense.

AP: But it has been said that 12 Group was reluctant to send squadrons as top cover for 11 Group's airfields.

DB: No, the problem was that they always asked for us too late.

AP: So Leigh-Mallory would assist whenever he was asked?

DB: Oh Christ yes! He was longing to be asked, so was I.

AP: Sir Douglas Bader, thank you.

Certain areas of the interview require discussion. Firstly, how can Sir Douglas say that he had no knowledge of the controversy? We know that he was present at the Air Ministry throughout the meeting on October 17th, which even Lord Douglas describes as an 'unnecessarily heated argument' between the two AOCs concerned. Even though Bader himself had been so outspoken to the politicians Sinclair and Balfour, perhaps he was unaware of just how much trouble he had caused for both Dowding and Park; equally, Bader might never have had knowledge of the protection the politicians consequently gave him. Air Chief Marshal Dowding was convinced that Bader was not directly involved in complicity against him personally. Nevertheless, Dowding blamed Bader for much of the trouble, and this is quite fair. Instead of seeking the 'Bubble Reputation', Squadron Leader Bader should have done his job as the commander of a 12 Group squadron, and reflected loyalty to the Commander-in-Chief; equally his AOC should never have acted contrary to Dowding's wishes. It has been said that in his sporting days, Bader was not a team player but a gifted and aggressive individualist. I find it surprising that he could not even be contained by such a team as the RAF.

Secondly, the subject of the Wittering Wing. Harry Broadhurst was five years older than Douglas Bader and had transferred from the Royal Artillery to the RAF in 1926. In 1937 he was awarded the AFC, and received a DFC after destroying a lone raider in bad weather conditions in early 1940. By May 28th 1940, Broadhurst was a Wing Commander and Sector Commander at Wittering. By that time, his flying hours amounted to 2,599.50. Wing Commander Broadhurst, who did not double as the Sector Controller as did Wing Commander Woodhall at Duxford, managed to fly virtually on a daily basis. On June 30th, Wing Commander Broadhurst wrote in his log book 'Leading 229 Squadron in Wing formation'. Again, however, this was immediately after the Dunkirk en masse flights and cannot be considered to be of any significance to the Big Wing argument. Throughout July and August, 'Broady' frequently flew to 12 Group HQ at Hucknall, presumably to liaise with the AOC. In view of the Wing Commander's extensive fighter experience and seniority, if Air Vice-Marshal Leigh-Mallory really had considered Big Wings before Squadron Leader Douglas Bader's suggestion, as many have claimed, why did he not formally create a Wing under Broadhurst's leadership, instead of the relatively *ad hoc* Duxford operation?

The majority of flights recorded by Broadhurst in July and August 1940 were either between various stations or night interception patrols in his personal Hurricane, P2823. On September 15th, however, he wrote 'Wing Patrol over the Estuary', and on September 24th, 'Wing Patrol over Duxford'. At this time, both the Hurricanes of 1 Squadron and the Spitfires of 266 were based at Wittering, so one would assume that these squadrons comprised the so-called Wittering Wing. However, referring to September 15th, their respective ORBs relate:-

.....both flights were patrolling over the Duxford Sector during the afternoon.

Six aircraft patrolled Duxford in afternoon.

Although no mention is made of joint squadron operations, if 1 and 266 Squadrons flew together on the afternoon of September 15th the formation consisted of only some 18 fighters. Also, from the evidence available it seems that the Wittering squadrons were sent to protect Duxford whilst the Big Wing was in action further south. No mention is made of patrolling the Thames Estuary, well into 11 Group territory. Does Broadhurst's log book therefore provide evidence of another 12 Group freelance fighter sweep over 11 Group?

On September 24th, the 1 and 266 Squadron ORBs respectively state:-

Red Section scramble and patrolled Cambridge at 20,000'.

Six aircraft on operational duty at Duxford.

This represents a total of nine aircraft, not even a squadron, let alone a Wing.

The operational flights of both the Wittering squadrons throughout September and October 1940 involved training flights and local interception patrols. Interestingly the latter were largely at either Section (3 aircraft) or Flight (6) strength.

The day after the Air Ministry meeting, on October 18th, Broadhurst flew to Hucknall; on October 25th he recorded 'Wing Patrol, Duxford - North Weald'. On that day, 11 Spitfires of 266 Squadron had proceeded to Duxford and undertook one operation with the *Duxford* Wing; 1 Squadron was engaged in gunnery practice at Sutton Bridge and other training flights. One must assume, therefore, that instead of Wing Commander Broadhurst leading his own formation, he actually flew as part of the Duxford Wing, led on that day by Squadron Leader Bader.

From November 10th onwards, after the Battle of Britain, the two Wittering squadrons flew an increasing number of Wing formation practices or Wing patrols over the Thames Estuary. During the latter period, 1 and 266 Squadrons were often led by the Duxford Sector's 19 Squadron. On November 10th, the CO of 19 Squadron, Squadron Leader Brian Lane, wrote in his log book, 'Wing Patrol. Wet nursing 1 and 266 from Wittering. My God!' On November 14th, the 19 Squadron ORB recorded:-

Last patrol with the Wittering Wing. Nearly last patrol with any Wing! AJAX Leader led his squadron straight into us from the sun as we climbed to meet them. Created quite a shambles!

It is clear from the foregoing evidence that not even an *ad hoc* Duxford-like Wing existed at Wittering during the Battle of Britain. Another point, of course, is that the Wittering squadrons had both served their time in 11 Group, unlike those at Duxford which had been jealously guarded by Air Vice-Marshal Leigh-Mallory. The question that has to be asked, is why was Acting Squadron Leader Douglas Bader permitted to lead the 12 Group Wing when such an experienced officer and pilot as Wing Commander Broadhurst was available? Firstly the special relationship between Bader and the AOC has to be a significant factor, and secondly I believe this to be further evidence of just how little thought was given to the Duxford Wing at the time.

The crux of the Big Wing argument is represented by Sir Douglas Bader's statement that 12 Group should have been called upon to 'get the buggers whilst they're forming up'. As we have seen, simple mathematical calculations, given aircraft performance, time and distance, not to mention the limitations of RDF, prove that this was impossible. This cannot be overemphasised. Turning to the claim that the Battle of Britain should have been controlled from HQ Fighter Command, this was, of course, totally contrary to the System and especially Air Chief Marshal Dowding's policy of tactical delegation to his Group Commanders. As Sir Keith Park said when told by Group Captain Peter Townsend of this suggestion, 'Well, that really beats the band!'

Rightly or wrongly, the Big Wing certainly enabled Squadron Leader Bader to make a more active contribution to the Battle of Britain. The combat claims of 242 Squadron led to the award of 10 decorations to Bader and his pilots, and inevitably the media seized upon the opportunity to make a morale boosting story based upon the legless fighter 'ace'. This coverage, coupled with the natural Bader charisma, led to Douglas Bader being projected as *the* Battle of Britain 'ace'. That viewpoint was, of course, cemented in the hearts and minds of the general public during the 1950s when 'Reach for the Sky' became a box office success. Even today if you ask a passer-by to name one of the Few, the chances are he will answer 'Douglas Bader'. It appears as though the names of other fighter pilots once in household use are now long forgotten. Understandably, many pilots, particularly those who served in 11 Group and therefore saw much more action than Douglas Bader, object to the all-consuming Bader exposure; Wing Commander HR 'Dizzy' Allen:-

> I am constantly bemused why Group Captain Sir Douglas Bader and the Battle of Britain should be considered synonymous. If he had served in the front line of No 11 Group, based essentially in Kent and Sussex, he might have realised that the Big Wing concept was balderdash - for the front line anyway - and that was the line that mattered.
>
> This is not to denigrate Douglas Bader's sheer determination in getting himself back into the RAF with tin legs, nor his distinguished record on the fighter sweeps of 1941. But I do wish that he would not allow himself to be pressed continually as the epitome of the Battle of Britain pilot. That is not his place in history, but he carved his own niche elsewhere.

The facts support Wing Commander Allen, although the Bader interview reflects a surprising degree of modesty. Perhaps his critics have never considered that Sir Douglas Bader had no personal control over what the press chose to write, regardless of the facts; having had some experience of this, I can sympathise. As others have indicated in this book, Bader's contribution was to the propaganda as well as the military war, and he certainly epitomised Britain's 'fight on against all odds' attitude.

Nevertheless, there remains an imbalance of credit. The contribution of *Fighter Command* should never be overshadowed by one man, and the evidence suggests that Group Captain Bader himself would have agreed with this. Even now any Bader-related story can grab a headline, and not all of them in context; having recently discussed with a reporter my concerns that the names of Dowding and Park are now unknown to many, I was unhappy that the consequent headline read 'Bader Not True Hero of the Skies', which was totally out of context with the point I was making. I am convinced that the problem today arises largely because many people, including journalists, just do not appreciate what the Battle of Britain was - an aerial conflict lasting 16 weeks; could any one pilot, therefore, legitimately claim to be the 'Hero of the Skies'? The fact remains, however, that such controversial headlines are attention grabbing and more likely to both sell newspapers and be noticed by the various press agencies.

To many, Douglas Bader is beyond criticism owing to his disability, but I think there are several other factors to consider. Firstly, whilst he has our unwavering admiration for returning to a fighter aircraft's cockpit despite his disability, having no legs has *nothing* to do with the Big Wing. Indeed, Air Chief Marshal Dowding himself touched upon this when he said that Squadron Leader Bader's disloyalty to him had 'nothing to do with gallantry in the air'. Once that has been accepted, it becomes easier to appreciate without emotion an accurate historical analysis. Of course we must not forget that Douglas Bader himself was determined to be judged as an equal alongside able-bodied men. Group Captain Bader's tireless post-war work for disabled people, although unconnected with the content of this book, remains an inspiration for which he was deservedly Knighted in 1976. This marvellous example to the disabled lives on under the auspices of the Douglas Bader Foundation, a registered charity of which Lady Bader herself is an active President. The Foundation is obviously a most worthy cause which I would urge all readers to support (further information can be found elsewhere in this book).

Research indicates that even today, few people realise the significance of the Big Wing Controversy. After Douglas and Leigh-Mallory succeeded Dowding and Park respectively, their tactical thinking was influenced by the performance of the Big Wing in 1940; we now know that contemporary reports are inaccurate in recording *confirmed* victories, and so it can only have been dangerous indeed to formulate the offensive policy of 1941 against such questionable statistics.

For the record, recent research published by an American, John Alcorn (see Bibliography), provides the following data for those Big Wing squadrons which did not serve in 11 Group during the Battle of Britain:-

19 Squadron:	Claimed 60.5, confirmed 26: accuracy 43%
242 Squadron:	Claimed 69, confirmed 22.5: accuracy 33%
302 Squadron:	Claimed 25, confirmed 5: accuracy 20%
310 Squadron:	Claimed 43, confirmed 14: accuracy 33%
611 Squadron:	Claimed 18, confirmed 10.25: accuracy 57%

In total, these units claimed 215.5 victories, of which 77.75 can be substantiated, representing an overclaiming factor of 2.77.

An interesting comparison exists between the foregoing figures and those of an *ad hoc* selection of 11 Group units:-

17 Squadron:	Claimed 42.5, confirmed 23.5: accuracy 55%
85 Squadron:	Claimed 60, confirmed 29, accuracy 48%
257 Squadron:	Claimed 19, confirmed 16.25: accuracy 86%
501 Squadron:	Claimed 100, confirmed 43.5: accuracy 44%
603 Squadron:	Claimed 76, confirmed 57.8: accuracy 86%

Checking the scoreboard: 611 Squadron.

Mr Benes, the Czech President in Exile, decorates Squadron Leader Blackwood and Flight Lieutenant Jefferies at Duxford

Congratulations! The Big Wing collects more gallantry decorations. Having received the DFC, an unknown pilot (who is not look-alike Frantisek Dolezal) congratulates 310 Squadron's Flight Lieutenant Jefferies whilst, to the latter's left, 19 Squadron's Flying Officer Haines and Flight Lieutenant Lawson look on.
(Top: Author, Middle & Bottom: Author via Mr WA Kirk)

Total number of 297.5 victories claimed, 170.05 substantiated: overclaiming factor of 1.74.

The accuracy of the 12 Group squadrons, operating in larger formations, are all lower than those 11 Group units detailed.

After the Battle: Squadron Leader DRS Bader and 242 Squadron pictured at Duxford; when the awards were handed out, 242 collected the lion's share.
(Author via Douglas Bader Foundation)

On December 20th 1940, two 66 Squadron Spitfires strafed a French coastal airfield (believed to have been Le Touquet). On January 9th, 1941, five RAF fighter squadrons swept across north-east France. Sensibly, the German Controllers did not respond, but the following day saw the first 'Circus' operation when 11 RAF fighter squadrons escorted six 114 Squadron Blenheims to Forêt de Guines. The idea of such complex operations was that as the Germans would be unable to ignore the presence of bombers, the enemy fighters would be scrambled but met by a numerically superior force of (mainly) Spitfires. Significantly, the only 12 Group fighter squadron participating in this first such operation was Squadron Leader Bader's 242 Squadron, all other fighter squadrons involved being from 11 Group (now commanded by Air Vice-Marshal Leigh-Mallory). During Circus No 1, the RAF fighters came off 'second best', losing two fighters; not a single Me 109 was damaged.

In March 1941, a new operational post was created, Wing Commander (Flying), and such Wing Leaders were appointed to all Sector Stations. Douglas Bader became Wing Leader at Tangmere, near Chichester, in 11 Group on March 18th. At Tangmere, Leigh-Mallory soon assembled the old 'team' with 'Woody' Woodhall's promotion to Group Captain and appointment as Tangmere Sector Commander and Controller.

Circus No 1, however, had set the scene for the 'Non-Stop Offensive'. There were no targets in France vital to the German war effort and so the *Luftwaffe* only needed to respond when tactical conditions were favourable. The Me 109, of course, was being used in the defensive role for which it had been designed, whereas the Spitfires and Hurricanes were now employed in an offensive manner, at the extremity of range, for which they were unsuited. It has been argued that, so soon after the Battle of Britain, the Non-Stop Offensive represented a 'little miracle', but it was an expensive one: by the end of 1941, Fighter Command was losing the day fighter war by 2:1. Amongst the high RAF losses were many experienced men, whose failure to return was ill afforded; Wing Commander Bader was to lead the Tangmere Wing in his typically aggressive style until being captured near St Omer on August 9th, 1941. The Non-Stop Offensive had been unashamedly influenced by politics: from June 1941 onwards the daylight operations over France increased in tempo as an expression of support for the Soviet Union. That might have been so, but the reality was that the *Kanalfront* remained held by just two *Jagdgeschwadern*, 2 and 26, until 1944.

Group Captain AB Woodhall (left, note Czech pilot's qualification badge) pictured when Station Commander and 'Boss Controller' at Tangmere during the Non-Stop Offensive of 1941. Air Vice-Marshal Park's replacement as AOC 11 Group, Air Vice-Marshal Leigh-Mallory, looks on (centre).
(Author via Mr Martin Woodhall

Wing Commander DRS Bader DSO DFC: Tangmere Wing Leader, captured August 9th, 1941.
(Author via Mr B Mabbett)

As previously indicated, some authors have claimed that the night blitz was a significant factor in Dowding's dismissal. That might have been so to some extent (although a lesser reason than the effects of the Big Wing Controversy), for amongst the shadowy figures in the background was Viscount Trenchard who was actively campaigning for Dowding's replacement. It has also been mentioned that Air Chief Marshal Dowding was awaiting new weapons with which to defeat the night bombers, and knew that until they arrived, little could be achieved given his current resources. In any case, the change in Air Officer Commanding-in-Chief of Fighter Command did nothing to halt the *Kampfgeschwarden*. Air Chief Marshal Douglas started 'Fighter Nights', the idea being to fill the night sky with so many day fighters that some bombers had to be caught. In practice neither the Spitfire nor Hurricane were good night flying aircraft, for which they were not in any case designed, and of course they lacked Airborne Interception radar. 'Fighter Nights' were futile in the main, although *occasionally* a raider would blunder into an orbiting RAF fighter. Air Chief Marshal Dowding had, however, previously rejected such sorties. The night blitz therefore continued largely unchecked until May 1941, when Hitler's territorial ambitions turned eastwards and in that direction went many *Luftwaffe* units.

Many of the Few still feel keenly the poor treatment of their leaders, Air Chief Marshal Dowding and Air Vice-Marshal Park. Dowding was not only temporarily exiled to America, on a mission for which he was unsuited, but eventually left the service in 1942 without promotion to Marshal of the RAF (MRAF). This always hurt him deeply, and also his 'Chicks'.

Flight Lieutenant Wallace Cunningham:-

Lord Dowding is the big success story - a strong man who had resisted political pressure to throw away a lot more fighters in France for a battle already lost. He was preserving Fighter

Command for the battle to come. Again a success story in the Battle of Britain. Clearly his was the credit for the strategy. He listened, said little but acted decisively. I had direct experience of his quick and clear thinking when our 20 mm cannons were performing badly; he visited the squadron, and within hours we were re-equipping with machine-gun Spitfires. So treasure the memory of 'Stuffy' Dowding - do not sell him short. His was the victory in directing and sustaining his 'Twelve Legions of Angels'.

The service has argued that the rank of MRAF is reserved for those who have served as the CAS, but neither MRAF Lord Douglas of Kirtleside nor MRAF Sir Arthur 'Bomber' Harris ever served in that exalted appointment. Instead, Air Chief Marshal Dowding received a peerage in 1943, becoming Baron of Bentley Priory. Lord Dowding spent the rest of his life away from the RAF, becoming increasingly concerned with spiritualism and such causes as the prevention of cruelty to animals. In 1968, he visited the sets of the *Battle of Britain* film at both Pinewood Studios and Duxford; at the latter location, Group Captain Douglas Bader insisted on pushing the 'Old Man' around in his wheelchair. In 1970, Lord Dowding died at home, aged 87. At that time, Douglas Bader said of his old Commander-in -Chief:-

Lord Dowding's simple marker in Westminster Abbey's Battle of Britain Chapel.
(Both: Author via Lady Odette Dowding)

Air Chief Marshal Dowding pictured with His Majesty, King George VI at Bentley Priory during the Battle of Britain. The AOC-in-C had this photograph made into a Christmas card.

Lord Dowding is probably unknown to most of the younger generation. Yet it was because of him as much as any other man that they have been brought up in the English way of life, speaking the English language. They might have been speaking German. Without his vision, his planning, his singleness of purpose, and his complete disregard for personal aggrandisement, Fighter Command might have been unable to win the Battle of Britain in the summer of 1940. What rankled most with the fighter pilots of 1940 was that he was never made MRAF. Seldom in our history has a man deserved so much of his fellow countrymen but wanted and received so little. He surely earned his place alongside Nelson and Wellington and other great military names in our history.

Lord Dowding's ashes were buried in Westminster Abbey, where a tablet records simply: 'He Led the Few in the Battle of Britain'. But there was no public tribute in the Capital until 1988, when the Queen Mother, wartime Queen and Royal Patron of the Battle of Britain Fighter Association, unveiled a bronze statue of Dowding outside the RAF church of St Clement Danes. The Battle of Britain Fighter Association was itself formed after the war and Air Chief Marshal Dowding was President; the former AOC 11 Group was Vice-President. That the commemorative project was initiated, organised and to some extent funded by Dowding's 'Chicks' themselves, would no doubt have deeply moved their old Commander-in-Chief.

As if by way of a postscript to Lord Dowding's story, on February 20th, 1997, the *Times* reported that following public pressure the RAF was considering the *posthumous* promotion of the great man to MRAF; if this ever transpires, what a tragedy that it was not done during his Lordship's lifetime.

Air Vice-Marshal Keith Park: the 'Defender of London'.
(Author's Collection)

And what of Air Vice-Marshal Park? After his exile to Training Command, he was appointed AOC Malta during the anxious period in which the defence of the island was conducted with such grim determination. His Battle of Britain experience proved invaluable, as initially Park's fighter force consisted of a meagre Hurricane force until the arrival of Spitfires. Eventually the Mediterranean was cleared and the garrison saved. Interestingly, Malta's chief fighter controller was Group Captain 'Woody' Woodhall, who had achieved the reputation of being the fighter controller 'par excellence' of the Second World War.

German files captured after the war indicate that the enemy respected Keith Park, to whom they referred as the 'Defender of London':-

Park is regarded as efficient and having great personal courage. Not a theorist, but a man of action who understands his work. He does not think a great deal of General Staff work. It is expected that he will make the Air Forces in the Eastern Mediterranean more active.

Of Air Chief Marshal Sir Trafford Leigh-Mallory the enemy wrote:-

Leigh-Mallory is considered as a pedantic worker with a preference for administrative questions, who gives his subordinates little room for personal decisions. He is therefore known as the 'Flying Sergeant'.

In January 1944, Air Vice-Marshal Park became AOC-in-C Middle East, and a year later Allied Air C-in-C of the South East Asia Command, ironically the appointment Leigh-Mallory was flying out to accept when he was killed. In 1946, Air Chief Marshal Sir Keith Park GCB KBE MC DFC DCL retired from the RAF and later returned home to Auckland where he became a City

Councillor. His nephew, Keith Park, remembers:-

The family of Keith Park were not only proud of him as a great airman and commander. He was also regarded with great affection for his human qualities. On his first visit to us, in 1946, after lunch he entertained the children and amused himself for half an hour pushing them on their swing - immediately captivating a boy aged five and his sister aged three!

The 'Defender of London' died on February 6th 1975, aged 82.

On Friday, 12th September 1975, a Thanksgiving Service took place at St Clement Danes in memory of Air Chief Marshal Sir Keith Park. The Lesson was read by Air Commodore ARD MacDonell CBE DFC, Chairman of the Battle of Britain Fighter Association. The Address was read by Group Captain Douglas Bader CBE DSO DFC. Tactfully, the Battle of Britain Fighter Association had 'unanimously' invited Bader's involvement. Douglas Bader said:-

The awesome responsibility for this country's survival rested squarely on Keith Park's shoulders. Had he failed, Stuffy Dowding's foresight, determination and achievement would have counted for nought. This is no sad occasion. Rather it is a time during which we can let our memories drift back to those halcyon days of 1940 when we fought together in English skies under the determined leadership of that great New Zealander we are remembering now. Keith Park was one of us. We all shared the great experience. That is what we remember today. British military history of this century has been enriched with the names of great fighting men from New Zealand, of all ranks and in every one of our services. Keith Park's name is carved into that history alongside those of his peers.

Group Captain Sir Douglas Bader himself died suddenly of a heart attack in 1982, aged 72.

*Generalleutnant Adolf Galland and Group Captain Douglas Bader
meet again as friends in America long after the war.*
(Author via Wing Commander PB Lucas)

What of other Big Wing 'notables'?

In June 1941, Squadron Leader Brian Lane left 19 Squadron and served on staff duties in the Middle East. The following year he returned to the UK and, after a Spitfire refresher course, reported as supernumerary to 167 'Gold Coast' Squadron at Ludham. On December 13th, 1942, his first flight with the squadron was a 'Sector Recce'. The second, made later that day, was a Rhubarb over the Dutch coast; Lane's section was intercepted by two FW190s and this gallant

25-year-old failed to return. Research indicates that he was shot down by *Oberleutnant* Walter Leonhardt of 6/JG1. In all probability, during his long spell away from operations, the exceptional Lane had lost the 'edge'; his name is recorded on the Runnymede Memorial, a tribute to those British and Commonwealth airmen with no known grave.

On August 28th, 1941, 19 Squadron provided the escort for Blenheims engaged in a low-level attack of shipping in Rotterdam harbour, another futile operation. The CO, Squadron Leader Walter 'Farmer' Lawson DFC was shot down into the North Sea by an Me 109 of 6/JG53, his name also being recorded at Runnymede. Flight Lieutenant Wallace 'Jock' Cunningham DFC was hit by flak and forced-landed on the beach south of Amsterdam, becoming a prisoner of war. As Cunningham's Spitfire descended, his No 2, Pilot Officer Peter Stuart, 'a fine Canadian', called over the R/T 'Cheerio Jock, Good luck'. Sadly Stuart was killed the next day when Acting Flight Lieutenant Arthur Vokes led the squadron on a patrol over the North Sea, searching for their missing comrades. The Spitfires engaged a formation of 6/ZG76 in a ferocious combat; four Spitfires and their pilots were lost against one Me 110 '15%' damaged. A week later, Arthur Vokes was dead, killed in a flying accident near Langham aerodrome; they buried the 24-year-old at Great Bircham.

The CO of 616 Squadron, Squadron Leader Howard 'Billy' Burton, went on to become Bader's right-hand man during the heady Tangmere Wing days of 1941. He later led a Kittyhawk Wing in North Africa, returning home, together with Air Commodore Harry Broadhurst and other officers, for a conference in England in May 1943. Whilst returning to North Africa, the unarmed Hudson, in which 27-year-old Wing Commander HF Burton DSO DFC was travelling with other distinguished RAF officers, was shot down over the Bay of Biscay by *Leutnant* Heinz Olbrecht of 15/KG40. Another name carved in stone at Runnymede.

By 1945, other Big Wing survivors had also been killed on active service or captured. Fortunately, the majority survived, amongst them Denis Crowley-Milling, in 1940 the impressionable young Pilot Officer captivated by his charismatic CO; their friendship truly lasted a lifetime, and for many years Air Marshal Sir Denis Crowley-Milling was the enthusiastic Chairman of the Douglas Bader Foundation. Sadly the Air Marshal died after a long illness in late 1996. The careers and fates of other survivors are well documented in various publications listed in the Bibliography of this book, so I will not duplicate that information here.

Duxford itself, a working airfield now owned by the Imperial War Museum, still reverberates to the mighty Merlin's roar and is established as *the* aviation museum in Europe. Visitors can see an outstanding collection of over 140 aircraft ranging from Spitfires to Concorde, and should not miss the opportunity to see the Duxford Sector Operations Room, scene of some of the drama related in this book. Nearby Fowlmere Farm has largely returned to more agricultural purposes than in 1940, but light aircraft still operate from the former Duxford satellite. I hope that this book will increase the appreciation and enjoyment of any visit to the area.

Fowlmere Farm as it appears today; the Few have gone, but their spirits remain.
(Andrew Long)

THE GREAT EXPERIENCE

In conclusion, I have to say what a fascinating experience it has been to research and write this book, especially as the *evidence* transpired to be so frequently at odds with previously published accounts. History is deserved of an accurate record, and as I believe that this now exists, it is with some satisfaction, therefore, that I now prepare to put down my pen. Also, the names of Air Chief Marshal Dowding and Air Vice-Marshal Park will now be brought to the attention of a new generation, as will the courage and gallantry of those men and women, both on the ground and in the air, who shared, as Group Captain Bader describes it, 'the Great Experience'; to *all* of them we owe a debt too great for words alone to repay.

Over 57 years later, the Battle of Britain continues to both fascinate and inspire: Dilip Sarkar gazes out from Sheerness across the Thames Estuary towards Southend, the sky above which, being the seaward approach to London, was the scene of bitter combats throughout the summer of 1940.
(Mark Postlethwaite)

Index of Royal Air Force and
Fleet Air Arm Personnel

For the purposes of standardisation those individuals referred to during the Battle of Britain period are listed with their ranks at the end of the Battle, or if killed, at the time of death.

In view of the frequency of reference to the following key figures, it has been decided to omit their names from the index:-

Air Chief Marshal Sir Hugh Dowding
Air Vice-Marshal W Sholto Douglas
Air Vice-Marshal T Leigh-Mallory
Air Vice-Marshal KR Park
Wing Commander AB Woodhall
Squadron Leader DRS Bader

Aeberhardt, RC, P/O, *50*, 85
Allen, HR, P/O, 201

Ball, GE, F/L, *40*, *54*, 80, 109, 119
Batt, LG, Sgt, 116, *117*
Beamish, FV, W/C, 73, 77
Bergman, V, P/O, 107, *108*, 109, 133, 187, 189
Blackwood, GDM, S/L, 59, *59*, 60, 94, 134, 139, 141, 153, 187, *203*
Blake, AG, Sub/Lt, 108, *108*, 125, 126, 175
Boddington, MCB, Sgt, 96
Bodie, CAW, P/O, 122
Boulton, JE, F/O, *59*, 107, *107*, *108*, 109, 198
Brand, Sir Quintin, AVM, 87, 93, 105, 116, 117, 145, 162, 168, 170
Brimble, GW, Sgt, 80
Brinsden, FN, P/O, 35, *35*, *50*, 74, 85, 109, 150, 192
Broadhurst, H, S/L, 199, 200, 209
Brothers, PM, F/L, 104, 120, 193, *193*
Brown, MK, P/O, 42
Brown, MP, P/O, 66, 122, 124
Burge, C, F/L, 28
Burgoyne, E, P/O, 85, 90, *90*, 143
Burnell-Phillips, PA, Sgt, 107
Burton, HF, S/L, 135, *135*, 139, 145, *145*, 209
Bush, CR, P/O, 141

Campbell, NN, P/O, *54*, 133
Casson, LH, P/O, 135

Chance, J, Cdt, 31
Charnock, HW, Sgt, 118
Chesney, F/O, *94*
Chlopik, F/L, 127
Christie, GP, F/L, 80
Clarkson, F/L, 34
Clouston, WG, F/L, *50*, 57, 85, 87, 103, 108, 133
Clowes, AV, P/O, 77
Cooper, S, S/L, 63
Coote, Patric, Flt Cdt U/O, 31
Copeland, P, Sgt, 142
Cork, RJ, Sub/Lt, 80, 99, 100, *100*
Coward, JB, F/L, 85
Cox, David, DGSR, Sgt, 51, 56, *56*, 73, 85, 92, 109,121, 143, 191, *192*
Cresswell, F/O, *102*
Crook, DM, P/O, 96, *96*, 105
Crowe, HG, G/C, 139, 162
Crowley-Milling, D, P/O, *40*, *41*, 54, *54*, 79, *100*, 101, *101*, 126, 141, 174, 188, *188*, 209
Cunningham, W, F/L, 51, *51*, 57, 102, 109, 126, 133, 137, 186, 191, 205, 209
Cutts, JW, F/O, 77

Darley, HS, S/L, 162
Davies, PO, Sgt, 77
Day, Harry, F/L, 31, 32
Deere, AC, F/L, 195
Devitt, PK, S/L, 87

INDEX

Dewey, RB, P/O, 122, 124

Doe, RFT , P/O, 93, 98

Dolezal, F, P/O, 103, 134, *134*, 203

Donaldson, E W, S/L, 24

Duke-Woolley, RMBD, F/L, 138

Dundas, HSL, F/O, 135, *145*

Duszynski, S, Sgt, 116

Edge, GR, F/L, 82, 181

Edmunds, D, *44*

Ellams, WA, AC1, 47

Ellington, Sir Edward, MRAF, 9

Evans, D, 42, 101

Evill, Sir Douglas, AVM, 30, 31, 52, 53, 74, 97, 130, 145, 146, 153, 168, 179, 184, 193

Farmer, JNW, F/L, *111*

Fechtner, E, P/O, *108*, 133, 174

Fejfar, S, F/O, 107, 109, 127

Fenton, HA, S/L, 116, 162

Field, Cdt, 31

Forshaw, F/O, 91

Freeborn, JC, F/L, 112

French, E, 36, *36*

Furst, B, Sgt, 103, *103*, *108*

Gardner, RE, Sub/Lt, *100*, 101, 181

Gaunce, LM, F/L, 182

Gaunt, GN, P/O, *96*

Gillies, KM, F/L, 122

Girdwood, AG, Sgt, 174

Gossage, EL, AM, 8, 14, 15, 23

Goth, V, P/O, *108*

Gracie, EJ, F/L, 77

Haines, LA, F/O, *50*, 88, 90, 125, 133, 137, 181, *203*

Halahan, FC, AVM, 31, 33

Hall, RMD, P/O, 105

Hancock, NPW, P/O, 77

Hannah, J, Sgt, 131

Harris, Sir Arthur, MRAF, 206

Hart, N, P/O, 80, 120, 133, 181

Hess, A, S/L, 59, *59*, 86, 127

Hill, HP, P/O, 133

Hodgkinson, CW, S/L, 34

Hogan, HAV, S/L, 76

Holden, K, P/O, 142, *142*

Holderness, JB, F/L, 99

Homer, MG, F/O, 141

Horn, KC, S/L, 63

Howard-Williams, PI, P/O, *50*

Hradil, F, P/O, 181, *182*

Hubacek, J, Sgt, 127

Hughes, DP, F/L, 116

Hughes, PC, F/L, 93, 96

Hyde, RJ, Sgt, 48

Janouch, S, P/O, *94*, 99

Jefferies, J, F/L, 59, *94*, *107*, *108*, 127,131, 133, *203*

Jennings, BJ, Sgt, *50*, 57, *57*, *84*, 90, *92*, 102, 112, 142, 143, 182, 186, 192

Johnson, J E, P/O, 87, 91, 97

Jones, RL, P/O, 118, 144, 191, *191*

Joubert de la Ferte, Sir Philip, AM, 162

Karwowski, WE, P/O, 132

Kaucky, J, Sgt, *94*, *108*, 141

Kirk, W, 60, *60*

Kominek, J, F/Sgt, 141, 142

Kopriva, J, Sgt, 88

Kowalski, J, F/O 133

Kowalski, J, Sgt, 128,

Kredba, M, P/O, 86

Lane, BJE, F/L, *50*, 51, 52, 53, 56, 57, 72, 87, 91, *92*, 93, 94, 96, *102*, 112, 121, 123, 125, 137, 143, *145*, 174, 182, 186, 192, 200, 208, 209

Lapka, S, P/O, 127

Latta, JB, P/O, 141, *141*

Lawrence, KA, P/O, 98

Lawson, GM, A/C,15, 146

Lawson, WJ, F/L, *50*, 90, 91, *92*, 93, *102*, 108, 121, 134, 137, 181, *203*, 209

Leach, JM, F/L, 33

Leather, WJ, F/L, 122, 124

Leigh, RHA, S/L, 31, 34, 35, 38, 40, 48, 67, 75, 88

Lester, W/C, 64

Levenson, SA, Sgt, 48, 112, 122, 124

Livivosk, S/L, 63

Lloyd, DE, Sgt, *102*, 118, 133

Lonsdale, RH, Sgt, 80, 109

Lucas, PB, W/C, 48, 95

Ludlow-Hewitt, Sir Edgar, AVM, 10, 13, 15

Lund, JW, P/O, 66, 122, 124

Lyne, Michael, F/O, 37, *92*

Lywood, OGWC, A/C, 162

Macdonald, P, F/L, 39, 42, 136, 162

MacDonell, ARD, S/L, 208

MacFadyen, D, F/L, 30, 31

Macfie, CH, F/L, *145*

Maclean, D, F/O, 30

Malan, AG, S/L,110, 111, 112, 113, 162, 195, 197

Maly, JM, P/O, *108*, 174

Markiewicz, A, Sgt, 187, *187*

212

Marsden, S/L, 63

Matthews, PGH, F/O, 77, 78

Maybaum, F/L, 78, 79

McComb, JE, S/L, 45, *45*, 66, 74, 75, 86, 106, 107, 112, 121, 122, 123, 124, 132

McEvoy, TN, W/C, 162

McKnight, WL, P/O, *54*, 79, 109, 133, 144, 181,

Meaker, JRB, P/O, 122

Merchant, HJ, Sgt, 76

Mermagen, HW, S/L, 32, *32*, 38

Milne, J, LAC, 49, *49*

Morris, DR , 88

Morten, HE, F/L, 63, *63*, 73, 103, 118, 149

Mortimer, PA, P/O, 120

Mumler, M, W/C, 111

Newall, Sir Cyril, AM, 5, 10, 24

O'Neill, DH , F/O, 122, 124

Oulton, W, AVM, 31, 32

Oxspring, RW, F/L, 192, 196

Paterek, E, Sgt, 133, 134,

Pearson, WJ, F/O, 30

Pemberton, DA, S/L, 76, 78, 79, 80

Pepper, J, 64, *64, 65, 65*

Pilch, ER, P/O, 132

Pinkham, PC, S/L, 52, *52*, 53, 87, 88, 89, 90, 91, 93

Plzak, S, Sgt, 90, 134, 143

Pollard, P/O, 122

Portal, Sir Charles, AM, 12, 33, 162, 165, 169

Potter, JA, Sgt, *50*, 57, 126, *126*

Poulton, HRG, P/O, 110

Powell-Shedden, G, F/L, 40, 101, 120

Prchal, EM, Sgt, 127, 133

Puda, R, Sgt, *94*

Rayner, R, F/L, 119

Rechka, J, Sgt, 127

Rimmer, RF, F/L, 120

Roach, RJB, P/O, 113

Roberts, F, LAC, 37, *84*

Russel, BD, F/O, 127

Rypl, F, P/O, 107

Sadler, HS, F/Sgt, 122, 124

Salmond, Sir John, AM, 12

Satchell, WAJ, S/L, 111, *111*, 127

Saul, R, AVM, 185

Saundby, AVM, 138

Sclanders, KM, P/O, 109

Shepherd, FER, Sgt, 113

Sinclair, GL, F/L, 59, *59*, 60, 92, 94, *94*, 107, *107*, *108*, 142, 143, 198

Slessor, JC, AVM, 162

Smith, DS, P/O, 142

Stainforth, GH, W/C, 34

Staniforth, F/L, 31

Stansfeld, NK, F/O, 80, 101, 126, 144

Steere, H, F/Sgt, *50*, 103, 125, 133

Stephenson, GD, S/L, 25, 31, 34, 35, 37, 38, 53

Sterbacek, J, P/O, *59*, 86

Stevenson, DF, AVM, 10, 13, 154, 157, 160, 162

Stoddart, KM, F/L, 122, 124, 188

Stuart, P, P/O, 209

Tamblyn, HN, P/O, 109, 121

Thomas, EH, F/O, *50*

Thomas, S/L, 31

Thomson, JA, F/L, *111*, 187, 188

Townsend, PW, S/L, 193, 201

Tracey, OV, S/L, *44*

Trenchard, P/O, *84*

Trenchard, Viscount, MRAF, 4, 5, 12, 183, 205

Tuck, RRS, 197, 198

Turner, PS, F/O, 39, 40, *40*, 99, 141, 144

Tyrer, E, Sgt, 120

Unwin, GC, F/Sgt, 25, *50*, 85, 88, *88*, 91, *92*, 102, 112, 121, 125, 131, 132, 133, 144, 181, 186, *186*, 190

Vokes, AF, P/O, *50*, 65, 109, 125, *126*, 128, 149, 209

Walker, JR, P/O, 122

Walker, WLB, P/O, 69

Ward, Sgt, 87, 91

Watkins, DH, F/O, 66

Watson, P/O, 37

Welford, GHE, P/O, 55

Wells, PHV, F/O, 182

Welsh, Sir William, AM, 23

West, B, Warrant Officer, 42

Whitbread, HL, P/O,136

Wilkinson, KA, Sgt, 189, *189*

Wilkinson, RL , S/L, 53

Williams, F/O, 122, 124

Zima, R, Sgt, *108*

Zimprich, S, P/O, 107, *108*

Zurakowski, J, P/O, 93, 96

Acknowledgements

O ver the years, many friends have kindly helped, either directly or indirectly, towards my research for this book. Firstly the following Big Wing pilots, although sadly, as time marches ever on, the Few are getting fewer and some did not live to see publication:-

Air Marshal (the late) Sir Denis Crowley-Milling KCB CBE DSO DFC*
Group Captain (the late) Sir Hugh Dundas KB DSO DFC* DL
Wing Commander BJ Jennings AFC DFM
Wing Commander Sir Kenneth Stoddart KCVO KStJ JP LLD
Wing Commander (the late) PI Howard-Williams DFC
Wing Commander (the late) FN Brinsden
Wing Commander GC Unwin DSO DFM
Wing Commander DGSR Cox DFC*
Wing Commander JA Thomson
Wing Commander (the late) GDM Blackwood
Wing Commander GL Sinclair DFC
Squadron Leader V Bergman DFC
Squadron Leader LH Casson DFC AFC
Flight Lieutenant W Cunningham DFC
Flight Lieutenant RL Jones
Flight Lieutenant R Puda
Flight Lieutenant KA Wilkinson
Warrant Officer AL Markiewicz

Other pilots who have helped are:-

Air Vice-Marshal JE Johnson CBE DSO* DFC*
Air Vice-Marshal MD Lyne CB AFC
Air Vice-Marshal FDS Scott-Malden CB DSO DFC
Air Commodore PM Brothers CBE DSO DFC
Air Commodore JB Coward AFC
Air Commodore (the late) EM Donaldson CB CBE DSO
Air Commodore (the late) HA Fenton CBE DSO DFC
Air Commodore HW Mermagen CB CBE AFC
Group Captain GR Edge OBE DFC
Group Captain (the late) PW Townsend CVO DSO DFC
Wing Commander RFT Doe DSO DFC
Squadron Leader RMD Hall DFC
Squadron Leader (the late) GHE Welford AE
Squadron Leader (the late) CW Hodgkinson
Squadron Leader TA Stevens DFC
Squadron Leader PHV Wells DSO
Flight Lieutenant LG Batt
Flight Lieutenant KA Lawrence DFC
Flight Lieutenant HRG Poulton DFC
Flight Lieutenant R Rayner DFC

Supporting personnel:-

Flight Lieutenant HE Morten
Mrs J Nielsen
Miss M Balfour
Mr D Evans
Mr DR Morris
Mr F Roberts
Mr J Milne
Mr EW French
Mr WA Kirk
Mr WA Ellams

Regarding my specific research into Group Captain Sir Douglas Bader, I am grateful to Lady Bader, Keith Delderfield of the Douglas Bader Foundation, and Dr Alfred Price.

Odette, Lady Dowding was most kind in allowing access to family photographs and records, as did Mr Keith Park, nephew of Air Chief Marshal Sir Keith Park, and Mrs Jean Allom (widow of Wing Commander HF Burton DSO DFC). Mr Martin Woodhall kindly allowed me access to the unpublished Duxford related memoirs of his late father, Group Captain AB Woodhall; all quotes from the Group Captain in this book were extracted from that source (see Bibliography). Mr Ben Longridge kindly supplied photographs of his uncle, the late Air Chief Marshal Sir Trafford Leigh-Mallory. Lady Broadhurst kindly allowed access to her late husband's flying log book, as did Mr Jim Pinkham regarding that of his late brother, Squadron Leader Philip Pinkham. Many years ago, Mrs D Green kindly passed into my care the personal papers and flying log book of 19 Squadron's Flight Lieutenant AF Vokes; arguably the research for this book commenced on that day back in 1988.

As ever, Wing Commander NPW Hancock OBE DFC, Honorary Secretary of the Battle of Britain Fighter Association, helped with tracing the Few. A further debt is owed once again to the Keeper and Staff of the Public Record Office, the RAF Museum, and the Imperial War Museum (in particular Frank Crosby at Duxford). Mrs Jean Buckberry, College Librarian & Archivist of the RAF College Cranwell also kindly supplied information.

Once more the wartime aviation enthusiast movement rallied to the cause:-

John Foreman, Norman Franks, Ernie Hardy, Alan & Sue Gosling and Richard Smith, all of the Purfleet Heritage Centre, Larry McHale, Mark Postlethwaite and Ivor Linsdell.

Dr Dennis Williams: my trusted friend and right-hand man, only ever a telephone call away to offer advice and encouragement. Dennis again undertook all photography work for this book.

Every publisher requires a professional and reliable printer, and Ramrod Publications remains indebted to 'Aspect Print & Design' for another excellent end result.

My previous books have acknowledged my wife's support (who also type-set this volume), but on this occasion I must also mention our children, James (5) and Hannah (2) who apparently understand that 'Daddy writes books *and* goes to work'. Our parents, Janet & Trid Sarkar JP, and Roy and Tilly Mayo, are to be commended for their baby-sitting services!

Bibliography

PUBLISHED SOURCES.

'High Commanders of the Royal Air Force', Air Cdre Henry Probert, HMSO, 1991.
'Dowding & the Battle of Britain', Robert Wright, Corgi, 1970.
'Dowding & Headquarters Fighter Command', Peter Flint, Airlife 1996.
'Sir Keith Park', Dr Vincent Orange, Methuen, 1984.
'The Second World War' (6 volumes), Sir Winston Churchill, Cassell, 1948-54.
'Big Wing: the biography of ACM Sir T Leigh-Mallory', Bill Newton Dunn, Airlife, 1992.
'Years of Command' MRAF Lord Douglas of Kirtleside with Robert Wright, Collins, 1963.
'Full Circle', AVM JE Johnson, Chatto & Windus, 1964.
'Reach for the Sky', Paul Brickhill, William Collins Sons & Co Ltd, 1954.
'The Bader Wing', John Frayn Turner, Midas Books, 1981.
'Bader: The Man & His Men', Michael Burns, Arms & Armour Press, 1990.
'Flying Colours: the Epic Story of Douglas Bader', 'Laddie' Lucas, Stanley Paul Ltd 1981.
'Fight for the Sky', Grp Capt Douglas Bader, Sidgwick & Jackson, 1973.
'Wing Leader', AVM JE Johnson, Chatto & Windus 1956.
'Flying Start', Grp Capt Sir Hugh Dundas, Stanley Paul Ltd 1988.
'Fighter Pilot', Wg Cdr Bob Doe, Spellmount Ltd, 1991.
'Aces High', Chris Shores & Clive Williams, Grubb Street 1994.
'Men of the Battle of Britain', Ken Wynn, Gliddon Books 1989.
'The Battle of Britain Then & Now Mk V', edited by WG Ramsey, After the Battle 1989.
'The Blitz Then & Now' (Vols I & II), edited by WG Ramsey, After the Battle, 1989 & 1990 respectively.
'Spitfire the History', Eric Morgan & Edward Shacklady, Key Publishing 1987.
'The Hawker Hurricane', Francis K Mason, Aston Publications, 1987.
'RAF Squadrons', Wg Cdr CG Jefford, Airlife 1988.
'Battle of Britain Day', Dr Alfred Price, Sidgwick & Jackson Ltd, 1990.
'The Hardest Day', Dr Alfred Price, Macdonald & Jane's, 1979.
'One Hurricane One Raid', Geoff Rayner, Airlife, 1990.
'RAF Fighter Squadrons in the Battle of Britain', Anthony Robinson, Arms & Armour, 1987.
'The Battle of Britain', Richard Townsend Bickers, Salamander Books Ltd., 1990.
'The Battle of Britain: The Jubilee History', Richard Hough & Denis Richards, Hodder & Stoughton, 1990.
'Target England', Derek Wood, Jane's, 1980.
'Duel of Eagles', Grp Capt Peter Townsend, Corgi, 1972.
'The Battle of Britain', Basil Collier, Fontana, 1969.
'Battle of Britain: The Forgotten Months', John Foreman, Air Research Publications, 1988.
'Battle Over Britain', Francis K Mason, Aston Publications, 1990.
'Fighter: The True Story of the Battle of Britain', Len Deighton, BCA, 1977.
'The Battle of Britain: the making of a film', Leonard Mosley, Wiedenfeld & Nicholson, 1969.
'1941: Part 1' & '1941: Part 2', John Foreman, Air Research Publications, 1993 & 1994 respectively.
'The Narrow Margin', Derek Wood & Derek Dempster, Arrow Books, 1969.
'Spitfire Squadron', Dilip Sarkar, Air Research Publications, 1990.

'The Invisible Thread: A Spitfire's Tale', Dilip Sarkar, Ramrod Publications, 1992.
'Through Peril to the Stars', Dilip Sarkar, Ramrod Publications, 1993.
'*Angriff* Westland', Dilip Sarkar, Ramrod Publications 1994.
'A Few of the Many', Dilip Sarkar, Ramrod Publications 1995.
'Bader's Tangmere Spitfires: the Untold Story 1941', Dilip Sarkar, PSL 1996.
'JG26: Top Guns of the Luftwaffe', Don Caldwell, Orion Books 1990.
'The JG26 War Diaries 1939-42', Don Caldwell, Grub Street, 1996.
'Der Riterkreuz Träger Der Luftwaffe 1939-45, Volume One - Jagdflieger, Ernst Obermaier & Verlag Dieter, 1966.
'The Luftwaffe War Diaries', Cajus Bekker, Macdonald & Co Ltd, 1966.
'*Zerstorer*: The Messerschmitt 110 and its Units in 1940', JJ Vasco & PD Cornwell, JAC Publications, 1995.
'Messerschmitt Bf109: Into the Battle', Michael Payne, Air Research Publications, 1987.
'Clouds of Fear', Sqn Ldr RMD Hall, Bailey Brothers & Swinfen Ltd, 1969.
'One of the Few', Grp Capt JA Kent, Corgi,1971.
'Nine Lives', Grp Capt AC Deere, Hodder Paperbacks, 1959.
'Spitfire Pilot', Flt Lt DM Crook, Faber & Faber, 1942.
'A Flying Memoir', Flt Lt LG Batt, private.
'The Man Who Holds the Watering Pot', Air Cdre HA Fenton, private.
'The People's War', Angus Calder, Granada, 1969.
'Pilot's Notes: Spitfire Mk IIA & IIB Aeroplanes', HMSO, 1941.
'Battle of Britain Top Guns', John Alcorn, article appearing in Aeroplane Monthly magazine.

UNPUBLISHED SOURCES:-

Taped interview of Grp Capt Sir Douglas Bader by Dr Alfred Price.
'Soldier, Sailor, Airman Too', unpublished memoirs of Grp Capt AB Woodhall.
Original, unedited manuscript of 'Spitfire Pilot' by Flight Lieutenant DM Crook DFC.
Author's extensive personal correspondence and taped interviews with survivors.

PILOTS' FLYING LOG BOOKS:-

Air Marshal Sir Denis Crowley-Milling.
Air Vice-Marshal Sir Harry Broadhurst.
Group Captain Sir Douglas Bader (RAF Museum).
Wing Commander GC Unwin.
Wing Commander BJ Jennings.
Wing Commander HF Burton.
Squadron Leader BJE Lane (PRO).
Squadron Leader WJ Lawson (PRO).
Squadron Leader PC Pinkham.
Flight Lieutenant DM Crook (PRO).
Flight Lieutenant AF Vokes, (Author's Archive).

PUBLIC RECORDS OFFICE.

In addition to the foregoing Flying Log Books indicating 'PRO', numerous other documents were consulted at the Public Records Office; the main references are as follows, all of these

BIBLIOGRAPHY

records being available to any reader with a valid ticket:-

Operations Record Books of the following squadrons (all in AIR 27):-

1, 17, 19, 56, 74, 151, 222, 242, 257, 266, 302, 303, 310, 501, 607, 609, 611 & 616

Also consulted were the Combat Reports of all foregoing squadrons, and numerous individual Combat Reports. In addition, reports by Squadron Leader P Pinkham, and various correspondence regarding 19 Squadron's cannon armed Spitfires, and Intelligence reports regarding both German bomber tactics and crashed German aircraft in the UK were also consulted.

The following AIR 2 files:-

5246, 7281 & 7355,

AIR 16:-

25, 78, 98, 131, 132, 212, 216, 217, 281, 330, 341, 367, 635, 735, 842, 846, 901, 1067, 1136,

Also, the official narratives concerning the Air Defence of Great Britain (various volumes) provide essential information, as do the Daily Summaries of Air Operations and reports to the War Office.

The
Douglas Bader Foundation

Sir Douglas Bader was a legend in his own lifetime. His bravery in overcoming the trauma of losing both legs to become a hero as a WW2 fighter pilot has been well chronicled. Following the cessation of hostilities Bader became very successful in his professional life. He developed considerable·golfing skills and devoted much of his personal time to helping others with similar disabilities to his own, encouraging them by example to *FIGHT BACK*.

After his death the Douglas Bader Foundation was established to further promote and develop the philosophies of this great man in helping the disabled community in whatever way it could. In 1993 *THE DOUGLAS BADER CENTRE* was opened, the Foundation having fully funded the building and equipping costs as well as the first two years of its operation. Having now completed phase one of its work and having secured the future of the Centre, the Foundation has embarked on the second phase of its development by establishing *THE DOUGLAS BADER GRANT SCHEME*.

This unique and innovative project enables those with disabilities to continue their social rehabilitation and reintegration once the traditional clinical processes have ceased. The scheme is being implemented selectively by allocating grants in specific areas such as the arts, sport, education or small business and set to given budgets. Furthermore, the Foundation is keen to assist research projects and programmes that directly benefit the disabled community.

WE NEED YOUR HELP to enable as many disabled people as is financially possible to take advantage of this scheme and to offer them a *"way back"* leading them to making their own contribution to the community and their own families.

"The more we raise, the more disabled people we can help"

For further information or to make a donation please contact:-
Keith Delderfield, Director of Operations

THE DOUGLAS BADER FOUNDATION
THE DOUGLAS BADER CENTRE
ROEHAMTON LANE
LONDON SW15 5DZ
Tel: 01817 881551 or Fax: 01817 895622
CHARITY REGISTRATION No 800435

"A disabled person who fights back is not handicapped........ he is inspired"
DOUGLAS BADER

219